J. W. Hitch
Seymour
Co

May 7, 1872

Given by the Library Asso.

AD CLERUM:

ADVICES TO A YOUNG PREACHER.

AD CLERUM:

ADVICES TO A YOUNG PREACHER.

BY

JOSEPH PARKER, D. D.,

Author of "Ecce Deus."

BOSTON:
ROBERTS BROTHERS.
1871.

CONTENTS.

Ad Clerum:

ADVICES TO A YOUNG PREACHER.

PART I.

CRITICAL LETTERS.

I.

DISCIPLINE.

MR. WASHINGTON has, in my opinion, done well to draw your attention to the ministry, though I feel that both he and you have thrown no little responsibility upon me in asking an answer to the many serious inquiries contained in your interesting letter. In accepting that responsibility (which is done with extreme reluctance), you must understand that throughout my correspondence I shall assume that you feel yourself called of God to the work of preaching the gospel, and that you are daily striving to live in the spirit of Jesus Christ. I wish to be very clear upon this point; for though I may take occasion to express myself somewhat playfully on many questions which will arise, yet I deeply feel that without a spirit of reverent and contrite humiliation before God, and a constancy of loving and trustful desire towards the Saviour, no man is fit to have part or lot in the Christian ministry; when, therefore, I avail myself of satire or raillery, it will relate to the weakness or eccentricity of human usages, and never to the vital and solemn realities of the Divine vocation. Our place, as aspirants to the highest ministry, is at the Cross, where alone the oppression of our own unworthiness is relieved by the completeness of Jesus Christ's grace and truth. All this must be assumed; if we are wrong here, we shall be wrong everywhere;—the gift of prophecy and tongues, and the understanding of all mysteries, will be only temptations and snares, and our ministry will be as a plague in the church.

You have been very frank in the statement of your difficulties, and I regard your frankness as an invitation to your confidence; I shall therefore speak with the familiarity of friendship, being assured that you will not make me "an offender for a word." Shall I condole with you upon your trials before the committee of the college? You complain that though you went before the committee with the simple desire to become a preacher of the gospel, one of the gentlemen horrified you by requesting that you would decline "*Hircus*, a he-goat," on the spot, and that having declined it in the only way which you knew, viz. with much bashfulness and civility, another gentleman asked you to show that if two triangles have their homologous sides proportional they are equiangular and similar. You ask me, in a somewhat impatient tone, what such pagan inquiries have to do with preaching the gospel? You also complain that you were not asked to preach *to* the committee, but to preach *before* the committee; on this point I merely say in passing that you really could not have preached *to* the gentlemen, because if you had addressed them as saints some of them might have been startled, and if you had spoken to them as sinners some of them might have been offended. The gentlemen, you must know, were not exactly hearing for themselves, but were rather congregationalizing by proxy, and giving the preacher a foretaste of the polite treatment which is in reserve for him. As to the Latin noun and the geometrical theorem, I can sympathize with your present dissatisfaction, yet I cannot but hope that growing experience will convince you that they may have some good influence upon your preparation for the ministry. You will probably forget that in an isosceles triangle the angles opposite to the equal sides are equal to one another, yet the discipline of demonstrating it will enable you to humiliate any rash heretic who may hereafter seek to poison your church members with the deadly doctrine of necessitarianism. You thus observe, my dear sir, that what we have in view is discipline; the strength of arm which you get by turning a grindstone may be turned to excellent account in felling a tree; and the discipline which is imposed by proving that some x's are some y's, and that other x's are all y's, will enable you to pulverize any hot-headed deacon who may hereafter attempt to prove that you had better be looking out for another pastorate. So you see we seek to whet you on hard subjects that you may the better cut easy ones, just as we whet a knife upon stone that it may the more readily cut the smoking joint. Pray, therefore, look upon your technical studies in the light of *discipline*,—say, if you please, in the light of dumb bells,—which may force you to breathe though they never breathe themselves. Besides this, you must remember that it would be very awkward if you could not meet your people on their own ground, and chastise some of them with their own whips. Only think how embarrassing it would be if a deacon's son knew more than you did about the Law of excluded Middle; how could that young man listen with any confidence to your exhortations from the pulpit? Would not the *principium exclusi medii, vel tertii*, on which he had broken you to pieces, deafen him to your most urgent appeals? Think again, if your lot should be cast among a seafaring population, how utterly quenched you would feel in dining with a captain if he discovered that you could not calculate the varying values of the semidiameters of the sun and moon; and though he might excuse your ignorance of the laws of oblique sailing, do you suppose he would ever ask you to dine again, if, having given you a lunar distance, you could not find its Greenwich date? Or if there was a dentist in your congregation, do you imagine he would pay his pew-rent with any satisfaction if he knew that you could not distinguish the cusps of the chimpanzee from the incisors of the gorilla? So, my dear sir, you must regard your apparently out-of-the-way studies strictly in the light of discipline, and remember that everybody expects a minister to know everything, and for this moderate expectation they urge the conclusive reason that "he has been at college."

I fancy your saying that this is all very well, but you want to know whether you could not have the substantial advantages of the discipline by studying subjects which are probably quite as difficult, yet more fruitful of practical results in actual preparation for the ministry. You think that instead of seeking help from the proposition that every straight line perpendicular to the directrix meets the parabola, and every diameter falls wholly within it, you might thrust your sickle into a richer field, and so with little loss of time become prepared for the work of preaching the gospel. The fact is, I am a good deal of the same opinion, though I have a just regard, not only for the parabola, but for conic sections in general; still you must remember that many great and good men would very strongly disapprove of this opinion, not only as weak, but as positively mischievous. Those great men have a right to be heard, because they have undergone the discipline, and (if the expression may be allowed) are living monuments of its advantages. I say distinctly, of its advantages, as a hundred instances could testify. A neighbor of mine, whose face is, metaphorically speaking, written all over with the words "scholium" and "lemma," was called to officiate at a wedding, and hastily snatching the marriage service, appeared at the altar just in time to save his reputation for punctuality; the reverend and learned man opened his book, and to his horror found that it was a volume of Martino's "Elementa Sectionum Conicarum"! But you see he had the advantage of discipline; and if the blushing bridegroom had stepped into the vestry, the learned minister could have shown him how to find any number of points in a parabola almost without having given either the focus or axis; and is not this infinitely better than the empty humdrum of a wedding service? Another neighbor, if I may call a man a neighbor who spends most of his time in a vain search for pure hyponitrous acid, has shown the advantages of discipline by giving a chemical turn to such expressions as "of the earth, earthy," and representing the doctrine of the resurrection by the formula C_4 H_3 O, HO, which formula he distinguishes as rational, in opposition to empirical. I could point to several other gentlemen equally learned, who carry with them the air of inexorable discipline; my great trouble with those men is to draw from them a sensible and straightforward answer to any question, and in this respect I have found their discipline extremely offensive. Their discipline has of course made them very *exact*, and their love of exactness is such that they will never positively declare what the day of the month is, or commit themselves to a distinct opinion of the time of day; they have a special horror of confounding the *Noumena* with the *Phœnomena*, and they look daggers at any unhappy man who is ignorant of the doctrine of concepts. It is amusing to watch the signs of suspicion upon their faces when an unknown interlocutor invites them to conversation; they evidently think that the treacherous intruder intends to trip them up by an Undistributed Middle, or to cheat them by a subtle perversion of the quantified predicate, and therefore they equip themselves with the Law of Contradiction. All this, you see, comes of high discipline, and therefore you ought to take kindly to the dry and tedious studies which seem to your inexperienced mind to have no connection with the work of the Christian ministry.

You must understand me as being thoroughly in favor of discipline; at the same time it is right to point out that in my opinion even discipline itself may be too dearly paid for. Discipline is too costly, for example, when it removes its subject from the common experiences and sympathies of men. I have had occasion to trace the cause of not a few failures in the ministry, and am bound to say that pedantic discipline has largely contributed to many unhappy results. There is a tendency in such discipline to create contempt for the ordinary pursuits of life, to withdraw men from the thoroughfares of the world and immure them in monastic solitude, and so to impoverish their ministry of the very qualities which could adapt it to the immediate and most pressing wants of their hearers. Pedantry always underrates reality, and is always impatient of practical service. It has, too, a contemptuous tone, which lingers with empty dignity upon the hackneyed inquiry, "Am I to come down to my hearers, or are my hearers to come up to me?" Infinite impertinence! *Up* to you? Where *are* you? Is it not always the teacher's place to come down, that he may take up his scholars? Is it not the duty of the strong to stoop to the weak and fallen, that they may be lifted? Does the mother stand by the cradle of her sick child, and say it is not my business to come down to you, but your business to come up to me? Did not God's own Son come down that He might find that which was lost? Who are *you*, then, with your half-educated head and uneducated heart, to talk such idiotic sublimity about people coming *up* to you! No, such lofty men are never gone up to; they are left in their frosted elevation: sinning, sorrowing men leave them; and in the course of seven years the learned nobodies either quit their denomination, or write their honored names in the long list of unappreciated though illustrious men, whose splendid fame had just begun to twinkle and flicker over nearly half a street!

It must not be forgotten that these remarks are applied solely to pedantic discipline. There is another discipline to which every earnest man will gladly and thankfully submit himself. You will find ministers of competent learning, who are really human, tender, and practical; ministers whose sermons are adapted to all known experiences, and whose prayers are rich in sympathy and spiritual power. Instead of pushing their learning to the front, they keep it in reserve; their accomplishments are not used to throw into contrast the disadvantages of less favored brethren; they act upon the gracious rule, —

> "Men must be taught as if you taught them not,
> And things unknown proposed as things forgot;"

and their reward in the confidence and love of their people is great and lasting. I am anxious that *you* should take your place amongst such ministers, and that you may do so it is essential that you should add to your intellectual training the constant and vigilant cultivation of your heart in the loving fear of God. Beware of having a trained intellect and a neglected heart; where they co-exist, the light is darkness, and the darkness is death; and under such a ministry as may be expected from the unnatural combination, every living virtue will languish and expire. Let me exhort you, with all love, to watch the life of your heart; goodness is strength; friendship with God is as a spring of water which can never fail; to walk in the grace and power of the Holy Ghost is to go from strength to strength, and to attain an influence which is infinitely better than the dying renown which may attach to greater powers than those with which you may be entrusted. I confess to a deep concern upon this point, as the permanence of your ministry will depend upon the depth and tone of your piety. To a man whose heart is not right before God, there will arise many temptations to escape the toil and disappointment incident to pastoral life; and in the course of his attempts to rid himself of a necessarily burdensome work, he will be driven to offer pleas and excusatory representations of his ministerial position which will often imperil his morality. On the other hand, where the pastor lives in God, and so yields himself implicitly to the guidance of the Holy Ghost, daily growing in the image of his Master, all such temptations will be successfully resisted, and their very existence will urge the pastor to deeper humiliation and a still profounder trust in God's grace. For the present, accept a loving farewell: I shall hope great things of you so long as you cultivate with devout and patient care the strictly religious side of your life; but if ever you neglect it, I shall be constrained to regard all your gifts and attainments as only so many flowers which may at once decorate and conceal a grave. "I would not, for ten thousand worlds, be that man who, when God shall ask him at last how he has employed most of his time while he continued a minister in His church and had the care of souls, should be obliged to reply, 'Lord, I have restored many corrupted passages in the ancient classics, and illustrated many which were before obscure; I have cleared up many intricacies in chronology or geography; I have solved many perplexed cases in algebra; I have refined on astronomical calculations, and left behind me many sheets on these curious and difficult subjects, where the figures and characters are ranged with the greatest exactness and truth: and these are the employments in which my life has been worn out, while preparations for the pulpit, or ministrations in it, did not demand my immediate attendance.' Oh, sirs, as for the waters which are drawn from these springs, how sweetly soever they may taste to a curious mind that thirsts for them, or to an ambitious mind which thirsts for the applause they sometimes procure, I fear there is often reason to pour them out before the Lord, with rivers of penitential tears, as the blood of souls which have been forgotten, while these trifles have been remembered and pursued."—*Dr. Doddridge.*

II.

EARNESTNESS.

Be *earnest;* be *natural;* be *as unlike a book as possible*, — that is about all I have to say upon the science of homiletics. These are only heads, however; and, after the manner of preachers, you will look for a little expansion.

As to the first head, it is happily unnecessary in your case that anything should be said merely in the way of exhortation. Your young heart glows with love to Jesus Christ, and with many a vow you have committed yourself to the holy work of publishing His name. This is the best of all beginnings. If you had begun elsewhere, you would have accomplished a swift journey to a failure as mischievous to others as it would have been humiliating to yourself. Your earnestness is my chief joy. The Cross is the strength of your heart, as it is to be the theme of your ministry; it is, you say, increasingly the solution of the mystery of life; it comes to your aid as an interpreter of all sorrow, and gives you views of sin which stir you with irrepressible desire to warn men to flee from the wrath to come. The manner in which you speak of the Cross is, to my own mind, the best assurance of the success which awaits your ministry; your apostolic enthusiasm shall not be wanting in apostolic results; he who uplifts the Cross shall surely share the exaltation and blessedness of his Lord. This holy earnestness will affect for good your entire relation to the life and service of the sanctuary, making you covetous of time, impatient of all trifling, sincere in sympathy, at once dauntless and tender in the exposition of truth, a watchful servant, and a brave soldier. There are men who unhappily imagine that it is necessary to be fussy in order to be earnest, and who wear a label on which is written, in colored letters, "This is an earnest man!" When a man is really earnest, he needs no label; he is a living epistle; his whole life is his commendation. The most earnest men whom I have ever known, whether in business or in the ministry, have made their earnestness *felt* rather than *heard;* to be within the circle of their influence was to know that there was going out of them a constant and heavy expenditure of life, and that all their powers were steadfastly set in one unchanging direction. They have made this *felt*, not by the production of diaries or memoranda of service and engagement, but by an influence at once penetrating and inexplicable. It is very remarkable, too, that such men have been able to secure a tranquillity which has led heedless observers to infer that they were but little in earnest about anything, — they were so quiet, so methodical, so unhurried! On the other hand, there have been fussy and effusive men who have acquired a great reputation for earnestness, when they should justly have had a name for making a great noise and a great dust. Such men have generally lost themselves in petty details; they have no clear plan, no broad and far-reaching lines of movement; their programme is made up of hop, skip, and jump, whimsically varied with jump, skip, and hop; you will have no difficulty in identifying the men when you have to suffer from the noise and dust in which their shallow lives are wasted, but you may have a momentary difficulty in clearing your way of their vexatious intrusion. The fact that there is a spurious as well as a genuine enthusiasm leads me to detain you with a few remarks, not so much upon earnestness itself, as upon three methods of it with which you ought to be familiar: these three methods may be described as the Dental, the Porous, and the Cordial.

The *Dental* method of earnestness goes a long way with people who keep their eyes shut. The Rev. Mr. Osted was an eminent example of this method some twenty years ago. That active and most garrulous man never, to the best of my belief, spoke one word from his heart; and this is saying a good deal, for the words which he spoke were as the sand upon the sea-shore, innumerable. He could have preached four times not only on Sunday, but on every day of the week; and could have visited all sorts of people between the services, without so much, as drivers say, as having one turned hair. Never a word came from beyond his teeth. With a scrupulous equity worthy of a better cause, Mr. Osted spoke in the same key whether at a wedding or a funeral, and with an impartiality truly severe accosted age and infancy with the same monotonous civility. Words! why, sir, they never failed; when the apostle said "whether there be tongues they shall cease," he did not know that Mr. Osted was among the blessings of the future, though he might have suspected this fact when he predicted that "knowledge shall vanish away." You have seen a hailstorm? Yes, but no hailstorm was ever a match for Mr. Osted's tongue; and yet never a word came from beyond his teeth! I have seen him in a sick room every day for a month, but never a word came from his heart, — all dental, dental, dental! Whilst he was addressing the patient, his dry and eager eyes would be examining everything in the room, and the sweetest, tenderest words of all God's promises would almost stiffen on his freezing lips; in fact, they ceased to be promises, and became mere expressions, without unction or emphasis. Often have I turned from him with ill-disguised detestation; yet the attendant ladies, having listened to his insipid commonplaces, have blessed him for his earnestness, and said to me in his absence, "He is such a *good* man; he comes every day, wet or fine." My enforced silence under such circumstances was excellent self-discipline;

I knew that Mr. Osted's service cost him nothing either in heart or brain, — not a nerve throbbed for it, not a pulse beat the quicker for it; and yet the unsuspecting ladies cherished his name with the most affectionate thankfulness. I could have denounced the sham in fitting terms, but for fear of injuring the venerated sufferer beside whose bed I had to sit and weep many a day. When Osted read the Scriptures, there seemed not to be any message in them for all the sorrow of our home, nothing as if it had been written on purpose for us; and when he prayed there never came any great expectation into the heart of the listener: words, words, words; O for one tone of the heart, one sigh of sympathy! but that luxury was denied us in the person of our pastor. Sometimes I asked another minister resident in the town to call upon the sufferer, and the beaming of his benign countenance was to me like the coming of a long-looked-for morning. He was with us as the servant of God; under his reading the holy book became *our own* in a most special sense, and when he prayed God seemed to be quite near. Yet this better man was never so popular as Mr. Osted; for when was the deep, true, great heart any match for a garrulous and untiring tongue? I felt that Osted could have spoken quite as easily into an empty barrel, if he had been paid for it, as ever he spoke to his congregation; and I do not hesitate to say that he would have gone quite as comfortably to a funeral as to a wedding, provided that the effect upon his pew-rents would have been the same in both cases. He was a *very* earnest man was Mr. Osted, — *very!* "Most unremitting in his attendance upon the sick," "never tired," "always had a word in season," "never off his legs," — such are the words which you may hear about him in the houses of those who attended his dental ministry. Mr. Osted was a devoted denominationalist; in fact, he was somewhat of a bigot; he was great on committees, so great that he could wear out the strongest of his rivals. He was keen, too, in committee law, so keen as to be quite the terror of young members. Twenty times in the course of one meeting would the watchful Osted dentally interpose, "Mr. Chairman, I rise to order," "Mr. Chairman, I *do* contend," "Mr. Chairman, I *must* be allowed to explain," "Mr. Chairman, I beg to move as an amendment"; and by this fussy and meddlesome method of interrupting everybody, he earned for himself the reputation of being a very *earnest* member of the committee! No man of ordinary shrewdness was ever deluded into the notion that Mr. Osted was a *legislator;* but for moving amendments, seconding resolutions, suggesting expedients, nominating deputations, and pestering secretaries, he was generally acknowledged not to have an equal in the county which he honored with his dental service.

Now, sir, this is the dental method of earnestness; and I need hardly add that you ought to be on your guard against it. Suspect the men who practise this method, and avoid them! They will make a tool of you; they will conduct experiments with you; and if you go too near the fire they will let you drop in, and then turn upon their heel as if they had always thought you a fool. My heart aches when I think of the possibility of warm-hearted young ministers falling under the influence of such men. They are quite without nobility of feeling, they can say the brotherly word without the brotherly trust, their civility is as measured as if it were determined by Act of Parliament, and their patronage would be intolerable but for the condescension which is so overdone as to render itself both harmless and laughable. I have had much to do with such men. Having leaned upon them, I know them as broken staves; having watched them in the storm, I know with what ease they can set themselves to the wind; and having carefully examined their work, I can assure you it is not pleasant to look below the surface. Once for all, I repeat, suspect and avoid the Dental method of earnestness.

The *Porous* method is not illustrated so frequently now as it was a quarter of a century since, though a few very conspicuous examples occur to me at this moment, — examples of living and accountable persons, whose enthusiasm is simply a question of porousness. My fancy turns at once to a very ponderous brother, whose voice is like a clap of thunder, and whose vast bodily amplification has caused some one to say descriptively, that "he carries all before him." For the sake of easy reference, I shall call him Mr Bodens. The manner in which that earnest gentleman exhausts himself in the pulpit is little short of alarming. No ploughman ever gasped as he gasps; no iron-founder ever sweltered at his furnace as Mr. Bodens swelters in the pulpit. His eloquence is a continual attempt at suicide, and his climaxes constantly suggest the possibility of a coroner's inquest. You will understand this when I tell you that his introduction always brings out handkerchief number one; his first head never fails to cover his face with the most varied streaks, which handkerchief number two vainly attempts to remove; the first subdivision under the second head brings on a style of breathing which can be accounted for only by internal agonies of the extremest poignancy; and the "one word more in conclusion," which always comes in immediately before "finally," drops in faint accent from a man whose earnestness has reduced him to a state of semi-liquefaction. His repute for earnestness is very high. He is spoken of by the gentler members of his congregation as "never sparing himself," "extremely energetic," "deeply devoted," and so forth. "Poor man," they say, "he does labor so when he preaches"; "dear man, he never seems to consider *himself*, he quite *wrestles* with his hearers, he is so *very* earnest"; and all this they say with sincere esteem for Mr. Bodens and his preaching. I have heard it again and again, and answered with a most ambiguous sigh. From this description you will infer that Mr.

Bodens is a hard-working man, but I am bound to deny the generous inference. There is not a stroke of hard work in him. To begin with, you cannot call him a hard reader; for beyond a few volumes of "skeletons," he has no library; you cannot call him a hard student, for he has often said that he never "meditates" but when in bed; and how far he is capable of meditating there you may judge from the fact that in his opinion "steaks and oysters are a supper for a king," and that he enjoys the said supper as often as his funds will allow. But though Mr. Bodens is neither a hard reader nor a hard student, there is a sense in which he does a good deal of work, and this ought in bare justice to be distinctly pointed out. As one of his congregation once observed to me in a tone of much satisfaction, "Mr. Bodens, you see, sir, is always *on the move;*" the good man evidently thought that to be "always on the move" was the perfection of industry, and that silent contemplation was "a sort of mental disease like, you know, and all that sort of thing," a lucid theory which had a remarkably soothing effect upon his own active mind. I was struck with the theory so very forcibly that I made it the beginning of a conversation.

"I am told, Mr. Bodens," said I, "that you are always on the move?" I purposely heightened the last word so as to throw the report into an interrogative form.

"Why, you see, sir," he replied, rounding himself to his full compass, and speaking with instantaneous emotion, "my forte, I may say without boasting, is calling upon the flock."

"You *like* it?" I replied, in a light questioning tone.

"I look upon it, sir, as one may say, in the light of duty combined with pleasure."

"That's it, is it?" said I, without committing myself to any particular opinion.

"It *is*, sir, it *is*. You see, my brother," Mr. Bodens continued, in the style of a lecturer on homiletics, "it helps the preaching, it makes my discourses practical and useful."

"Don't see it," said I.

"Don't see it, sir? Why, the thing is patent, sir, quite patent; how can you help seeing it?"

"*Prove* it," said I, quite in a challenging manner.

"Prove it? Ah, my dear sir, no young minister would have said that at the time when I began my ministry, and that will be five and thirty years ago next midsummer; my old professor always told me to visit the flock, and I should be sure to succeed in my work."

"Come now, Mr. Bodens," said I, "tell me plainly what good all this visiting does."

"Good? Why, sir, look how it promotes a happy union between the pastor and his flock!"

"Then do you mean to say that your people like that sort of thing?" I inquired.

At this point Mr. Bodens took from his pocket handkerchief number one, and then replied, "Sort of thing, sir? what sort of thing are you talking about?"

"Why, visiting," said I; "do you seriously say that your people like it?"

"I say more than that, sir," Mr. Bodens haughtily replied, drawing handkerchief number one across his pudgey and wrinkled brow; "I say, sir, that they not only like it, they positively *demand* it." Mr. Bodens pronounced the word "demand," as if it involved a subpœna, and then looked at me with a steady and piercing eye.

Not wishing to go too far with the old gentleman, and observing already a faint foreshadowing of the streaks which accompany the demonstration of his first head, I fell into a conciliatory and appreciative tone, which quite pleased him.

"I should infer, then," said I, with winning blandness, "that you have a hospitable people?"

This was the right word; you should have seen the glitter of his half-buried eye! He turned round, as if to assure himself that we were alone, and then laying his hand upon my shoulder, he said, impressively,—"Brother, they *are!*"

I nodded vehemently, as if I had received an ample explanation.

"Hospitable?" Mr. Bodens continued, without changing his attitude, "can you take a word in confidence? In confidence as between brother and brother, or, as one may say, between father and son?" He then retired a pace, as if to see how that idea affected me generally.

"No doubt of it," said I, "provided it is nothing very alarming, and provided the vow is not binding after your death."

"Then," said he, "look here: just by way of curiosity I kept a memorandum of one week's hospitality; now read *that*, if you wish to know the terms upon which I live with my dear people."

"Will you read it, sir, as I am not good at making out other people's writing?"

Mr. Bodens read. There was unction in Mr. Bodens' voice; there was light in Mr. Bodens' eye; in one word, Mr. Bodens was *himself*. I quote the memorandum:—

"*Monday:* dined at H.'s; everything in season was on the table; opened a new lot of white wine. *Tuesday:* tea and supper at B.'s; a splendid game pie to supper, that would not cost a penny less than three pounds; Mrs. B. had set aside a few prime Whitstables for my special benefit, a kind creature. *Wednesday:* lunched with F., who insisted upon opening a small barrel of natives; F. is very unselfish and amusing, and would insist upon my having an extra dozen in honor of an event which had taken place in his house on the previous day. *Thursday:* paid eight visits, and supped with D. at the club; D. is a liberal friend, nothing cold would do for him, everything was steaming hot. *Friday:* took an early dinner in the Park; the table was quite a picture; a finer display of choice meats I never saw. *Saturday*, of course," Mr. Bodens added, "was spent at home."

"Well," said I, "there's no sign of famine in your note-book."

"What's the consequence?" said Mr. Bodens, as if about to establish a moral.

"Probably *bursting*," I replied, suggestively.

Mr. Bodens was shocked at this levity; he evidently regarded it as quite out of season. That earnest man never laughed. Life was too serious a business with him to admit of any pleasantry, however mild its form. Under the influence of my flippant answer, he turned himself quite round, so as to give me a complete view of his magnificent back, and personal inspection enables me to say authoritatively that in all respects it was worthy of the memorandum-book. I felt the force of the reproof, or rather I saw it; to have *felt* it would have been death upon the spot.

"Pardon me," said I, "it was quite a slip of the tongue; tell me what the consequence really is."

Mr. Bodens looked at me with much doubtfulness, as if unable to forgive the hard-hearted suggestion all at once.

"Seriously," I continued, "I wish to know the consequence."

"Consequence is, sir, according to the old proverb, a house-going minister makes a church-going people; and I can prove that to be the case, for there is not a seat in all our chapel to be let, not one, sir, even if the king himself wanted it!"

"But, Mr. Bodens, if you will excuse me, may I ask when you find time to study?"

"Study, sir?" he replied, "who wants so much study? Study your people, say I; go amongst them as a shepherd among the flock; study their ways;

make yourself acquainted with their wants; and you can easily write out a skeleton or two on Saturday night."

"Is it right, then," I inquired, "to eat so many fat things, and to pay for them with a skeleton?"

That was a fatal imprudence on my part. Mr. Bodens gave me a stern and devouring look, and went away as rapidly as so vast a personage could move. I watched his conspicuous figure until it was out of sight, and that, as you may suppose, was a considerable part of a lifetime. You will not wonder after this that Mr. Bodens liquefied a good deal in his preaching, nor will you readily believe that he perished as a martyr to the cause. Last of all, however, Mr. Bodens died also, died of the memorandum-book. To the very end he was spoken of as an earnest preacher, and even to this day there are old members of his congregation who reverently recall the occasions when Mr. Bodens was so exhausted with preaching as hardly to be able to get into the vestry in the customary manner of solid bodies. When he died he left a great blank.

By the *Cordial* method of earnestness is meant, of course, the method of the heart. We must be earnest as *Christians*, before we can be earnest as *ministers*. How can our work be right if our heart be wrong? And how can our heart be made right but by constant watching at the Cross? Though we are ministers of Jesus Christ, yet we are poor sinners; our salvation is not in ourselves, but in the Son of God; and if for a moment we imagine that our ministry involves an exemption from the lowliness and contrition which become guilty men, we fall from grace, and our strength is withered. When we come from the Cross heart-broken, and yet glad in the salvation which has been wrought for us, our words will be simple, our manners will be natural, and our tone will be none the less persuasive because it falters with the emotion of thankfulness for our redemption. Truly, our weakness is our strength; when we feel our own nothingness, the grace of Christ is most magnified in our hearts; and when the shallow channel of our invented eloquence is quite dry, God gives us His word as a well of water whose springs never fail. Out of this earnestness will come a simplicity which cannot be misunderstood, a candor which is above suspicion, and an independence as superior to flattery as it is scornful of intimidation. "Keep thy heart with all diligence, for out of it are the issues of life." To fail there, is to fail altogether! "Take heed to thyself, and keep thy soul diligently, lest thou forget the things which thine eyes have seen, and lest they depart from thy heart all the days of thy life." See how we are thus urged to personal consecration! What is our standing before God? Is our love deep as our life, or is it but a transient impulse? Is Jesus Christ merely a theme to be talked about, or is He the strength of our heart and our portion forever? Is our Christian experience a luxury with which we pamper our selfishness, or does it constrain us to abundant service such as no hireling would ever undertake? These are questions which call us into the secrecy and terribleness of Divine judgment.

III.

NATURALNESS.

Be *natural*, and be *as unlike a book as possible*, are the two heads which are now to be discussed. To be natural is to be *yourself* in look, in speech, in action; provided always that you have a self upon which nature has stamped her own simple and graceful impress. If the expression may be allowed, some preachers seem to have a very unnatural nature; in their case a good deal of grinding and polishing may have to be done before they can be safely trusted with the advice to be themselves. An illustrative case occurs to me at this moment: a ministerial acquaintance of mine is entirely innocent of imitating any one, yet a more unnatural speaker never addressed an audience — never; "only himself can be his parallel"; for fluency, pomposity, and inflation he stands alone. He can talk by the hour together in a most deafening and terrifying manner, and when he has done, the acutest hearer may be safely challenged to repeat, or even hint at, one sentence which has been uttered. No mill-wheel was ever so monotonously energetic; no barrel organ was ever so incapable of being worn out; no furnace fire ever tore up the chimney at so desperate a rate. The manner of my reverend acquaintance is nobly independent of the spirit or importance of the subject which he undertakes to discuss; he holds such discrimination in dignified abhorrence; with a lofty impartiality he creates an equal volume of smoke around every theme which he attempts to expound, and in doing so assumes the air of a righteous man. My unnatural acquaintance is quite as eloquent in giving his opinion whether a ministerial dinner should cost one and sixpence or one and ninepence, as when describing the creation of man or the battle of Armageddon. Can anything be finer in the way of even-handed justice? Does an express train care a pin whether it is carrying one passenger or ten, except that it may go fastest when it has least to do? Certainly not; and my acquaintance is exactly an express train without passengers, but not without a furious driver. I have heard him give a public announcement of a tea-meeting, tickets ninepence each, in a manner quite as solemn and urgent as if in one hurried breath he had been announcing that there was a flood in England, a fire in Scotland, and an earthquake half over the continent of Europe. The consequence was, that no timid persons ventured to go near the tea-meeting, and not more than half a dozen adventurous youths took a ninepenny ticket each, in order to see what was going to happen! He cannot be easy; he cannot lower his pompous tone to an ordinary key; if he were to ask a chambermaid for a candle, he would leave upon her mind the impression that the morning would rise upon the smoking ruins of the house. No doubt of it, there is a frightful emphasis in his manner, which makes havoc of the common mind. In private life his grandiloquence is overpowering, so much so that when I see him in the distance I thankfully avail myself of the next turning to the left, wherever it may lead to.

"Well, madam," he said, addressing my wife one day late in April, "the days are gradually attaining a very agreeable continuity."

With a most reprehensible simplicity my bewildered wife merely answered, *Yes.*

"The services, madam," he continued, "which are now in contemplation will be sustained under auspices of a character decidedly flattering to our denominational status."

With scandalous absence of mind my wife amiably replied, "Indeed."

"Quite so, madam; not only the worshipful the mayor, but also the whole corporation, arrayed in full official costume, will condescend to honor us with their patronage, and I do fervently hope that we may be favored firmamentally as well as municipally."

Now, when a man talks in this manner about the anniversary of a ragged school, what may you expect when he begins to preach? Happily, in this case you have nothing worse to expect, for the impartial speaker pursues an undeviated course of grandiloquent declamation. He knows nothing of the charm of variety, nothing of the distribution of light and shade, nothing of the graceful undulation which at once relieves and delights the mind. Let this man, then, be a caution to you; in that way he may even yet be turned to a good purpose, the only good purpose I am afraid which he can now serve. You will not understand me as undervaluing the integrity and earnestness of this unfortunate brother. I have reason to believe that he writes two sermons fully out, even to the Amen, every week, and that he sets them to the lively tune of the whirlwind, and that every Monday he complains (and not without reason) of being fatigued; and I have understood that a feeling of "Mondayishness" is not uncommon with the congregation as well as with the preacher. Under all these circumstances, it is only proper that hard work should be spoken of with all deserved respect.

Another acquaintance of mine exhibits quite a different phase of unnaturalness, — a phase which would be immoral, if it were not so intensely farcical. Mr. Dexter (such is the name destined to a splendid renown) feels himself called upon to attempt a reproduction of Mr. Binney, for the advantage of his rural congregation. Mr. Dexter is Mr. Binney upon a miniature scale, very miniature indeed! Though Mr. Dexter's sight is as good as yours, he thinks it part of his vocation to use an eye-glass set in a gold frame; said eye-glass is thought not only to give a knowing look to young preachers, but to convey a profound impression about late hours, deep studies, and ministerial martyrdom, — in fact to present, without undue ostentation, a bird's-eye view of what may be called the tragic side of student life. Mr. Dexter knows how Mr. Binney's eye-glass is occasionally used; consequently, before announcing his text, he does a little polishing upon that optical instrument, during which he darts his furtive glance at the congregation, partly in an observant and partly in a threatening manner. Mr. Dexter knows how Mr. Binney occasionally says more by the significant motion of his hand than could be said in so many words; consequently Mr. Dexter finishes his introduction with a grotesque flourish of his hand, and completes the third head by extending his first finger in the direction of the northwest angle of the meeting-house. Under this graphic attitudinizing the rural hearers often quail, because, as they say, it leaves so much to be understood.

"That's it, sir," said one of his hearers to me; "you see his thoughts are too great for words, and when that finger of his goes up you may be sure something is meant."

"You know that for a fact?" said I.

"Known it long enough, sir; in fact, we have all known it. Why there's my little boy, only five years old, gets on the table and mimics Mr. Dexter to perfection."

"And you really think that such gestures do good, do you?" I inquired.

"They do good in this way, sir, you see," he answered; "they set people a-thinking; our people begin a-saying to one another, 'now whatever did Mr. Dexter mean when he shot out his hand in that way, so sharp and sudden like?' And then one says one thing, and another says another, and so they keep coming and coming, and watching and watching, d'ye see?"

"Then Mr. Dexter does that sort of thing pretty regularly, does he?"

"Every Sunday, sir; it would n't be like Sunday if he did n't do it; my word, but sometimes he does come out with jerks and twitches that are capital; he like lays his hand upon something, and clutches it as if he would never let go!"

Thus Mr. Dexter caricatures and debases the original. He forgets that what may be natural in Mr. Binney, with his lofty stature and beaming countenance (a countenance of rare dignity and expressiveness), may be absurdly grotesque in anybody else, and especially absurd in a man little more than five feet high, with a face that was intended to adorn a very small haberdashery establishment, in a very small back street, in a very small market town.

"Why, they tell me," said one of his admiring hearers, "that our Mr. Dexter is very like the great Binney!"

"Indeed," said I; "did you ever see the great Binney?"

"Oh, no, no; but them as has seen him has told me so more nor once."

"In what way, then," I inquired, "is Mr. Dexter thought to be like Mr. Binney?"

"Why, in his way o' going on, a-pointing and a-twitching, and such like."

Such is the penalty of popularity! Dogs paint themselves tawny, and then set up for lions; dwarfs buy high-heeled boots, and give themselves out as giants. There are many who imitate Mr. Binney's mannerism who know nothing of his wonderful insight and spirituality; they think that when they have borrowed his hat, they have also borrowed his brains. Yes, that is their trick. You have heard of maiden ladies who have lived by themselves in lonely houses, setting a number of men's hats upon the hall tables at nights, so as to give any intruder the notion that the house was full of burly defenders: even so do the Mr. Dexters of the pulpit; they borrow all Mr. Binney's old hats, and then boldly challenge the world to touch their ministerial reputation.

I have said that some men require a good deal of grinding and polishing before they can be safely entrusted with the advice to *be themselves.* Much, however, will depend upon the way in which the business is gone about. Let me at once advise you to be on your guard against professors of elocution, if you wish to be natural, easy, and effective as a public speaker. I remember the case of a few youths who were very ambitious of being orators, and who accordingly availed themselves thankfully of an offer of the services of a professor who undertook their instruction at the rate of five shillings per lesson. Happily, their exercises had no view to the pulpit. They felt the importance of being able to speak readily at tea-meetings and other exciting assemblies of their fellow-townsmen, and consequently went into the study of elocution with great spirit. Their professor thought himself a very able man; he buttoned his coat in military fashion; and while his head always looked as if he had just hit upon a new and daring figure of speech, his protruding eyes generally seemed to be fixed defiantly upon an imaginary opponent. He had a nice smart way, too, of waving a little cane which he always carried, a way which seemed to advertise its owner as no common man, though at that particular time he had not reached the happy and convincing climax of paying twenty shillings in the pound; but this, said the waving cane, was more his misfortune than his crime. The professor was unquestionably a great rhetorician, in his own estimation; so great that no other man knew what he himself knew, viz., the secret of opening silent lips in copious and eloquent speech. The professor's system was strictly secret; "of course so," said he, "for, gentlemen, that secret is nothing less than my *bread!*" and down came the cane by way of emphasis.

"Gentlemen," the professor would say, "to-night we assemble as rhetoricians; your esteemed, and I will add, though without one particle of flattery, your able fellow-student, Mr. Binton, has consented at my special request to embody our idea of a few emotions; gentlemen, I propose that we first take an embodiment of the emotion appropriate to admiration, mingled, if you please, with somewhat of surprise and even bewilderment: Mr. Binton be kind enough, sir, to give us your notion of the proper gesture."

Mr. Binton, who had had ample notice that he would be called upon to act this part, and who had secretly gone through several rehearsals in his own bedroom in front of the little tenpenny shaving glass which was nailed above the mantel-piece, then stepped into the middle of the room, and set himself in a well-studied posture.

"Gentlemen," the conductor continued, "what criticism have you to offer?"

"In my opinion, sir, the head is not sufficiently drawn back."

"The eyes should show more white, sir," a very mild young member suggested.

"Go on, gentlemen; your criticisms are extremely discriminating."

"Sir, I think Mr. Binton's left hand should be horizontal and his right hand perpendicular."

"Try that, Mr. Binton, and let us see if the effect be pleasing," the conductor added.

"But, sir," a practical member interposed, "don't you think Mr. Binton should *say* something? I mean, something appropriate to the attitude."

"Excellent suggestion, sir," the conductor replied; "now let me see what would do for that purpose. It must be something brief, abrupt, and striking; come, now, let me see; yes, just so, nothing better: Mr.

Binton, be kind enough to exclaim, 'Bless my soul, the creature is beautiful!' Your tone must be clear and startling, expressive of surprise as well as delight."

Mr. Binton, with his well-combed head drawn back, his eyes nearly rolled away somewhere under his eyebrows, his right hand perpendicular, and his left hand horizontal, began, "'Bless my soul—— ;' I forget the rest, sir," he said, with humiliation; and when the surrounding rhetoricians laughed, Mr. Binton turned round to "confound" them, and in that single moment he became a most natural and effective speaker.

The professor frowned. Who had any right to laugh in *his* presence? That question has never been satisfactorily answered to this day. It took a full half-hour to recover the needful composure. The young rhetoricians, pledged to five shillings a lesson, bitterly regretted their untimely laugh, and promised amendment.

"Gentlemen, our second lesson will supply us with a contrast. Mr. Turner" [apprenticed to a boot-maker, and who had his head examined by every travelling phrenologist who came in his way] "has kindly consented to assume the gesture which he considers appropriate to the sensation of *horror*, and to accompany that gesture with the pathetic exclamation, 'O, save my drowning father!'"

Mr. Turner felt himself to be nothing short of a born orator. His neighbors indeed, who were extremely plain people, without the slightest regard for literature or the arts, got up a rumor that young Jonas Turner was crazy; and when called upon to substantiate that serious charge, they referred to his howling in his bedroom, and to the strange shadows which appeared almost every night upon the white calico window-blind of that elevated apartment. They said he sometimes talked as if he was scolding about twenty people all together, and sometimes he shouted as if he was calling somebody who was a mile off, and that he was always most outrageous the night before there was a tea-meeting at the

Young Men's Club. On that particular night, they said, his voice was often quite threatening, and he would keep up his bawling so long that decent people quite despaired of getting to bed before morning. Such was Jonas Turner.

Jonas now appeared as a personification of *horror*. He had studied the part carefully. The born tragedian extended his arms in a clutching manner, strained his eyes until they were almost lying on his cheek, opened his mouth to its utmost stretch, threw himself forward into a beseeching attitude, and in a voice whose filial pathos was intended to be heart-rending, exclaimed, "O save my drowning father!" The rhetoricians looked upon the agonized tragedian with amazement, mingled with envy.

"How will *this* do?" Jonas himself inquired, in a tone not at all dissatisfied.

"Gentlemen," said the delighted professor, "don't prolong the torture of your friend; criticise at once."

"Don't you think the left leg should be a little further drawn back, sir?"

"The word 'father,' sir," said an envious critic, "would admit of a little more pathos."

"The word 'O,' sir, should be more piercingly pronounced. Mr. Turner makes it too round."

"Mr. Turner's hair, sir, should look a little more wild and scattered, and the clutch of the right hand should be more expressive of desperation."

"I think, sir, the eyebrows should be a little more elevated, and the upper lip should writhe as if in agony, and a sprinkling of foam around the mouth would add to the effect considerably."

"Try the exclamation once more, sir," the professor demanded, with dignity.

A loud shriek was then uttered by Mr. Jonas Turner.

"Come, gentlemen, there is vigor, and no mistake; what may it please you to say to *that?*"

"He should have said '*my*' more affectionately."

"The first syllable of '*father*' should have been much more penetrating."

"There was not soul enough in the word '*drowning*,' sir; it strikes me that 'drowning' is the most important word in the sentence."

"Say you all so, gentlemen?"

"No, sir."

"How say you then? Let each student give his opinion fearlessly."

The young men then contradicted one another flatly, no two agreeing which was the most important word in the sentence. Each maintained his own opinion stubbornly, and the professor looked on without attempting to decide the fierce debate.

Side by side with these rhetorical abominations let me place the following letter addressed by David Garrick to a young preacher: —

"My dear Pupil,—

"You know how you would feel and speak in the parlor to a dear friend who was in imminent danger of his life, and with what energetic pathos of diction and countenance you would enforce the observance of that which you really thought would be for his preservation. You would not think of playing the orator, of studying your emphasis, cadence, or gesture. You would be yourself; and the interesting nature of your subject, impressing your heart, would furnish you with the most natural tone of voice, the most proper language, the most engaging features, and the most suitable and graceful gestures. What you would be in the parlor, be in the pulpit; and you will not fail to please, to affect, to profit.

"Adieu ——."

Yes, *that* is rhetoric! Be earnest, and you will be eloquent; let your soul speak, and your words will be wise and good. When I venture to put you on your guard against professional rhetoricians, you must not understand that I am cautioning you against friendly and sensible criticism. We cannot see ourselves as others see us; hence many an ungainly action or offensive habit may be modified, if not quite removed, through the good offices of judicious critics. Court the judgment of your professors, and receive their hints with thankfulness; they are, of course, deeply interested in you, and if they wound your vanity their wounds are inflicted, not with ill-nature, but with faithfulness and even generosity. Invite the knife, if you would be strong and useful; fret at criticism, if you wish to lose a lifetime rather than endure temporary mortification. What I do warn you against is *the wickedness of taking any studied gestures into the pulpit.* I denounce this as iniquity in the sight of God, as the consummation of heartlessness, as a hypocrisy as transparent as it is audacious. Abandon all selfish notions of popularity when you stand before men as the messenger of God; and that you may be enabled to do this, watch and pray, and fast if need be, and God will accept your sacrifice; look upon all self-consciousness in your ministry as a temptation of the devil, and cry mightily to God that he may break the damning snare: for what have you to do with your personality, and with human opinions about your appearance and styles, when your Lord is waiting to speak His living word through your lips? Know you not that you preach in God's hearing as well as man's? Will you cheat your hearers with an attitude, when you should give them a gospel? Will you perplex them with a riddle, when you should call them to salvation? Will you attract their eyes by a grimace, when you should fix their vision upon the uplifted Saviour? May God in His mercy strike us dumb rather than allow us to preach *ourselves;* but rather may He fill us with His love that our preaching may be all of Christ!

IV.

DELIVERY.

We have discussed the first two divisions named in the opening of the second letter, and now we approach the third. When I advise you to be as unlike a book as possible in the method of your delivery, you will understand that I wish to dissuade you from the unnatural and evil practice of reading your sermons in the ordinary course of your ministry. You will say that this is strong language; so it is, but it is the language of strong conviction. Having tried both methods, the method of free speech and the method of reading, I can give an opinion founded upon experience, and I now give it as entirely favorable to free speech. The pulpit will never take its proper place until the habit of reading sermons on ordinary occasions is entirely abandoned; it is official, pedantic, and heartless, and ought to be put down. Let me try to win *you* to the side of free speech; in other words, to the side of earnestness, reality, and power.

I am aware that one or two objections have to be encountered at the outset, yet I fancy they are not very formidable. For instance, it has been contended that the very presence of a manuscript is itself an evidence that careful preparation has been made: the manuscript could not have been written without labor, and therefore, as the minister spreads it boldly out before the eyes of the whole congregation, he mutely announces himself as a painstaking servant of the church. Be it so. I wish this fact to be stated with all due effect, because I will not yield to any man in hearty appreciation of hard work. You will altogether misconceive my meaning if you infer that in condemning the reading of sermons, I also condemn the writing of them. On the contrary, I insist upon the most critical and zealous preparation for the pulpit; I would have the minister live *in* his work, and *for* his work, and toil as in the presence of Jesus Christ, under the unquenchable inspiration of Divine love, and in the happy assurance of complete success. A terrible malediction awaits the indolent minister! Let me pray you, then, to acquit me of the suspicion of self-indulgence in recommending you to preach the gospel rather than to read it, for I dare not incur the responsibility even of appearing to tempt you to waste one hour of the life which is too short for the accomplishment of all its holy work. If you will follow my advice, I think you will not complain of having nothing to do. Do you wish to know the method of preparation which I recommend, in view of free delivery in the pulpit? You shall have it in full. Take as your text a paragraph from the apostolic writings. Read it carefully in the original language; trace the various meanings which may be attached to its principal words in other parts of the New Testament; having satisfied yourself as to the grammar and meaning of the passage, commit your decision to writing, and then take the opinion of two or three of the most critical expositors, and see how far your judgment accords with theirs. Having thus secured a firm standing-place (which is often quite unattainable without rigid criticism), you may write in regular order the principal thoughts which the passage suggests to your mind, and this memorandum will be the skeleton of your discourse; now proceed to elaboration, writing upon wide lines so as to leave room for erasure and interlining. Having completed a full draft of all your divisions, begin at the beginning, and strike out all the long words and all the superfine expressions; let them go, without murmuring! Particularly strike out all such words as "methinks I see," "cherubim and seraphim," "the glinting stars," "the stellar heavens," "the circumambient air," "the rustling wings," "the pearly gates," "the glistening dew," "the meandering rills," and "the crystal battlements of heaven." I know how pretty they look to the young eye, and how sweetly they sound in the young ear; but let them go without a sigh: if you have spoken of God as the Deity, put your pen through the word "Deity," and write "God" in its stead; if you are tempted to tell your hearers that Jonah spent a portion of his life under the care of a "submarine custodian," don't hesitate to say plainly that it was only a whale; if you should so far forget yourself as to write the word "pandemonium," put it out and write the monosyllable over its ruins; and if in a moment of delirium you should write "my beloved, come with me on the pinions of imagination," pause and consider soberly whether you had not on the whole better remain where you are. This process being completed, greatly to the disfigurement of your manuscript, re-write the discourse with the most watchful care, determined that everybody who hears you shall not be left in doubt of your meaning; write as if every line might save a life; and when you have made an end of writing, put the manuscript away, and go to your public work with the assurance that all faithful and loving service is accepted of the Father, and will be crowned with His effectual blessing. Work thus diligently at the beginning of your ministry, say for the first five or seven years, and the advantage of the discipline will show itself down to your latest effort as a preacher. You will see, then, that my advice to speak freely in the pulpit gives you no license to go up with an empty head and an unbridled tongue; it does not permit you to trifle with your opportunities, or to give your hearers a stone when they perish for lack of bread; it binds you to the severest preparation, and holds you guilty before God if you keep back any "part of the price." What is said by Henry Rogers upon prose composition generally, may be said with equal truth respecting the composition of sermons in particular. Let me lay before you his weighty words: "Perhaps it may not be superfluous to remind the young minister that if he would attain more than correctness, or even a fluent facility; if he would impress upon his compositions that individuality without which they cannot live, he must ever keep in mind that prose may be possessed of nearly as various excellence as poetry, and as much requires sedulous self-culture, profound meditation of the subject-matter, familiar acquaintance with the best models (models sufficiently numerous to prevent that mannerism which results from unconscious imitation if there be too familiar converse with some one), and that '*limæ labor*,' that patient revision, which is the condition of all excellence, literary or otherwise." Believe this, and your sermons will never fail of the simplicity, condensation, and pungency without which they will do little good. As I use the word "simplicity" I am reminded of Lord Jeffrey's happy expression: "Simplicity is the last attainment of progressive literature; and men are very long afraid of being natural, from the dread of being taken for ordinary." You will forgive the momentary digression for the sake of the profound wisdom.

You will probably suggest in favor of sermons that are read that they secure for the preacher great accuracy, refinement, and variety of expression. No doubt this may be so; at the same time it may be worth while to consider whether such advantages may not cost too much; that is to say, whether they are not often secured at the expense of the instruction and edification of many hearers. Everything, in the settlement of such a question, depends upon the preacher's position. If his position be so exceptional as to give him the advantage of addressing well-trained men who can follow the course of a close argument and appreciate the niceties of refined expression, he is bound to be faithful to the claims of his position; if, on the other hand, as will be found to be generally the case, he is called upon to minister to a miscellaneous congregation, of which probably not more than one person in ten may have received other than a common school education, he is bound as the servant of Jesus Christ, who pleased not Himself but endured the deepest humiliation, not to consider his own cultivated tastes and the cultivated tastes of half-a-dozen of his people, but to study carefully what is best adapted to the capacity, the habits, and the wants of the congregation as a whole. Is he the servant of the few or of the many? Luther said of himself as a preacher, that he took no notice of the doctors who heard him, of whom there were about forty, but preached to the young men and servants, of whom there were about two thousand. You will not hesitate to say that Luther was right. He was right, too, even so far as the doctors were concerned, because as learned men they did not need mere criticism or brilliance of expression, while as sinners before God they did continually require to hear the gospel of Jesus Christ. For whom, then, are you anxious to secure all the technical accuracy and finish which are supposed to be the excellences of read discourses? Your congregation will, to a large extent, be composed of persons who have all the week been engaged in some department of business, who have been tried by many disappointments, perhaps too tormented by many temptations; you will have heads of houses, whose lives are troubled with many anxieties; you will have youths who are fast becoming entangled in the snares which beset inexperienced feet, and little children whose every look is a wonder which should be lovingly answered: such will be your congregation; what will you supply in the way of teaching? You may prepare two elaborate essays weekly, which are sublimely indifferent to all the troubles and burdens of common life; you may play the philosophic theologian twice a week in the presence of men who have no heart to follow you in your mocking speculations; you may display your scholastic trinkets upon your pulpit-board, to the amazement of the vulgar and the disgust of the thoughtful; you may write the most faultless sentences, and elaborate the most skilful paragraphs, and you may become absorbed in the idolatry of your own genius: but, my dear sir, in doing all this are you the servant of our Lord Jesus Christ, whom the common people heard gladly, and who made Himself of no reputation? Are you a preacher of the Cross? Are you inspired by an ardent desire for the salvation of men? I think I know your answer. You will say that in writing your sermons you will write simply and earnestly, under the impulse of Christian love, and with a single eye to the great object of the gospel ministry; you will write practically; you will instruct, exhort, appeal, with all prayerful earnestness, and your composition shall be more marked by your Christianity than your scholarship. I rejoice in such a resolution, yet I adhere to my advice,— be a *Preacher*, not a *Reader*, of the gospel! Remember the pungent but truthful words of Sydney Smith: "Pulpit discourses have insensibly dwindled from speaking to reading,—a practice of itself sufficient to stifle every germ of eloquence. It is only by the fresh feelings of the heart that mankind can be very powerfully affected. What can be more ludicrous than an orator delivering stale indignation, and fervor of a week old; turning over whole pages of violent passions, written out in German text; reading the tropes and apostrophes into which he is hurried by the ardor of his mind; and so affected at a preconcerted line and page that he is unable to proceed any further!" It is but poor eloquence that comes of such a process, and its very vehemence only confirms one's suspicion of its artificialism. Why not address your people in a free, natural, and hearty manner? Why preach *at* them, when it is your business to preach *to* them? From these questions you will rightly infer that in my opinion your sermon should always be *part of yourself;* instead of saying "I *have* my sermon," you should say "I *am* my sermon," and then you will speak livingly and fearlessly. I am acquainted with a minister who reads the most eloquent papers (sermons he would incorrectly term them) to his people; they are elaborate, rhetorical, sensational, highly polished in expression, and always ready for the press. In reading those papers my friend works himself into the intensest excitement; he swings his right arm in a threatening manner, and jerks his left hand as if it were always in an inconvenient place; occasionally he stamps his foot, and throughout his effort there are many signs of excitement. I have looked at him with wonder; but my admiration has always suffered considerably as I have thought that if the manuscript could be removed he would not be able to keep the attention of his hearers for five minutes. I object to being *read at* when I go to hear the gospel. Why, I ask again, don't ministers speak to their people as if the sermon came from the heart, and was meant to do them good? I am aware that my friend's sermons are not unfrequently spoken of as "very finished," "wonderfully thought out," "very elaborate," and "highly eloquent"; but I never hear a sentence quoted, nor am I aware that the hearers are ever compelled to forget the speaker in his subject. On the other hand, I can point you to a man who never takes a note into the pulpit, whose sermons are never praised as elaborate or finished, yet whose words are quoted all the week long, and whose prayers linger in the memory as blessings and helps to the whole life. Truly, this man's sermons are not prepared for the press; they are prepared for the understanding and the heart alone; and long after the voice of the artificial rhetorician has been forgotten, the sharp, clear, penetrating words of the natural orator will abide in grateful recollection.

It may be worth while to remind you, in this connection, that God has been pleased to bless, in an extraordinary degree, a kind of preaching which, in point of technical value, has been almost contemptible. Look at Whitefield's sermons, — where is the logic, the profound doctrine, the accurate criticism, the instructive exposition, which are so justly esteemed by thoughtful Christians? Yet those sermons, without any pretence to learning or ingenuity, stormed the nation. Mr. Spurgeon has never been regarded as what is generally understood as a "*finished*" preacher. He is no pulpit essayist; he is not a cunning contriver of pretty sentences; yet he has done a work in the Christian pulpit which can never be forgotten. The principle so strikingly illustrated in these marked examples has been almost as fully illustrated in the case of the great Methodist preachers, as also in the case of the popular ministers of Wales. Whitefield and Spurgeon cannot be ranked with educated men; neither of them can be said to have had any proper theological training; yet both of them are names which can never perish from the most conspicuous page of the history of the British pulpit. It seems as if God had always used things that are base and weak, and things that are not, to bring to nought things that are; and that in all high and Divine concerns He had determined that the stone which the builders rejected should become the head stone of the corner. Many ministers will tell you that sermons on whose composition they have expended their strength have hardly ever been referred to as the means of awakening or edifying their hearers, whilst sermons in whose structure and elaboration there was neither genius nor eloquence, have brought many to thoughtfulness and decision. Undoubtedly this fact may be abused by the self-indulgent hireling, but let not that man think that he shall receive anything of the Lord, — he shall be as a withered branch, not as a green and fruitful tree. I once asked Mr. Binney what he thought was the best method of preaching, and he replied, "To gather your materials, and set fire to them in the pulpit." Think of this: the words are full of meaning; to "gather your materials" means to work hard, to turn all things into mental and spiritual riches, and to be thoroughly furnished; to "set fire to them in the pulpit" means to have that elevation and holy enthusiasm of Christian love which cannot be depressed by fear of man, nor be made indifferent to the claims of truth. In a word, then, no essays in the pulpit! I know what can be said about accuracy, polish, variety, culture, and so forth; yet, in full view of it all, I repeat, no essays in the pulpit, — no pathos, scientifically punctuated and paragraphed, — no entreaty exquisitely polished, — no theatrical pedantry under the guise of Christian earnestness.

At the risk of what may look like an unjust suspicion of your memory, I must remind you of my abhorrence of unprepared sermons. The question before us is not whether sermons shall be *prepared*, but how they shall be *delivered* after they have been prepared. I have ventured to set you some hard work in the preparation, and now I may seem to call you to equally hard work in the delivery of your discourses. Be it so: hard work is good for us all; in all labor there is profit, especially in the labor which is spent for God. As your pastoral work increases, and the claims upon your public service become more urgent, you will not find time for the toilsome preparation which has been recommended for your early years; you will then require some readier method of arranging your material for the pulpit; and in view of this necessity it may help you to decision if you are made acquainted with the practice of two or three eminent speakers.

In his review of Curran's biography, Lord Jeffrey says: "He is here said to have spoken extempore at his first coming to the Bar; but when his rising reputation made him more chary of his fame, he tried for some time to write down, and commit to memory, the more important parts of his pleadings. The result, however, was not at all encouraging; and he soon laid aside his pen so entirely as scarcely even to make any notes in preparation. He meditated his subjects, however, when strolling in his garden, or more frequently while idling over his violin, and often prepared in this way those splendid passages and groups of images with which he was afterwards to dazzle and enchant his admirers. The only notes he made were often of the metaphors he proposed to employ, and these of the utmost brevity. For the grand peroration, for example, in H. Rowan's case, his notes were as follows: 'Character of Mr. R.: *Furnace — Rebellion — Smothered — Stalks — Redeeming Spirit.*' From such slight hints he spoke fearlessly, and without cause for fear. With the help of such a scanty chart, he plunged boldly into the unbuoyed channel of his cause, and trusted himself to the torrent of his own eloquence, with no better guidance than such landmarks as these. It almost invariably happened, however, that the experiment succeeded; 'that his own expectations were far exceeded; and that, when his mind came to be more intensely heated by his subject, and by that inspiring confidence which a public audience seldom fails to infuse into all who are sufficiently gifted to receive it, a multitude of new ideas, adding vigor or ornament, were given off; and it also happened that in the same prolific moments, and as their almost inevitable consequence, some crude and fantastic notions escaped, which, if they impeach the author's taste, at least leave him the merit of a splendid fault which none but men of genius can commit.'"

Let me call your attention to three points arising out of this statement. First of all, cultivate to the fullest extent the great gift of *mental composition.* In my estimation, the value of this gift cannot be overstated. It not only saves the drudgery but the *time* demanded by writing, and it sets the speaker at liberty to take the exercise which is essential to the preservation of health. One of the most distinguished preachers, whose name is universally honored, told me that he could compose a sermon from beginning to end without ever writing a word! Why, some of us, poor slaves, cannot compose a dozen sentences, unless we are shut up in the silent study, and have the best writing materials at command. In confidence I may tell you that of all such slaves I may almost claim to be chief. Many a time I have gone into the quiet lanes with a steady determination to compose a sermon; but before I have got far enough to require a semicolon, my truant mind has taken up with some more tempting though less profitable subject. Then would come shame, and then renewed courage; another sentence would be boldly begun, but alas! the very next horse that passed me would carry away my thoughts with it, and I would be left in deeper humiliation. Take warning from this example, and if you have any such gift as Curran had, do allow me to urge you to cultivate it with the most painstaking diligence. Its exercise will almost double your life, and will certainly impart to your speech a freshness and strength which are unattainable, except in very rare cases, by the monastic penman. The second point arising out of the statement is the awkward difficulty which is often occasioned by the brevity of one's memoranda. In Rowan's case Curran jotted down the word "*Furnace*," but imagine his embarrassment if on coming to that word he could not have recalled the train of thought which it was intended to suggest! Many a time, on looking over the notes which have been prepared for the pulpit, I have asked, "Whatever did I mean when I wrote *that?*" and therefore, in recollection of my own embarrassment, let me advise you to be explicit in your notes, so that your invention may not be hampered by a faithless memory. —The third point is the possibility of violating good taste in the rapidity of extemporaneous speech. You cannot be sure that the right word will infallibly come at the right moment. The speaker has fully committed himself to his work; he cannot hesitate or pause to correct himself, he must go on; and under this tyrannous necessity he may again and again offend good taste, a fact of which he is even more painfully aware than his most fastidious hearer can be. It is, then, a question of comparison of advantages; a written speech may of course be always correct, whereas an extemporaneous (though well-considered) oration may be marred by hasty and ill-regulated expressions. On the whole, however, having regard to the great object of preaching, free speech in the pulpit is in my opinion infinitely preferable to the most finished written composition.

Whitefield, if he can be said to have had any method of preparation at all, adopted a course which it would be unsafe to recommend indiscriminately. On this point Cornelius Winter has given us the benefit of his personal recollections: "The time Mr. Whitefield set apart for preparations for the pulpit, during my connection with him, was not to be distinguished from the time he appropriated to other business. If he wanted to write a pamphlet upon any occasion, he was closeted; nor would he allow access to him but on an emergency, while he was engaged in the work. But I never knew him engaged in the composition of a sermon until he was on board ship, when he employed himself partly in the composition of sermons, and reading very attentively the History of England written by different authors. He had formed a design of writing the history of Methodism, but never entered upon it. He was never more in retirement on a Saturday than on another day, nor sequestered at any particular time for a period longer than he used for his ordinary devotions. I never met with anything like the form of a skeleton of a sermon among his papers, with which I was permitted to to be very familiar; nor did he ever give me any idea of the importance of being habituated to the planning of a sermon. It is not injustice to his great character to say that I believe he knew nothing about such a kind of exercise. Usually for an hour or two before he entered the pulpit he claimed retirement; and on a Sabbath morning more particularly he was accustomed to have Clarke's Bible, Matthew Henry's Comment, and Cruden's Concordance within his reach. His frame at that time was more than ordinarily devotional. I say more than ordinarily, because, though there was a vast vein of pleasantry usually in him, the intervals of conversation evidently appeared to be filled up with private ejaculation connected with praise. His rest was much interrupted, and his thoughts were much engaged with God in the night. He has often said at the close of his very warm address, 'This sermon I got when most of you who now hear me were fast asleep.' He made very minute observations, and was much disposed to be conversant with life, from the lowest mechanic to the first characters in the land. He let nothing escape him, but turned all into gold that admitted of improvement; and, in one way or another, the occurrence of the week or the day furnished him with matter for the pulpit."

Can you wonder, other things being equal, that such a man was the most attractive preacher of his day? Could any one have stolen George Whitefield's sermon? Can you imagine him looking round on Sunday morning for his black book, and showing a little nervousness because he could not lay his hand upon it in a moment? Can you fancy him fretful because the fogginess of the morning would probably interfere with his comfort in reading his manuscript? Why, George Whitefield *was* the sermon: it was *in* him as part of his very life; and his word was therefore with living power. If you ask me what I mean by being as unlike a book as possible, I answer, look at George Whitefield, the natural, devout, fervid, and impressive preacher. I cannot find what may be termed a bookish sentence in any of his sermons; everywhere there is the vivacity, the point, the abruptness of free and earnest speech. Take the peroration of his sermon upon "The Kingdom of God," and say whether you can imagine such an appeal to have been written as books are written: mark the simplicity, the directness, the stormy yet tender vehemence of the exhortation: —

"My dear friends, I would preach with all my heart till midnight, to do you good, till I could preach no more. Oh, that this body might hold out to speak more for my dear Redeemer! Had I a thousand lives, had I a thousand tongues, they should be employed in inviting sinners to come to Jesus Christ! Come, then, let me prevail with some of you to come along with me. Come, poor, lost, undone sinner; come just as you are to Christ, and say, If I be damned I will perish at the feet of Jesus Christ, where never one perished yet. He will receive you with open arms; the dear Redeemer is willing to receive you all. Fly, then, for your lives. The devil is in you while unconverted; and will you go with the devil in your heart to bed this night? God Almighty knows if ever you and I shall see one another again. In one or two days more I must go, and perhaps I may never see you again till I meet you at the judgment-day. O my dear friends, think of that solemn meeting; think of that important hour, when the heavens shall pass away with a great noise, when the elements shall melt with fervent heat, when the sea and the grave shall be giving up their dead, and all shall be summoned to appear before the great God. What will you do then, if the kingdom of God is not erected in your hearts? You must go to the devil — like must go to like — if you are not converted; Christ hath asserted it in the strongest manner: 'Verily, verily, I say unto you, except a man be born again, he cannot enter into the kingdom of God.' Who can dwell with devouring fire? Who can dwell with everlasting burnings? Oh, my heart is melting with love to you. Surely God intends to do good to your poor souls. Will no one be persuaded to accept of Christ? If those who are settled Pharisees will not come, I desire to speak to you who are drunkards, Sabbath-breakers, cursers, and swearers, — will you come to Christ? I know that many of you come here out of curiosity: though you come only to see the congregation, yet if you come to Jesus Christ, Christ will accept of you. Are there any cursing, swearing soldiers here? Will you come to Jesus Christ, and list yourself under the banner of the dear Redeemer? You are all welcome to Christ. Are there any little boys or little girls here? Come to Christ, and He will erect His kingdom in you. There are many little children whom God is working on, both at home and abroad. Oh, if some of the little lambs would come to Christ, they shall have peace and joy in the day that the Redeemer shall set up His kingdom in their hearts. Parents, tell them that Jesus Christ will take them in His arms, that He will dandle them on His knees. All of you, old and young, you that are old and gray-headed, come to Jesus Christ, and you shall be kings and priests to your God. The Lord will abundantly pardon you at the eleventh hour. 'Ho, every one of you that thirsteth.' If there be any of you ambitious of honor, do you want a crown, a sceptre? Come to Christ, and the Lord Jesus Christ will give you a kingdom that no man shall take from you."

This is not what you would call a finished literary style; it is too exclamatory and hortative to be expressed fully in type; but let the words be spoken with melodious power of voice, and accompanied by all the signs of earnestness which characterized George Whitefield's ministry, and one can conceive the effect which they would produce upon a mixed congregation. The people would feel that the minister was intent upon their salvation, and that everything was made subordinate to that end. There is a marked personality in the appeal; the preacher seems resolved to address his hearers actually by name, lest any man should imagine himself excluded from the happy invitations of the gospel. "He had," says Cornelius Winter, "a most peculiar art of speaking personally to you, in a congregation of four thousand people, when no one would suspect his object," — a wonderful power, yet one that should be constantly under the control of the severest prudence.

A very different man was Frederick William Robertson, yet he furnishes a striking illustration of what is meant by being as unlike a book as possible. "So entirely was his heart in his words, that, in public speaking especially, he lost sight of everything but his subject. His self-consciousness vanished. He did not choose his words, or think about his thoughts. He not only possessed, but was possessed by, his idea; and when all was over, and the reaction came, he had forgotten, like a dream, words, illustrations, almost everything. . . . He spoke under tremendous excitement, but it was excitement reined in by will. He held in his hand, when he began his sermon, a small slip of paper, with a few notes upon it. He referred to it now and then; but before ten minutes had gone by, it was crushed to uselessness in his grasp; for he knit his fingers together over it, as he knit his words over his thought." Why? Because he was intensely in earnest. I cannot see how a man who is thoroughly in earnest can content himself with reading a paper to his congregation. The man may unquestionably be pious, sincere, wishful to do good, and very industrious in all his ministerial habits; but how he can be bound down by his paper, and stand from year to year reading his literary productions, instead of crying out with irrepressible emotion that the kingdom of heaven is at hand, it is beyond my power to explain. "As every sound is not music, so every sermon is not preaching, but worse than if he should read a homily.

. . . What a shame is this, that the preachers should make preaching be despised! In Jeremiah xlviii. there is a curse upon them which do the business of the Lord negligently; if this curse do not touch them which do the chiefest business of the Lord negligently, it cannot take hold of any other. *Therefore, let every preacher first see how his notes do move himself, and then he shall have comfort to deliver them to others like an experienced medicine which himself hath proved.*" These are the words of the "silver-tongued" Puritan, Henry Smith. You will probably express a fear that you will break down if you attempt to speak in the way which has been recommended. Your fear does not deter me from repeating the advice. Break down in the right way, rather than succeed in the wrong one! Show yourself so deeply in earnest for the salvation of your hearers as to deliver yourself from the snare of so unworthy an apprehension; and if you should break down, pray God the Helper of the weak to make your failure a means of magnifying His own grace. When we are weak then are we strong. There is a breaking down which is mortifying to our personal vanity; there is another breaking down which brings us closely and tenderly to God, in humble and perfect trust. Are you not a servant of God? May you not draw from the fulness of His love? Will He not honor your secret labor with public success? Cease to think of yourself other than as the messenger of God, the ambassador of Jesus Christ; and you shall speak, probably with many technical imperfections, but with a simplicity and power which must do good to your hearers. The words of a celebrated writer are so appropriate to this point, that I am sure you will excuse the length of the quotation for the sake of the nobility and pertinence of the sentiment:—

"There are two ways of regarding a sermon, either as a human composition, or a Divine message. If we look upon it entirely as the first, and require our clergymen to finish it with their utmost care and learning, for our better delight, whether of ear or intellect, we shall necessarily be led to expect much formality and stateliness in its delivery, and to think that all is not well if the pulpit have not a golden fringe round it, and a goodly cushion in front of it; and if the sermon be not fairly written in a black book, to be smoothed upon the cushion in a majestic manner before beginning. All this we shall duly come to expect; but we shall at the same time consider the treatise thus prepared as something to which it is our duty to listen without restlessness for half an hour or three-quarters, but which, when that duty has been decorously performed, we may dismiss from our minds in happy confidence of being provided with another when it shall be necessary. But if once we begin to regard the preacher, whatever his faults, as a man sent with a message to us, which it is a matter of life or death whether we hear or refuse; if we look upon him as set in charge over many souls in danger of ruin, and having allowed to him but an hour or two in the seven days to speak to them; if we make some endeavor to conceive how precious these hours ought to be to him, a small vantage on the side of God after his flock have been exposed for six days together to the full weight of the world's temptation, and he has been forced to watch the thorn and the thistle springing up in their hearts, and to see what wheat has been scattered there snatched from the wayside by this wild bird and the other; and at last, — when, breathless and weary with the week's labor, they give him this interval of imperfect and languid hearing, he has but thirty minutes to get at the separate hearts of a thousand men, to convince them of all their weaknesses, to shame them for all their sins, to warn them of all their dangers, to try by this way and that to stir the hard fastenings of those doors where the Master himself has stood and knocked yet none opened, and to call at the entrance of those dark streets where wisdom herself has stretched forth her hands and no man regarded; thirty minutes to raise the dead in; — let us but once understand and feel this, and we shall look with changed eyes upon that frippery of gay furniture about the place from which the message of judgment must be delivered, which either breathes upon the dry bones that they may live, or, if ineffectual, remains recorded in condemnation, perhaps against the utterer and listener alike, but assuredly against one of them; we shall not so easily bear with the silk and gold upon the seat of judgment, nor with ornament of oratory in the mouth of the messenger; we shall wish that his words may be simple, even when they are sweetest, and the place from which he speaks like a marble rock in the desert, about which the people have gathered in their thirst."*

Let us hear the words of this strange but friendly watchman, and go resolutely and trustfully in the direction which they indicate. You will observe that the whole of my advice has proceeded upon the recognition of special occasions upon which the use of the manuscript may be justified; occasions, for example, on which the preacher may be addressing not only his equals but his superiors in culture and information, or occasions which demand a high effort in criticism or controversy. There may, too, be occasions on which it is important to restrain all passion, and to give a judicial statement of a difficult subject. Nay, more, I will go even further, and freely allow that a settled minister, whose duty it is to teach as well as to preach, may now and again ask his people to listen to an essay or a series of essays upon doctrines which they may be advanced enough to understand and appreciate. All this, however, is very different from the regular work of the ordinary ministry, and it is to this regular work alone that the most of my remarks have been directed.

*John Ruskin, "Stones of Venice," vol. ii., chap. 1, § 12, 13, 14.

You will of course remind me that Dr. Chalmers read his sermons, and that several eminent men are in the habit of doing the same. Quite so; but though Dr. Chalmers read, it does not follow that all who read are Dr. Chalmerses. Don't be startled at the suggestion that Dr. Chalmers and the eminent men referred to cannot in my opinion justly be called *preachers!* Call them effective *readers* of eloquent addresses; call them dignified or vehement *repeaters* of elaborate dissertations; but *preachers* in the apostolic sense of the term they certainly ought not to be called. They read well; their intensity was in their favor, so was their calm dignity; but they were not *preachers.* Peter and Paul were preachers; Knox and Bunyan were preachers; Wesley and Whitefield were preachers; Christmas Evans and John Elias were preachers; — may their mantle fall upon our rising ministry!

V.

SENSATIONAL PREACHING.

From the tenor of the last letter you may possibly infer that I am in favor of what is known as sensational preaching. Before contesting the justness of your inference, we must clearly understand what we respectively mean by that ambiguous expression. If you ask whether I am in favor of *sensationless* preaching, my answer will be a prompt and emphatic negative, but you will not be justified in regarding this negative as committing me to an affirmative upon the question now to be discussed. What do you mean by the term "sensational preaching"? I presume that you do not employ the expression abstractly, but that you have in your mind certain positive illustrations to which you refer as embodying its meaning. Unless I know what these illustrations are, I shall be arguing the question at a disadvantage. At the outset, therefore, I must be allowed to cross-examine you a little. By sensational preaching do you mean a kind of pulpit mountebankism, in which the irreverent mountebanks play all sorts of grotesque and ridiculous tricks, pulling off their coats, swaggering from side to side of the pulpit, setting up what they are pleased to call penitent forms, and treating with contempt all the decencies of public worship? You cannot seriously ask me whether I approve of such monstrous profanity. Like yourself, I detest such wicked exhibitions with all my heart. By sensational preaching do you mean a screaming noise, "an idiot's tale, full of sound and fury signifying nothing"? Then I am sure you will not attempt to degrade my understanding by asking whether I approve of it. By sensational preaching do you mean an incoherent raving about things in general and nothing in particular; a perversion of every text; an insult of common sense; a recital of anecdotes which are untrue, and a use of illustrations which are unmeaning? Is this the sort of thing you describe by the term "sensational preaching"? If so, I need not put my indignant answer into words. I would even say with Lord Bacon, "God forbid that every man who can take unto himself boldness to speak an hour together in a church, upon a text, should be admitted for a preacher, though he mean never so well." Boldness is not always moral courage; it is sometimes mere impudence, and only thought to be religious because it reaches the point of irreligion. Lord Bacon well says: "It may be justly thought, that amongst many causes of atheism, which are miserably met in our age; as schisms and controversies, profane scoffings in holy matters, and others; it is not the least that divers do adventure to handle the word of God which are unfit and unworthy." Today there are undoubtedly many who set themselves up to preach, who ought to become scholars in the infant classes of Sunday-schools, and who could be refused admission into those useful institutions only on the ground of discouraging the scholars by their ignorance, and corrupting them by their bad manners. They are wanting in every claim to respect; their emptiness, their vanity, their hilarious animalism, which mistakes a good digestion for Divine inspiration, their contempt of men whose shoe-latchets they are not worthy to unloose, their vulgarity which is only rendered harmless by its disgusting and repulsive intensity, must always mark such men as reckless intruders upon holy ground, and condemn them to the censure of all earnest and thoughtful people. I commit myself to this opinion with the full consent of my judgment: at the same time I cannot pause here as if the case were complete; there are other points which must be considered: there are discriminations to be marked; and in the discharge of this remaining duty our views may perhaps come into sharp collision.

If I look at the ministry of our Lord Jesus Christ, it was undoubtedly, in the highest and best sense, sensational. "The people were astonished at His doctrine, for He taught them as one having authority and not as the scribes." Such a ministry must have produced a sensation. "And they were all amazed, insomuch that they questioned among themselves, saying, What thing is this? what new doctrine is this? And immediately His fame spread abroad throughout all the region round about Galilee." You cannot regard this as a *sensationless* ministry. "And all bare Him witness, and wondered at the gracious words which proceeded out of His mouth. . . . They were astonished, and said, Whence hath this man this wisdom, and these mighty works? . . . Never man spake like this man. . . . They were astonished at His doctrine, for His word was with power. . . . And they were all amazed, and spake among themselves, saying, "What a word is this!" Can we have any doubt that such a ministry was sensational? Now we are called to preach the same word, and are distinctly promised that our Lord himself shall be with us alway. With such a doctrine and such a fellowship, how can we content ourselves with a spiritless ministry? We may be endued with power from on high, and have grace poured into our lips; we have an inspired volume to expound, and an inspiring Spirit to open our understanding and teach us the word of wisdom and power; why then should not our hearers say, "Did not our hearts burn within as he opened to us the Scriptures?" You will remind me of the difference between the disciple and his Lord, and I listen to the suggestion reverently; but let me remind you in return that our Lord thoroughly identifies Himself with His servants: He works in them; He has given them the Holy Ghost for the express purpose of leading them into all truth; all His influence is upon their side; they are the subjects of his intercession; He visits them in their holiest hours, and carries them forever as the burden of His tenderest love; should they not then be mightier than their enemies, and bring with them into the sanctuary the power of an endless life? We are right in believing that we can never carry the Lord's omnipotence in our poor dying hands, yet let us try not how *unlike* our Lord we can be, and yet be His ministers, but rather let us plead with Him until He makes us conquerors and princes in His kingdom. I cannot doubt the largeness of His answer to the prayer of ambitious love. It must touch Him to the heart to see one of His redeemed flock spending day and night in prayer, that he, a saved and thankful sinner, may be taught the wisdom of winning souls! Can the Lord withhold His chief blessing for such a suppliant? Will He not clothe him with power, and give him the rod with which rocks may be broken and seas be divided? We have restrained prayer before God; we have not gone to Him as if we would take His kingdom by violence; we have brought the least of our vessels to the fountain of His grace; and it is no wonder that our ministry has been without power and without signs following. May I ask you to beware of the dangerous place, where our feet well-nigh slipped?

If we turn to apostolic history, we find a ministry that was undoubtedly sensational. "These that have turned the world upside down have come hither also. . . . Long time abode they speaking boldly in the Lord, which gave testimony unto the word of his grace. . . . My speech and my preaching was not with enticing words of man's wisdom, but in demonstration of the Spirit and of power. . . . Our gospel came not unto you in word only, but also in power, and in the Holy Ghost, and in much assurance. . . . And now, Lord, behold their threatenings, and grant unto Thy servants, that with all boldness they may speak Thy word, by stretching forth Thine hand to heal, and that signs and wonders may be done by the name of Thy holy Child Jesus." Such a ministry must have been marked by extreme excitement, must have been sensational in an unparalleled degree. Of course it will be answered that the power of working miracles has been withdrawn, and that we address ourselves to a civilization which was unknown to the apostles. Let this be granted, and what then? This is not a question as to *the particular signs* which should follow our ministry, but whether our ministry should produce an appropriate effect upon our hearers. Should our words be heard as an idle tale, or as the messages of God? Should our preaching be languid or fervent? Should our ministry lie remote from the common experience of the world, or should it fall closely upon the whole daily life of our people? Should we preach merely as if we had learned a lesson, or as if we had seen God face to face, and received a message from his lips? We give but a poor account of the failure of our ministry when we say that the gift of miracles is withdrawn, and that the times have changed. Our complaint conveys the impression that Jesus Christ himself has changed, and that the truth is no longer what it was. If the times have changed, our ministry should be adapted to the altered circumstances; upon the indifference which may have lulled the public mind we should pour the terrors and threatenings of the Lord; in the hearing of the luxurious and effeminate we should preach the doctrine of the Cross; and on the attention of the worldling and the scoffer we should force the realities and claims of eternity. The gospel can be adapted to all ages; we believe that to the end of the world it will be the power of God unto salvation; and we are called to be watchmen, taking note of the signs of the times, and changing our voice with the varying aspects of the age. The tokens which accompany the preaching of the gospel, as the seal of God, may not be precisely the same in any two centuries; but the gospel itself is the same for ever, and I cannot but feel that as ministers we should look for the special token of Divine favor which may be adapted to the peculiar circumstances under which we labor. If we are faithful servants, God will not withhold His witness; and though that witness may not be given as fire upon Carmel, or as the signs and wonders of the apostolic age, it shall be so obviously accorded in the quickening and spiritual growth of our hearers as to leave no doubt that God himself is our inspiration and strength.

Passing from apostolic times, and looking into the lives of men who have done most to establish the character and power of the Christian pulpit, it will be found that they have been what may be justly called *sensational preachers*. Look, for example, at the case of Whitefield. "I hardly ever knew him," says Cornelius Winter, "finish a discourse without weeping more or less; his voice was often interrupted by his affections; and such was the scope he gave to his feelings sometimes, that he exceedingly wept, stamped loudly and passionately, and was frequently so overcome that for a few seconds you would suspect he never could recover. As soon as he was seated in his chair, nature demanded relief, and gained it by a vast discharge from the stomach usually, with a considerable quantity of blood, before he was at liberty to speak." I am not to be supposed to regard this as a model which young ministers should adopt; each man must of course work according to his temperament; yet he should in my opinion earnestly try the effect of discipline upon a temperament which is likely to make his ministry gloomy and frigid. Take away the element of joy from the gospel, and what is left? The gospel itself is then destroyed. Whitefield's spirit was stirred within him; the cold message never could have come from his tongue of fire; "in Europe, in America, on board ship, in the workhouse, in the jail, in the hall of nobility, in the parish church or dissenting chapel, in the street, the market place, or bowling green, pressing the gospel on the attention of soldiers, mariners, emigrants, outcasts, culprits, lords, and wits, and mixed multitudes, the man was the same, and his object was one — to save souls." When he returned to Bristol after a short absence, "the people blessed him as he passed along the streets. Though preaching five times a week, he could not appease the eager crowds. It was difficult for him to make his way through them to the pulpit. Some climbed upon the roof of the church, others hung upon the rails of the organ loft. . . . When he preached his farewell sermon, the irrepressible feelings of his hearers broke out into sobs and tears all over the house. They followed him weeping into the street. They kept him busy the next day, from early morning till midnight, in comforting or counselling them, and he had to escape from their importunities secretly, during the night, for London." And when he reached London, "constables were stationed at the door to restrain the multitude of hearers; churches were crowded on week days, and on the autumnal Sunday mornings the streets were thronged before dawn with people lighting their way by lanterns to hear him."* Or take the case of Joseph Alleine, the celebrated author of an "Alarm to the Unconverted." His biographer, the Rev. Charles Stanford, says: "'The king's business requireth haste,' was his constant feeling, and he could not stay to study the structure of sentences while dying men were waiting for the word of life. Had the young preacher of St. Mary's been advised to think more of verbal refinement, he would probably have replied in language like that of John Owen, 'Know that you have to do with a person, who, provided his words do but express the sentiments of his mind, entertains a fixed

* Stevens's History of Methodism, vol. i., pp. 89, 90.

and absolute disregard for all elegance and ornaments of speech.' His addresses had far higher elements of excellence. They all breathed a winning tenderness, and all revealed an amazing power of rapid, homely, shattering appeal. The thoughts were all impetuous with a rush of fresh and glowing life; and though there was the prophet's rough mantle, there was also his chariot of fire. Every meaning was clear, every stroke told, every gesture seemed to speak, — *vividus vultus, invidi oculi, vividæ manus, denique omnia vivida.* One of his hearers tells us that 'he never preached without a long expostulation with the impenitent, vehemently urging them to come to some good resolve before he and they parted, and to make their choice for life or death, expressing his great unwillingness to leave the subject till he could have some assurance that he had not fought against sin as one that beateth the air; and that much of his power arose from the point and seasonableness of his words, spoken as they were with an intimate knowledge of the individual cases of those who formed his auditory.' There was piercing directness; the shafts of living Scripture flew straight to their intended mark, and each swift sentence had an aim clear as had the arrow found on the ancient battle-field, bearing the motto, 'For Philip's eye.' . . . . With shouting voice, flashing eye, and a soul on fire with love, he proclaimed a completed and gratuitous salvation to all who were willing to accept it. The Spirit of God gave his message great effect, and multitudes, through all the days of heaven, will remember Taunton Magdalene as the place where they first beheld that great sight, — 'the Lamb of God who taketh away the sin of the world!'" Was this sensationless preaching? Take another illustration. Of William Burns, the missionary to China, it is said: "While preaching for his father, and very solemnly pressing upon his auditors the immediate acceptance of Christ, the whole of the vast assembly were overpowered; the Holy Spirit seemed to come down as a mighty rushing sound, and to fill the place: very many were that day struck to the heart; the sanctuary was filled with distressed and inquiring souls." Frederick William Robertson cannot have been a sensationless preacher: "It was always as great a mental exertion to recall as to think out a sermon; and he was frequently unable, if he waited till Monday, to write out the notes of what he had delivered on Sunday, unless it had been partially written beforehand. After some of his most earnest and passionate utterances he has said to a friend, 'Have I made a fool of myself?'" We ought to be very sure, in condemning sensational preaching, that we do not condemn such men as these; for while they are not by any means to be classed with the grotesque pretenders described at the beginning of this letter, they certainly cannot be classed with the heartless formalists who have turned the gospel into a metaphysical enigma, or a lofty speculation which has little or nothing to do with the sin and sorrow of the world.

This view of the subject permits a natural reference to what may be termed emotional preaching. I have a strong conviction that our sermons should be more and more marked by deep Christian *feeling*. The subject is one of extreme delicacy, without question; for nothing is more odious than an affectation of pathos, and nothing more likely to be resented than an artificial attempt upon the emotions of our hearers. You will not, however, understand me as advocating anything so hypocritical and abominable, so I need not waste your time in fencing my position. I wish to draw your attention to the suggestion that the emotion of our sermons is not equal to their information. At this moment, for example, there is lying before me a volume of really able sermons, in which I have not found one touch of natural pathos. The sentences have been carefully constructed; there is no appearance of any word having been hastily adopted; the logic is good;

the theology is sound: yet it would almost appear that either the preacher had no heart, or he preached to hearers who had none. Throughout the whole production there is a cold scholastic air; and in the effort after scientific precision the emotions have been quite overlooked. Surely this is not *Christian* preaching; it is vigorous and even eloquent talk *about* Christianity, but the spirit of sympathy, tenderness, and anxious importunity is not in it; the anatomy is good, but where is the loving and earnest *life?* There is, too, in these sermons a decidedly controversial tone; the preacher is always on the defensive: an evil spirit seems to be looking at him, and constantly threatening an assault; consequently the spirit of criticism is excited in the hearers, and one feels tempted to say, "Well, if he is going to be so desperately logical as all this, we must watch for his tripping." The hearer is never allowed to *rest;* his anxieties are stimulated; and even when the preacher ventures to assure him that the ground is safe, he gives the assurance in a tone which suggests that after all there is a little reason for uneasiness. In this way the gospel ceases to be good tidings, and becomes an unprofitable controversy. Is this right? Should not logic lead to something better than itself? If we fall short of love, do we not fail of the chief end of our ministry? Let us think of Jesus Christ, who, when He came near the city, wept over it; and let us be mindful of Paul, whose argumentative power has never been denied, who said, "many walk, of whom I have told you often, and tell you now even weeping, that they are the enemies of the cross of Christ," and who ceased not to warn his hearers day and night with *tears*. The gospel is adapted to the heart of the world; it seeks to bind up the broken-hearted, and comfort all that mourn, and therefore should be preached in a spirit kindred with its own. A harsh controversial statement of its doctrines may gain the preacher a reputation as a skilful debater, but it will never give him the high position of an apostle of Jesus Christ.

Perhaps I shall not have a better opportunity than in this connection of referring to a fallacious analogy which is sometimes attempted by the supporters of a very questionable sensationalism. It has been complained that the minister does not often compare favorably with the barrister; the appeals of the former are said to be inferior to those of the latter, and the effect is considered to suffer proportionately. Without going into the argument which might be justly founded upon the difference of subjects which engage the attention of the respective speakers, it may be enough to refer to two or three points which destroy the tenableness of the analogy. Are our hearers bound upon oath to listen to us, and to give their verdict before leaving the church? Set a barrister to expound an act of parliament eighteen hundred years old; let him address the jury upon it twice every week in the year; let each juror pay five shillings a quarter for a seat in the jury-box; let the barrister call upon the jury for a monthly collection to enable other barristers to expound the same act of parliament to other juries; when the court room falls out of repair, let the jury be called upon to pay for its restoration; and when the barrister has thus put himself upon an outside equality with the minister, let him have five years' work, then five more; let him double the ten and add five, and then we shall see how he compares for freshness, variety, and power with a painstaking minister of Jesus Christ.

VI.

THE HOMILIST: MAN AND BOOK.

Skeleton is a word which means different things to different people. When a timid lady says it, she shudders as if a cold hand had touched her heart; when a needy preacher says it, he glows with thankful delight. To him that hideous word means wealth; and the more other people are repelled by it, the more he secretly rejoices. You may have heard of a minister who, on being told of a volume of sermons which he had not seen, exclaimed, "I have preached three of the volumes, and now that there is a fourth, I feel as if I had suddenly fallen on great spoil." This was candid, if not ingenious and original. Now, without for a moment supposing that *you* will ever be a needy preacher, I may take the liberty of pointing out one or two sources of supply which are not unknown to many respectable brethren of large digestive and respiratory power. As the projector of the *Pulpit Analyst*, its editor for the first two years, and its most voluminous contributor up to the present moment, I may be permitted to say a word on its behalf. Probably its design surpasses its execution; yet, as furnishing *variety* of preaching, it is not unworthy of your attention. I am not aware that any one method predominates; it contains both native and foreign products, and so supplies the most varied illustrations of homiletic treatment.

Do you know David Thomas, of Stockwell, — editor of the *Homilist?* If you do not know him personally, you will find it to your advantage to know him editorially. The first time I heard him preach he was in his own pulpit, conducting an ordinary morning service. Immediately on his opening the vestry door, I was struck with his noble, animated, and expressive countenance, and felt predisposed towards him. David Thomas is a man, — physically and mentally, every inch a *man*. Beyond many even of his most flourishing brethren, he makes "a fair show in the flesh": his great head is like a rock; his immense black eyes are full of gentle lustre; and his mouth, if not very elaborately chiselled, is not without pleasant lines. There is nothing secret in all the open sunny face; perhaps, if anything, it is too open; there are no permanent shadows in which power may be *hiding* itself, no cavernous marks as if the soul had often been driven back upon itself and compelled to look out upon the world from secret places; the soul rather seems as if it had generally had its own way, — so boldly and shiningly does it express its dominance in the expansive and unsuspecting face. Yet the countenance is not without pensiveness; the eye has occasional shadowings which to me looked as if the soul was not altogether a stranger to melancholy, — as if now and again it saw the corruption, the distress and poverty, which lie under the world's fairest exterior. I can quite believe this to be the case. David Thomas has not forgotten other people's darkness in his own sunshine; to him human life is not altogether a wedding festival; he occasionally hears other sounds than the clash of rejoicing bells, and can heave a sigh when other men cannot understand his emotion. Understand? Why, whenever were such men as David Thomas understood? Sparrows cannot understand eagles, — can the minnow understand leviathan? David Thomas is intellectually qualified to be at the head of his denomination, and if his sectarianism had been equal to his genius, he would long before now have been as officially conspicuous as he has been mentally influential. How very hard those excellent servants of the world, called *committee men*, must have winked, not to have seen David Thomas! They must have blindfolded one another; they must have sealed one another's eyes; they must have actually put each other's eyes out! So much the worse for the committee men, — not for David Thomas! He has a most cordial dislike of societies, resolutions, amendments, and those infinite nuisances called sub-committees; and, as a reward for his dislike, he has been allowed to live without secretarial patronage and official promotion. Happily, the world is the better for this ostracism; David Thomas has exerted a greater influence (often indirect and unacknowledged) upon the British pulpit than any living man with whose name I am acquainted; and his influence will live for good when those who have done their best to keep him in the background are remembered no more forever.

What, then, you will say, — is David Thomas without fault, the perfect man and the upright, whom we are called upon by high authority to mark and behold? Probably, seeing that he is only a man, there may be somewhat of imperfection about him; it would not be unnatural, would it? David Thomas is human enough to be imperfect, but perfect enough to be above the reproach of many who are hardly human. Let us allow, for example, that he finds it very difficult to adopt the step of intellectually little men, and that he is impatient of their contradiction, their tardiness, or their timidity, — what then? Undoubtedly all this may be said justly of David Thomas; he *cannot* dwarf himself to the measure of ordinary society; he delights to take wing for the open firmament of heaven, while others may be content to sit in the window of a select conventicle; he aspires to know the universe, while others spend their lives in studying a footprint. This necessarily removes him from the common courses of the world, — it isolates and individualizes him, and gives him an appearance of scornful self-sufficiency which is really not in his nature. Let us further allow that when an idea fully lays hold of his mind he cannot accommodate himself to the cautiousness which suggests doubts of its practicability; he condemns it as little, contemptible, puerile, and absurd; he uses hard words about those who do not instantly accept his propositions, and work for them with an enthusiasm which ignores all difficulty and danger; let us allow, too, that in referring to his purposes and enterprises he employs a great many capital letters and a great many notes of admiration; — I grant all this, but what of it? We must get behind it all, if we would know the man; we must know how much of it is essence and how much accident, and not commit ourselves to the fool's error of mistaking a flourish of the hand for a habit of the soul. I have sometimes felt that David Thomas spoke with impetuous, unreflecting scorn of a certain class of his brethren; he had no patience with them; he derided them, and did not always stop to give them their due. On the other hand, he has been most generous in his recognition of incipient power, and done much towards its development; he has sought out the "village Hampdens" and "mute, inglorious Miltons," and encouraged them to put forth their strength; and no man has spoken more stimulatingly to some who have labored under difficulties which had daunted and unnerved them. Both these considerations must be taken into account in estimating the man. Having looked at them both myself, I give it as my opinion that the generosity of David Thomas far exceeds his severity. In a few rare cases indeed his generosity must have been regarded as somewhat embarrassing; as, for example, when he has extemporized a eulogium upon a Welsh minister who may have unexpectedly presented himself in the Stockwell congregation. The Welsh brother has occasionally been portrayed as a prodigy, "full of poetic fire," "his soul ringing with the music of his native hills"; the unhappy man has been described as melodious, tuneful, philosophic, and eloquent, overflowing with pathos and burning with zeal, and has then been publicly asked to preach on the spot! The martyr has had no escape,—preach he must! In two cases out of three his sermon has probably been one long stammer,—one continuous grotesque contradiction of every word which the pictorial doctor has said of him! What then? Why, of course, the doctor instantly replied to every disappointed objector that the preacher was all that had been said of him—*in Welsh!* To this neat answer no Stockwell man could ever return a contradictory reply. On this side of David Thomas's character no doubt there is a fault, but let him that is without sin cast the first stone.

Dr. Thomas's brain is remarkable for capacity, quality, and strength. Phrenologists would assign him an extraordinary *central* brain, giving evidence of unusual analytic and metaphysical power. This would be just, though Dr. Thomas has cultivated his analytic gift more highly than his metaphysical faculty. Probably this has arisen from the necessity which his work has imposed upon him; his *thinking* power has always been employed in working out results for the pulpit, rather than in abstract metaphysics, though in so working he has often, almost invariably indeed, worked quite as much as a psychologist as a theologian. Possibly Dr. Thomas has not had the advantage of the severest educational drill; possibly also his education has developed his more urgent faculties at the expense of faculties which, though latent, were neither narrow nor feeble. Circumstances may have compelled him to abandon purely speculative philosophy, and to turn his attention to concrete effects; yet even under such compulsion he has shown that if he had not been the first of textual analysts, he would have been amongst the foremost of abstract thinkers. His metaphysics are not scholastic; in fact, it may be doubted whether he is more than ordinarily read in formal metaphysics, because he always works from intuition rather than information, and his writings generally convey the impression that he owes less to acquisition than to nature. David Thomas seldom sees truths in their individuality; one truth is related to another; no principle works alone; the many worlds are one universe; the many waters are one sea; and all the lights which brighten the firmament are referable to one central and everlasting splendor: to discover their relations, to set them in order, and to show how they converge in glory upon the throne of God, and thence operate for the good of all creatures, is David Thomas's chief joy.

Yet David Thomas cannot be justly described as *imaginative*. I have spoken of him taking wing for the open firmament of heaven, and the figure is not exaggerated; yet while he is on the wing he is rather looking at the relations and proportions of things than singing "songs without words"; when he does sing, it is at the end of an argument; when he dreams, it is after the fashion of a syllogism. It may be doubted whether, in the proper sense of the term, he has much fancy; there is a finality about most of his statements which shows that he has reached his limit; there is no colored haze beyond, which may be concealing continents or seas; the reader feels that he can go all the way without ever losing sight of clear blue sky. David Thomas never ascends alone, striking with strong wing into circles inaccessible to every visitant except dreaming and contemplative fancy; he is often above, but always on well-known highways; the cloud never receives him out of our sight, nor does he ever hear things which it is not lawful to utter; he utters all that he hears, — in inspiring and tuneful language indeed, yet capable of being written in common ink. It may be want of expression rather than want of thought, but certainly David Thomas, from the one cause or the other, though fond of poetic language, is never absolutely carried away by poetic inspiration. He cannot poise himself on his wings and linger long in the light, as if detained by sights which held him by some subtle enchantment;

we can hear the flapping of his wings, and see him hurrying along the courses of the wind; and while we admire his strength, we cannot but feel that he has not trespassed upon the highest fields of poetry. David Thomas is characterized by ideality rather than by pure imagination; many of his homilies indeed are flecked with choice colorings of quoted poetry, but his own writing was never dictated by visions of the night; he would cross-examine the spirit of dreams, and know how far the stranger could justify himself by valid human reasoning. Nor is all this to be regretted. The servant of Jesus Christ should bear a plain message to the world; he has to confront the fact of sin with the fact of salvation; he has to answer the questionings of the heart with the revelations of God. In doing this work, Dr. Thomas speaks with the most modern accent, and never with "the holy tone" which the the Scotch desiderated in the preaching of Whitefield. His preaching is the New Testament translated into the language of to-day, — choice enough for the scholar, robust enough for the man of common business.

David Thomas will be known to a remote posterity by his great work, *The Homilist.* To that work he has been faithful through many years of hard toil and anxious care. The slovenly man (for he is slovenly in some things, notwithstanding his supposed liking for good tailoring) issued the first seven volumes without any *date*, — no date on the title-page, — no date at the end of the preface! The thing is so unbusiness-like as to be almost incredible. That David Thomas of Stockwell should never have thought of putting a date to his work is quite conceivable by all who know him; that the somnolent house of Ward & Co. should have omitted the date is not surprising; but how the *printers* came to omit the usual MDCCC., etc., is not easy of explanation. The omission is of great consequence, and will be increasingly so with the lapse of time. Suppose that a minister shall fifty years hence take up a volume of the

Homilist, wishing to know when it was written, that he may compare it with the current literature of its own day, — how perplexed he will be! He will not know from the volume itself whether it was written ten years ago, twenty, or fifty. This is to be regretted, for it is one of the little wheels on which good machinery so much depends.

The *Homilist* did not enjoy a very flourishing beginning. On the cover of one of the early numbers the despondent editor announced that it did "not pay," and that unless the circulation increased it must be given up. Happily the circulation *did* increase, and the *Homilist* has since, as a class magazine, commanded unexampled success. In my opinion this success has been honestly and most fully deserved. Nothing is due to trickery, sensationalism, or denominational prestige; all credit is due to perseverance, ability, and a happy adaptation of means to ends. Never was the saying "the laborer is worthy of his hire" more faithfully fulfilled than in the brightening and expanding history of the *Homilist;* nor has the saying "perseverance conquers obstacles" been more honorably exemplified than in the steadiness of its indomitable and fertile editor. When the *Homilist* made its appearance, men were becoming tired of dividing everything in heaven and on earth into first, second, and third, with three subdivisions under each head, three points of application, and with "finally, one word more, and lastly" for a melancholy peroration. At that dark time any brother who could make a suggestion bordering upon novelty was privily called for by the wise men, and diligently inquired of concerning the birth of the child. Under the old sermonic form scores of healthy congregations had languished and died; deacons had dropped into syncope, and treasurers had been found again and again with both hands in a state of catalepsy. The triangular division of the intellectual universe had thus been most ruinous in its effects, and the church sighed for a variation of the geometrical form. No doubt great boldness was required to beard the tyranny of traditionalism; the man who profanely declared that any text could be viewed in *four* aspects, and discussed without a single subdivision, would have been in peril of an attack from the very men who had been sighing for a change; what then would be thought of the adventurous young minister at Stockwell, who began his new magazine with "*A Homily on the Wants of the World, and the Weakness of the Church*," and concluded the first number with "Healthful Rays of Genius" from *Plato*, and *Carlyle?* What *could* be thought of such a man but that he was dying of some heretical pest, and corrupting the morals of the rising ministry? Elderly ministers bought the magazine as it were under protest, on the principle of the pious Quaker, who went to the races "just to see if any of our people were there"; college professors slyly hid it in their desks, and peeped at it stealthily while the students were (mistakenly) supposed to be absorbed in gerund-grinding, — yes, quite mistakenly, for the students themselves had put their pence together, after the fashion of a copper round robin, so that no one could tell who *began* it, and procured a copy of the dangerous magazine, which they read with most immoral avidity. "*That* was the sort of thing," they impetuously declared, without waiting for the soberer judgment of the college committee, or of a sub-committee appointed to "report on the *whole* case"; and forthwith every man of them threw his triangular "skeletons" into the fire, and began the higher geometry. The awakening churches said they were *startled;* the elder orthodoxy was *pained;* and the men who had comfortably slept for years through "first the fact stated, second the doctrine implied, and third the lessons which may be inferred," adopted a tone which in general terms may be described as *threatening*. This resentment was neither unaccountable nor unpardonable: it was not unaccountable, for masculine pewholders like to know that their own sentiments are being promulgated from the pulpit in the very words which they have used to their wives and children "many and many a time"; it is both comfortable and complimentary, as well as indicative of theological stability: in the next place, the resentment was not altogether unpardonable, for sentimental pew-holders who have shed rivers of tears over the tender words, "How doth the little busy bee," and "Twinkle, twinkle, little star," naturally shudder at the paganism of "instinctive beliefs," "moral intuitions," and "the empirical conscience." Such shuddering is in no wise to be wondered at; it is the protest of outraged nature against all new ideas and novel words, and on that account is to be highly esteemed.

In issuing the second volume of the *Homilist*, the editor felt "it due to those who take this volume in their hand with the intent to purchase, to declare some of its omissions, that there may be none of the regret of disappointment after the bargain." The "omissions" are thus stated: "First, the book has *no finish;* secondly, the book has *no denominationalism;* thirdly, the book has *no polemical theology.*" The statement is not properly qualified. As a rule, the opening homily of each number *has* "finish," it is elaborate, continuous, and complete; as to the second omission, it is generally safe to infer that when any man disclaims denominationalism he is about to constitute *himself* into a denomination, or else he has degenerated into the malevolent sectarianism of no sect; the third omission is stated pretty accurately, though the book is by no means without a controversial tone. The catholic editor does not agree with everybody; he can adopt an attitude either defensive or defiant, though as a general rule he is peacefully disposed towards those who let him alone. David Thomas is a lover of peace; he would knock a man down for peace; he would go to war for peace; no wonder, therefore, he avoids "polemical theology." It is a singular fact that the man who has written so many new sermons has never written a new *preface!* Year by year he has said, "As the old key-note will still rule the melodies of the *Homilist*, and no new specific description is requisite, the preface may be again transcribed." I draw your attention to this circumstance, that I may candidly point out that David Thomas's *homiletic method is decidedly wanting in variety.* It is perfectly true that one preface will do forever. First of all, the text is made to yield a *subject*, thus: take the text, "That which hath been is now" (Eccles. iii. 16), and the *subject* is, "The impotency of time, or the eternally permanent amidst the constantly fluctuating"; or the text, "Then he which had received the one talent came," etc. (Matt. xxv. 24), and the *subject* is, "The non-use of power in the feeblest." This is David Thomas's method with every text; he does not seem able to move until he has wrought it into a wide generalization, and in the great majority of instances the generalization is not only wide, but legitimate and profound. Not only is the text itself a subject, but each head, even of the most severely analytic division, is also a theme. As an illustration, take the main outline of the subject, "The trial-bearing Force of Spiritual Religion": I. Spiritual religion engages the supreme attention of the soul under trial; II. Spiritual religion recognizes God's superintendence under trial; III. Spiritual religion identifies man's will with God's under trial. Or take the main outline of the subject, "The Pool of Siloam, or the world in miniature" (John v. 1–9): I. The human world is greatly afflicted; II. The human world has alleviating elements; III. The human world is pre-eminently selfish; IV. The human world has a glorious Deliverer. So unvarying is the substance of his method, that any careful reader of one volume of his homilies may almost infallibly predict how David Thomas would discuss any text. His homiletic mannerism is unchangeably fixed. He never surprises readers who have familiarized themselves with his style, by sudden variation of method, unexpected adventures of fancy, or whimsical adaptations of architecture; everywhere you find order, logic, and proportion; he is never so borne away by his first thought as to forget his second; when he begins his journey all his appointments are complete, and when he returns he has accomplished his whole purpose. The man of whom this can be justly said must have unusual self-control, and, according to his capacity, must have completeness and equality of mental power. Still, this rigid regularity does become monotonous; mile after mile of unchanging architecture, however massive and stately, wearies the eye, and from this continuity of formal excellence the constant reader of the *Homilist* undoubtedly suffers. He cannot but wish that a few texts at least should escape the suspicion of being cunning riddles to which David Thomas alone can suggest happy answers; he gets tired of the boundless stretch of small capitals and emphatic italics, and almost sighs for a little change in the treatment of subjects. David Thomas deals largely in "germs," but the germs are nearly all of one sort; it may be very depraved moral horticulture on my part, but I should certainly like to see a few deciduous plants among the evergreens, and even the evergreens themselves might be selected with a view to a vivid and effective interspersion of coloring. Why not mix the peach-colored flowers of the almond with the splendid golden alder or the purple-leaved Darwinii? Why not alternate the cypress with the cistus? Why this "boundless contiguity" of cedar?

Variety is quite as much wanted in the *language* as in the *planning* of the *Homilist*. As a general rule, the language of the *Homilist* is specially clear and strong: yet its range is limited; it is local rather than cosmopolitan, certainly not rich in allusion, and seldom equal to the thinking which it is intended to express.

We rarely get any idea of the author's *reading* from the variety of his language; we do not find from the gorgeousness of one homily that the writer began it after a long spell at *Burke*, nor from the riotous impetuosity of another that it was written under the inspiration of *Macaulay;* we never exclaim, "Here is the quaintness of Trapp, the splendor of Hall, the sublimity of Charnock, the delicacy of Taylor": we feel, and feel deeply, that the book which the writer knows most about is the last volume of the *Homilist* itself! We do not want quotation, but inspiration; not garlands and chaplets, but perfumes gathered from many gardens, the aroma of the world's genius. We deprecate the absurd criticism which censures one man because he is not another; but we admire the universality of mind which can never be satisfied with its own resources, but must, with self-misgiving and most emulous determination, intermeddle with all wisdom. It may be said, if Burke has a style of his own, and Macaulay, Shakspeare, and Scott, and each of the other immortal writers of English, why not David Thomas? There is no reason why David Thomas should not have his own style, nor is there any reason why he should not be continually enriching and refining his style. Moreover, his is not so much a style as a mere *habit;* in a literary point of view, it has more *form* than *life;* provided the words will barely *cover* his idea, he cares nothing for their efflorescence and coloring. This is not altogether to be admired. The careful writer will sometimes pause before electing either of two synonyms; he will look at the fine shading, he will study the balance and cadence of the syllables, that his thought may have all the advantage of perfect rhythm: the *preacher*, too, will "seek out acceptable words," remembering that even in his sacred office there are many opportunities of profiting by the canon: —

"True wit is nature to advantage dressed,—
What oft was thought, but ne'er so well expressed."

In a standing notice, prefixed to every monthly copy, the editor of the *Homilist* says, "We want things, not words." The notice is bold, but is it discriminating? Is it not true that in some cases words *are* things? Is it not also true that there is adaptation between thought and language, as between the king and his chariot? "There would seem at first sight to be no more in Milton's words than in other words. But they are words of enchantment. No sooner are they pronounced, than the past is present and the distant near. New forms of beauty start at once into existence, and all the burial-places of the memory give up their dead. Change the structure of the sentence: substitute one synonym for another, and the whole effect is destroyed."* Perhaps in penning this notice the sagacious editor was preparing friends among the critics of unrighteousness, that in the day of his exposure they might receive him into their houses; or perhaps he admired the conciseness, without thinking of the justness, of his notice.

This you will regard as a candid criticism, not I trust the less valuable because of its discrimination. David Thomas has done a great work, and if there be a fault or a flaw in it here and there, who can wonder? We must not forget that if he were to review *our* work, he might be able to show that there is more in it to censure than to admire; it should therefore be under a sense of our own imperfection that we offer an opinion upon the capabilities and services of another man. The name of David Thomas will increase in honor and influence, in proportion as the ministry increases in intelligence and vigor; and long after his noble countenance has ceased to brighten our assemblies, his noble thoughts will stimulate our minds: there may have been a little envious mist thrown about his earlier course, but there is before his name an honored and a splendid future.

* Macaulay.

"When first the sun too powerful beams displays,
It draws up vapors which obscure its rays;
But even those clouds at last adorn its way,
Reflect new glories and augment the day."

In my opinion, the time for the completion of the *Homilist* has fully come. It may now with advantage coalesce with the *Pulpit Analyst*,—giving it the prestige of a unique history, and leaving it to supply some omissions which mark the service even of the strongest minds.

From all this you will correctly infer that I advise you to procure the entire set of the *Homilist*, now extending, I suppose, to something like twenty volumes. This advice I do tender with most cordial urgency, under the assured conviction that no young minister can study its method without gaining very much, both in stimulus and instruction.

Since writing this critique I have seen David Thomas, after a lapse of nearly ten years. Some changes have taken place in his appearance; time has just begun to set its mark upon him; and whilst the old contagious buoyancy still abounds, there is a tenderer mellowness in many of his observations upon men and things. He is still sermonizing, and is still justly proud of his *Homilist;* with the simplicity of a little child he boldly declares that it is as good as ever; and if for a moment you doubt it, he is prepared to give half-a-dozen of its latest outlines, which undoubtedly prove that his right hand has not forgotten its cunning. Life and peace be to him in exceeding measure!

VII.

TEXTUAL DIVISIONS.

It may be convenient now, considering that you are expecting shortly to take your place on the college preachers' list, to give some attention to the various methods of treating texts, a subject which has occasioned much diversity of opinion, and on which no man can give a final judgment. All I can hope to do is to cite a few examples, and to point out where, according to my own ministerial experience, they appear either to succeed or fail in giving the most effective expression to the truth of the text. In approaching this work, allow me to put you on your guard against the temptation to make what are called *clever* sermons. The temptation appeals very powerfully to the youthful mind; there is much plausibility in it; it stimulates genius; it calls up individuality of thought; it takes a man off the common ground, and gives him a standing place of his own; — all these considerations will present themselves; and if you be taken unawares, they will vitiate and debase your ministry. The young preacher often looks for strange texts, and having announced them, gazes upon his congregation with an expression which signifies, "There! what could *you*, or what could any man but *myself*, make of a text like *that?* Now let me show you how clever I am!" You cannot tell how deeply your thoughtful hearers will be grieved by such eccentricity: it may please the idle-minded and the vain, but it will distress all who come to worship God, and receive His word at your lips. Have you any sermons upon particularly striking texts? Take a friend's advice, to put them into the fire. Don't think I am cruel; the advice is really kind, and you will probably thank me for it in less than ten years; let all such sermons go into the fire at once; the loss will be a gain, the sacrifice will be made up to you if you offer it with a good motive. As a servant of God, a chosen messenger of Jesus Christ, you have little or nothing to do with detached expressions, broken sentences, and perverted accommodations; your business is with the whole revealed counsel of God, and you should give yourself day and night to its prayerful and anxious study. This is your wealth and strength as a Christian minister. The Bible is not to be looked upon as a mere repository of texts collected for professional convenience; it is the Word of God, with a meaning and a purpose which you must earnestly seek to understand. We shall often be at a loss what to say to our people if we draw only upon our own resources; Saturday will find us empty-handed, Sunday will be a day of painful bondage, and Monday an occasion of heartless joy. On the other hand, if the word of Christ dwell in us richly in all wisdom (Col. iii. 16); if we can say with Jeremiah (xv. 16), "Thy words were found, and I did eat them, and Thy word was unto me the joy and rejoicing of mine heart"; if we can say with Job (xxiii. 12), "I have esteemed the words of His mouth more than my necessary food," we shall never be at a loss for messages both instructive and comforting. The Holy Spirit will magnify His own word; He will make His statutes the songs of His people in the house of their pilgrimage (Ps. cxix. 54), and clothe His ministers with the garments of zeal. You will see, then, that I am more anxious about your knowledge of the Bible as a whole, than about particular texts and skilful methods of division. Think what a weapon God has put into the hands of His servants! "The word of God is quick and powerful, and sharper than any two-edged sword, piercing even to the dividing asunder of soul and spirit, and of the joints and marrow, and is a discerner of the thoughts and intents of the heart" (Heb. iv. 12). What more do you require? Don't spend your time in extracting mere particles of steel from this great weapon; let every text be a handle by which you lift the whole instrument for the working out of a particular end. Don't regard your text as complete in itself; it is only one of a series. Carefully collate the whole class, and bring, not the text only, but the entire *truth* which it represents, to bear upon the mind and heart of your hearers. You cannot do this without patient study of the word; but it is by such patience that men become mighty in the Scriptures, and rich in heavenly wisdom. As I shall have occasion to recur to this subject in another connection, we may proceed to the secondary matter of texts and their division.

You have selected a text, — now what is your first business? Not how to *divide* it; not to consider what particular purpose it may be strained to serve; not how to exercise your ingenuity upon it; but *to find out its exact critical and doctrinal meaning.* Does it contain any words of doubtful etymology? Have any of the words ever been used in different senses? What is the bearing of all the parallel passages? What is the meaning which the Divine Spirit intended the words to convey? You must be clear upon all these points before you think of division or elaboration. First have the *truth*, and then set about its treatment. Having got the truth into the mind, next get it into the heart; pray for a deeper and tenderer love; beseech God to stimulate your affection for the truth, to make it your own by happy experience, to shed its light over your whole life, and to bring you altogether under its influence. In this way God will cause His truth to become as it were part of your very being; and when you preach it, there shall be evidence that instead of merely repeating a lesson, you are speaking from a believing and thankful heart. So long as the text is only an external object, your discourse will be artificial and powerless; when it becomes a living reality in your own spiritual experience, it will come to your hearers with simplicity and effect. Let it be understood, then, that in offering an opinion about homiletic outlines, I take for granted that we are agreed up to this point; we must be at one about the foundation, before we discuss the best methods of scaffolding. Enjoying and loving the truth, you wish to know how to preach it most clearly and usefully: on this basis let us talk together freely and at large.

Some divisions are mere commonplaces, others are distinct propositions, and others again are cumulative and logical. I am not prepared to say that any one of these is best; each has its advantages and its drawbacks. It is remarkable that Mr. Robertson's divisions are generally very tame, giving no idea whatever of the rich suggestiveness of his teaching. Take his sermon upon the faith of the centurion (Matt. viii. 10); his main divisions are — I. The faith which was commended, and II. The causes of the commendation. Probably the poorest preacher in the world could not have conceived a less promising outline, yet the sermon is instructive and pathetic. Again, in his sermon on *The early Development of Jesus* (Luke ii. 40), he gives as his plan — "In the text we read of a threefold growth, (I.) In strength, (II.) In wisdom, (III.) In grace"; a less original plan never introduced any sermon, yet the discourse is by no means wanting in novelty or freshness. In a discourse upon an incident in the life of Elijah (1 Kings xix. 4), he gives as his division — (I.) The causes of Elijah's despondency, and (II.) God's treatment of it. Who could make anything out of such a plan! Apparently Mr. Robertson set little by the formal division; the merest hint was enough. This method of division has been common in all ministries, irrespective of denominational training. In a sermon on *Religious Meditation* (Gen. xxiv. 63), Richard Watson, the distinguished Methodist preacher, gives as his outline —

(I.) The greatness of its objects, and (II.) Its moral advantages. In an eloquent sermon upon *Excitements to Missionary Effort* (Eccles. xi. 1–6), he has a very ordinary outline: (I.) A large and liberal benevolence is enjoined upon us; (II.) Some interesting motives to the exercise of benevolence are here set before us; (III.) Several objections are implied in the text; (IV.) We have some reasons for diligence and constancy. Another distinguished Methodist preacher, Dr. Beaumont, was often as inexpressive in his method of division; for example, on *The more excellent Sacrifice* (Heb. xi. 4), he says, "In bringing before you the character of Abel, our attention is required to the following considerations: (I.) He is the first of whom it was affirmed that he was justified by faith; (II.) He was the first of whom it was stated that he offered an acceptable sacrifice to God; (III.) He was the first personal type of Christ; (IV.) He was the first martyr for the truth; (V.) He was the first whose redeemed spirit entered heaven. Again, in his sermon on the *Joyful tidings by Angelic Messengers*, he says: "(I.) Let us consider the matter of the tidings brought by the angel unto the shepherds; (II.) The quality by which these tidings are characterized; (III.) The extent of application to which they are destined." In a sermon on *The Lamb of God* (John i. 36), Dr. Guthrie has this outline: (I.) Behold Christ before He came to this world; (II.) Behold Christ on earth, in His humiliation; (III.) Let this Lamb of God be the supreme Object of our desires, and the sole Object of our faith. On *The Christian's Faith* (Matt. xv. 29), the same eloquent preacher has this plan: (I.) Her earnestness is an example, as her success in an encouragement to us; (II.) Observe the trials to which Christ put her earnestness and faith. William Jay, of Bath, had the reputation of being a skilful divider of texts. Some of his divisions are very commonplace. In his sermon on *The Gospel Jubilee* (Lev. xxv. 10), he merely says, "Let me explain the nature of the jubilee, make some remarks upon the design of it, and examine what there is in the gospel to correspond with it." These may be taken as examples of the commonplace method; and for the eminent men who adopted it, no doubt it was sufficient. Their gift lay rather in elaboration than in analysis: if you have their genius, you may adopt their plan; but if *not*, you will do well to seek a more excellent way. I venture to think that the following outline, given to me by a friend who brings a rare analytic power to his pulpit preparation, is much superior to any yet quoted. The text is Exodus iii. 14; we have here (I.) *The chief inquiry of man as a responsible agent*,—who sends me? what is His name? what account shall I give of myself? (II.) *The highest revelation to man as a speculative thinker*, God's name, "I AM"; not *atheism*, for God Himself speaks; not *pantheism*, for God's personality is declared; not mere *deism*, for God descends to take an immediate interest in the affairs of men. (III.) *The highest authority of man as a moral worker*,—I AM hath sent me, I am *God's* servant; this is inspiration, this is power. Another friend has favored me with a striking outline upon Job xiv. 10: "Man dieth, and wasteth away; yea, man giveth up the ghost, and where is he?" (I.) If he was a good man, he is where he has long *desired* to be; (II.) If he was a good man, he is where he was *prepared* to be; (III.) If he was a good man, he is where he will forever desire to *remain*. On the other hand, if he was a bad man, then (I.) he is where he never really desired to be; (II.) where he was prepared to be; (III.) where he can never wish to remain. This is a very happy method of division; but its treatment requires great care, because there is a strong temptation to study the *form* rather than the *truth*, and thus to degenerate into mere *cleverness*. The same skilful friend has a sermon upon 1 Peter v. 7, "Casting all your care upon Him, for He careth for you," in which he figures every man as a traveller carrying three bundles: (I.) the past; (II.) the present; (III.) the future. The preacher takes down the three bundles, and examines them: the first is full of sins, unhappy memories, neglected duties, etc.; the second is full of the troubles of daily life, the deceitfulness of riches, worldly engagements, etc.; the third is full of fears, anxieties, apprehensions, etc. The preacher then exhorts his supposed traveller to cast all these cares upon Divine strength. The method of division by distinct propositions embodying the spirit of the narrative is instructive, and not difficult either of construction or remembrance. As an illustration, take the narrative of the journey of Abram, given in the 12th chapter of Genesis, and regard it as setting forth the journey of a good man through life: we may then affirm that in his journey through life the good man (I.) reverently listens to the Divine voice; (II.) reposes implicit faith in the sovereignty and fatherhood of God; (III.) maintains his faith by continual worship; (IV.) often finds his blessings associated with trials; and (V.) sometimes feels that his faith is tried more severely by the less than by the greater affairs of life. This method is illustrated in a sermon by Dr. McAll on "the nature and causes of that joy with which the good man hails the return of every season wherein it is his privilege to approach to the house of God, and to mingle in the engagements of the sanctuary." (I.) There he is warranted to expect the peculiar enjoyment of the Divine presence. (II.) The gratification thus expressed on approaching to the house of God springs also from the happiness of a near and intimate association with our brethren in all the exercises of united devotion. (III.) The truly pious man will delight in approaching to the house of the Lord, because of those sacred and solemn employments, so congenial with his best feelings, there awaiting him. (IV.) Because of the progressive improvement in all our character there constantly experienced. I need hardly point out the wordiness of these divisions, except to put you on your guard against it. Be concise. Try how many words you can remove without obscuring the sense which you intend to convey. Take a single sentence from Dr. McAll's sermon, and see how many of the words you can safely take away: "We have learned from Scripture, and rejoice in the noble sentiment, that heaven, even the heaven of heavens, cannot contain him: that is, perhaps, that if we should ascend through the nearer and more limited regions of existence from this speck of earth into those that rise in magnificence above, vast as they are, and ever widening on the view; if we should pass through the heavens that we behold studded with stars, and gleaming with all the brightness of the firmament, into the loftier and more ethereal realms beyond them, soaring still, and still stretching forward on the wing to others yet more distant and more exalted, which are the heavens to them, encircling them within their glowing sphere, beaming forth on them, as these on us, the splendors of the Deity;—and if, still untired, we should mount to the third heavens, those fields of magnificence and glory which are yet undiscovered and unknown, and wherein there shines no light of sun or star, no other radiancy but the pure emanations of the Godhead: even then should we not have arrived at an expanse sufficiently capacious to include and shut within itself the illimitable fulness of His being." There is a defiant challenge to your pruning-knife! What long words, what ambition, what panting haste, what redundant expression, what useless speculation! Dr. McAll says that the third heavens "are yet undiscovered and unknown," yet he speaks of them as if he had seen them; how, if they are *undiscovered*, he knows that there is neither sun nor stars in them, and how, if they are *unknown*, he has come by the intelligence that they have "no other radiancy but the pure emanations of the Godhead," are points which we cannot determine; yet we can fancy how a carriage-keeping congregation would be thrown into ecstasies by this "ascending," "soaring," "stretching," "mounting" sentence, and how dizzy it would become when standing in "undiscovered and unknown fields of magnificence and glory." Yet Dr. McAll could write short, glittering sentences, and express himself with childlike simplicity. Imitate his conciseness, his refinement, his courage; but beware of his ascents to the third heavens! For a grander specimen of the same kind of verbiage, take the following magnificently finished balloon passage from the writings of Dr. Chalmers: —

"Or if, instead of viewing the Deity in relation to *time*, we view Him in relation to *space*, we shall feel the mystery of His being to be alike impracticable and impervious. But we shall not again venture on aught so inconceivable (yet the reality of which so irresistibly obtrudes itself upon the mind) as immensity without limits; nor shall we presume one conjecture on a question which we have no means of resolving, whether the universe have its terminating outskirts, and so, however stupendous to our eye, shrink by its finitude to an atom, in the midst of that unoccupied and unpeopled vastness by which it is surrounded. Let us satisfy ourselves with a humbler flight. Let us carry the speculation no farther than our *senses* have carried it. Let us take account only of the suns and systems which the telescope has unfolded; though for aught we know, beyond the farthest range of this instrument there might be myriads of remoter suns and remoter systems. Let us, however, keep within the circle of our actual discoveries, — within the limits of that scene which we know to be peopled with realities; and, instead of trying to dilate our imagination to the infinity beyond it, let us but think of God as sitting in state and high sovereignty over millions of other worlds beside our own. If this earth which we know, and know so imperfectly, form so small a part of His works, what an emphasis it gives to the lesson that we indeed know but a very small part of His ways. 'These are a part of His ways,' said a holy man of old; 'but how little a portion is heard of Him!' Here the revelations of astronomy, in our modern day, accord with the direct *spiritual* revelations of a former age. In this sentiment at least the patriarch and philosopher are at one; and *highest science* meets and is in harmony with *deepest sacredness.* Hence we construct the same lesson, whether we employ the element of *space* or the element of *time.* With the one the basis of the argument is the ephemeral experience of our little *day;* with the other, the basis of the argument is the contracted observation of our little *sphere.* They both alike serve to distance man from the infinite and everlasting God."

Dr. Chalmers, too, could write short and pregnant sentences, though he was more at home in mounting his aerial car, and joining McAll in a hazardous trip to the third heavens. In writing this, it occurs to me to suggest that it may be well for you to send me a sermon for criticism. Do so, pray, and give me permission to speak freely about it; don't be offended by a sharp word; it shall be spoken in honest love. I await your reply.

IX.

HARRIS AND BEECHER.

Are you suffering from the effects of the last letter? If so, probably you would be glad to have an opportunity of returning the compliment, which I have taken such pains to pay you. No doubt you have instinctively turned to your sword, because you have felt an abhorrent sense of a heartlessness and injustice which have baffled and defied your power of expression. You call me hypercritical; you see where I am wrong; you protest that I have misunderstood your meaning; in a word, you regard yourself as an injured man. Do you? Do you take my remarks good-humoredly, or do you burn with an indignant desire to lay hands upon a sermon of my own? By-and-by you shall have a chance of repayment; but not to-day, — to-day you are in a dangerous mood. Let us take a turn upon common ground, until your good temper is quite recovered.

You are too young to have known Dr. Harris, who was not, in my opinion, according to a statement in a former letter, a *preacher*, but a most pleasant and persuasive *reader* of sermons. I propose to quote the outline of an eloquent sermon of his upon *Christ weeping over Jerusalem*. "And when He was come near, He beheld the city, and wept over it, saying, If thou hadst known, even thou, at least in this thy day, the things which belong unto thy peace! but now they are hid from thine eyes" (Luke xix. 41, 42). Speaking of the Saviour as presented in this text, Dr. Harris says: —

"1. His comprehensive mind reverted to the *past;* He remembered the days of old, when Israel was holiness to the Lord." I think it is a mistake, in taste to say the least, to speak of Jesus Christ's "*comprehensive* mind." If the epithet, which is complimentary rather than reverential, had been omitted, the sentence would have been purer and stronger.

"2. With the self-denying love of a patriot, and the grace of a Saviour, He looked beyond the spectacle of *His own* sufferings, and fixed his eye upon theirs; He could look at them only through the atmosphere of compassion." This, too, seems to me to be pitifully complimentary. If the first thirteen words had been omitted, the sentence would have gained much.

"3. The exclamation, regarded as a sentence, was broken and incomplete; but who does not see that it is in effect eloquently completed by the tears which break it,—tears which are the natural language of compassion, and which express its intenseness beyond all words?" I cannot see why this should have been given as a separate head, though it is legitimate as a general remark. Homiletically, it is certainly not scientific; this is not unimportant to a student.

"From this amplification and general interpretation of the text, let us proceed next to consider its particular bearing on ourselves." I should have liked a less formal transition; a curve would have been better than a right angle.

"1. *There are things which pre-eminently belong to your peace.* 2. The period allotted to you for attending to them is definite and brief,—it is here called '*your day.*' 3. Should your day of opportunity close, and leave you unsaved, your guilt will be great and your condition remediless. 4. This is a spectacle calling for the profoundest lamentation. 5. Behold in the tears of Jesus a proof of His unextinguished compassion for them, and an inducement to apply to Him at once for salvation." The chief merit of these points is that nothing can be said against them, if indeed an exception may not be made as to the use of the word "you" instead of "us." A preacher should be careful how he separates himself from his hearers; by identifying his own spiritual condition with theirs, he disarms criticism and conciliates confidence, but by too marked a separation he exposes himself to the charge of priestliness and professional sanctimony. The whole sermon, of which the outline is now before you, is undoubtedly written with spirit; there is no want of pleading terms or urgent expostulation. Yet to my mind it is singularly ineffective, and it is so principally because of the impression that it is *manufactured;* the pathos seems to have been got up for the occasion, and to have been adapted to the requirements of artificial propriety; the appeal is entirely artistic, measured to order, and overshadowed by the imagined presence of the printer; while the very marks of exclamation carry with them a terrified look, as if they had just seen a critic. I miss the freedom, the elasticity, and the sympathy of *nature;* I cannot shed tears even when the preacher delicately intimates that such a sign of emotion would be timely and becoming; I cannot tremble with mortal fear when the preacher tells me to "reflect, *thirdly,*" that the day of visitation is hastening to a close. No, no, I cannot "reflect *thirdly*"; the preacher should have *constrained* me to reflect by his gentle, sympathetic, earnest portrayal of the Saviour's sorrow, and if his own grief had interrupted his smooth and rhythmic eloquence, I might have caught the infection of his tears. Away with this trimly cut pathos! if not to be condemned as blasphemy, it is to be abhorred as simulation; it looks like mere stock in trade which the sermon-writer keeps in his inkhorn for business purposes.

Lying before me is a sermon on the same text, by Henry Ward Beecher; and a greater contrast it is impossible to find. Beecher's sermon is full of life, spontaneity, and tender vigor; you feel throughout that the preacher derives his power over you from a deep acquaintance with the human heart, and a rich experience of Christian truth in his own soul; he talks *to* you, not *at* you; there is nothing artificial; every sentence is natural; the preacher seeks your salvation, and stands as if he would not go away until you receive the Saviour. Starting with the inquiry, "What is a Divine visitation?" he prosecutes an analysis of the influences which operate upon human life, showing at how many points God attempts to reach the sinner's soul. "It is a great mistake to suppose that only technically religious institutions and truths are God's instruments, and that the world is abandoned of good unless there are technically religious influences brought to bear upon it. It is an error to regard the world as a vast labyrinth of evil, in which religion alone is recuperative. For I understand that the whole system of the world, from the outside shell to the inside core and seed, from the centre back to the remotest circumference, is part and parcel of one great attempt of God for the development of the human race; that the revelation of the Lord Jesus Christ, although it is transcendently higher in its kind, is not more a part of religious culture than the revelation of God in the natural world, in social life, in business, in all the appointments in which man acts or in which he is acted upon. All these constitute, it is true, only subordinate parts, but nevertheless real and integral parts, of that general course of education and development which God superintends in this world. So that if a man had never seen a church, or never read a Bible, it could not be said that he was undeveloped or uneducated. He would be destitute of the best part of the educating system; nevertheless, he would not have escaped out of the great, spacious academy of education which this world affords, until he had escaped out of life itself!" Around this proposition he gathers arguments and analogies most pressing and apposite; then come parables, figures, as true as they are ingenious and beautiful. "If," says the preacher, "you look comprehensively, it may be said that the human soul lies in the body like the keys of a great organ, and that the great Organist has not left a single key untouched in the whole seven octaves, — touched, not once or twice, but many times; not in single melodies, but in the most massive harmonies; so that every person trained in a Christian family, brought up under Christian institutions, in Christian communities, in the midst of Christian visitations, has been the subject of special influences on every single one of his faculties, from the top of the scale all the way down to the bottom." Referring to the changeful experiences of the soul in regard to Divine visitations, Mr. Beecher gives the following simple but effective illustration: —

"I suppose every man passes, at some time, into a kind of scepticism. I know I have had such times; I suppose everybody has them. At my former mountain home in Lenox, there were days in August, when, although I knew there were mountains near, they were so hazy that I could not see them. I looked to the north, where old Greylock stood, and he had gone. I looked to the south for Mount Washington, and he had gone. I looked to the east for the range of mountains that rose up there, but they had stolen away. I looked to the west to see if any remained, but they too had hid themselves, and all were invisible. But when I slept and woke, all the mountains the next morning, washed by night showers, came back, so clear and distinct that the old crag upon the ten-mile-distant hill stood up, vivid as a line against the sky, and my eye could sweep over all the country round about, and the truant hills seemed to have travelled home again stealthily in the night. I think it is just so in the soul. There are times when a man goes grieving, saying, 'Where are those aspirations which I once felt? I am now sodded and stupid as a sponge. Where are those up-reachings that I once enjoyed? Where is all that old enthusiasm of honor? Where are all those mountings of desire? Ah! they are all gone! Man is after all but a superior animal; he is but a part of the material creation; he is but the highest form in which matter develops.' Man complains to himself, 'I shall live, and, like an autumnal leaf, wither and die; something else shall grow out of me, and in turn something else shall grow out of that.'

"But though there are, in every man's life, times of obscuration, of dulness, of deadness, that come over the soul, there is no man so bad, so worldly, so obstinately set in his philosophic errors, so bound up in unbeliefs, that he has not certain other brighter and revelatory moments, in which he rises superior to his common life, in which his immortal nature mounts mountain-like above him, in which he stands upon the tops of his own soul, and, looking out, exclaims: 'I born to fall like a sparrow and rot? I grow like a vegetable that goes back again into the earth? Never! This that is in me, so royally, shall live and mount far above the touch of decay!' He feels his affinity to God! He is, in his own consciousness, near heaven; and there is a throb of immortality in his soul!"

Again, what natural and charming talk is this: —

"It is remarkable, in respect to these visitations of God, that they do not follow the telescope; they are rather like comets, that come when they please; for when you search for God, 'by searching you cannot find Him out.' Often, when I have tried to prepare a sermon, and have ranged the heavens for higher conceptions of God, I could not find them; but at other times I have been walking along the street, never dreaming or thinking of God, when, coming in contact with some of my fellow-men, I would see some suggestive trait fall out among them, and all at once, from that little incidental circumstance, there would spring up such a luminous development of the Divine character that I have said to myself, 'Oh, if I could only have such a thought as that in the pulpit, I could then preach the truth of God!' But it came when I was out in the street, and where nobody would hear. I could only fill my own soul with it for a moment, and pass on, till it gradually faded away. Such thoughts have come to you unbidden, sometimes in your counting-room, or when you were on a journey, or on the sea; sometimes when you have been in your house all alone, your family in the country; sometimes in trouble and adversity; in various ways, — often coming, though never twice alike, as if the Divine phases had sought to present, at different times, different aspects to you. And if, all the way along, you had treasured up these times — precious times of great treasure! if you had treasured them as you have when you have made a good bargain, or gained a new honor; if you had treasured all these interior peculiarities as you have the exterior, you would find them, I think, almost within speaking distance all the way from childhood to manhood. And, although you had never such a consecutive view of the whole, yet really all along you have been subject to such impressions! And they have come again and again, from childhood clear down to manhood. There is not a man in this congregation that has not been dealt with in that way! You do not know yourself! You have been the subject of culture when you did not know it! You were unconscious of it, because it was silent and modest, because it did not report itself like a bell!"

This is preaching! When a preacher descends after this manner into the common experiences of life, his dullest hearer cannot escape his stimulating influence; he widens his pulpit until it includes the whole world, and simplifies his theology until little children even catch the meaning of God's living word. Apart from the richness and beauty of these quotations, does anything strike you as remarkable? It certainly strikes me that the preacher could not have *read* such passages; there is a freeness about the sentences which could hardly be attained by a writer; there is, if you will pardon a whimsical expression, an air of *spokenness* about these urgent and sparkling utterances. Harris's sermon is an essay, Beecher's is a speech; Harris *reads at* you, Beecher *speaks to* you; Harris is an artist, Beecher is an orator; Harris conducts you into a *conservatoire* of artificial flowers, Beecher leads you into a garden where all is life and bloom and fragrance. Most heartily do I commend Mr. Beecher's sermons as the best models of pulpit addresses with which I am acquainted. They are full of matter; they are instructively and popularly philosophical, without being distractingly metaphysical; they abound in allusions to common life and the universal experience of mankind; they are rich with illustrations drawn from all quarters; they are conceived in the very spirit of the gospel, and expressed with a pathetic sympathy which is often most subduing and persuasive. I have reason to speak gratefully of Mr. Beecher; his words, so natural, so human, yet so divine, have stimulated and blessed me, when the refined analysis of Bushnell, the vehement eloquence of Chalmers, the waxen beauty of Harris, and the perspirational rhetoric of Melville, were unsuited to my spiritual condition. Mr. Beecher's outlines are seldom striking; in fact, he does not, as a rule, care for a formal mapping of his subject; his mind and his heart are full of it, and this dictates his utterance. He has been accused of occasional extravagance, and not without reason; but such extravagance is the result of exuberant life, and is in my opinion much to be preferred, to the tame propriety which is the chief characteristic of many sermons. Mr. Beecher's extravagance appears to me to be only such extravagance as may be found in nature; the carved cabinet may be exact in its proportions and convenient in its design, yet it should not be cited to the disadvantage of the irregular but living tree. Homiletics has become too much of a cabinet-carving art; the square and compass have been too much in requisition; it is quite time that we should follow a little more closely the logic of life and the poetry of nature. Mr. Beecher does this in a remarkable degree, and is therefore an example to all young ministers whose aim it is to preach with simplicity and effect. I wish my space would allow me to present another contrast which Mr Beecher offers to Dr. Harris in a sermon upon Rom. i. 16. The sermon by Dr. Harris on this text contains many fine sentences, and a good deal of careful painting; it is evidently the result of the minutest painstaking, and undoubtedly it reflects great credit upon Dr. Harris as a devout and contemplative essayist. I heard Dr. Harris preach the sermon in 1852 at the opening of a chapel in the suburbs of London, and my recollection of the preacher's placid yet animated countenance, his sweet and tuneful voice, his grave and impressive manner, is very pleasant; his sermon was an admirable essay, admirably delivered. In a literary point of view, Mr. Beecher's discourse is inferior to Dr. Harris's, but as an address delivered to a miscellaneous assembly, it is, in my judgment, much superior to it. Its argument is close, its illustrations are vivid, and its appeal (as indeed is Dr. Harris's) very practical. Mr. Beecher in this instance, as in the former, has the obvious advantage of *speaking;* when will *all* ministers avail themselves of that advantage? You see how easily I am brought again to this point; it is because I attach to it an importance which cannot be exaggerated. Again and again, hoping that importunity will not be thrown away upon you, I urge you to be a *preacher*, and not a mere *reader* of the gospel. Be resolute, and you will surely succeed!

"Get the substance of your sermon, which you have prepared for the pulpit, so wrought into your head and heart, by review and meditation, that you may have it at command, and speak to your hearers with freedom; not as if you were reading or repeating your lesson to them, but as a man sent to teach and persuade them to faith and holiness. Deliver your discourses to the people like a man that is talking to them in good earnest about their most important concerns and their everlasting welfare; like a messenger sent from heaven, who would fain save sinners from hell, and allure souls to God and happiness. Do not indulge that lazy way of reading over your prepared paper as a schoolboy does an oration out of Livy or Cicero, who has no concern in the things he speaks; but let all the warmest zeal for God, and compassion for perishing men, animate your voice and countenance; and let the people see and feel, as well as hear, that you are speaking to them about things of infinite moment, and in which your own eternal interest lies as well as theirs."— (*Dr. Isaac Watts.*) This is the counsel of true wisdom. I grant that it is counsel which at first involves most serious difficulty to thoughtful and diffident preachers. There is a natural anxiety about the proper construction of sentences, the distribution of parts, and the unity of the whole discourse; and this anxiety is not favorable to the determined self-possession which is essential to effective public speaking. The young speaker (I do not mean the flippant gabbler) soon falls under the tyranny of fear; he is nervous about the next sentence, he is alarmed by the most trifling grammatical slip, and any unexpected circumstance distresses and enfeebles him. Yet this is only one side of the account; on the other must be put down the growth of power and its consequent ease, the development of sympathy with the varying conditions and moods of a congregation, and a happy independence of many possibilities which are the terror of artificial speakers. There is no finer sight than that of a great teacher addressing an assembly with a power self-conscious enough to secure perfect ease, yet self-misgiving enough to invest the speaker with the holy and tender charm of devout reliance upon a strength that is not his own. Does not such a sight enkindle your best ambition? The way indeed into this kingdom is narrow, and the gate is strait; but do not be discouraged on that account, for it is true of all kingdoms that are worth entering. You cannot have a broad way and a wide gate into any of God's kingdoms; he devil makes wide paths for his followers, otherwise he could never lure them into darkness; but God always sets the severity of discipline before the reward of glory.

X.

THE MINISTER IN THE PULPIT.

MICHAEL ANGELO is reported to have said, "Trifles make perfection, and perfection is no trifle." Under the patronage of this high authority, you will permit me to take note of sundry little things in connection with the higher matters with which it is now proposed to engage your attention. Nothing should be despised which contributes to the increase of legitimate influence, and nothing indulged which aids merely artificial effect. Everything connected with the ministry should at least be *real*. Now for particulars: —

1. *You have to go into the pulpit.* You smile at this trite remark perhaps; there are, however, two ways of going into a pulpit. To ascend the pulpit with a hurried step, or with any air of affectation, is indecorous, if not profane. Some ministers have an extraordinary way of *rolling* into the pulpit; others are severely perpendicular in their attitude; others are natural and solemn, without being either flippant or sanctimonious in their manner. Some ministers make their appearance at the vestry door with a bold and almost defiant look, others drop their eyes as if ashamed to hold up their heads; in both cases, perhaps, there is a little affectation: what you and I have to do is to be *natural*, *sincere*, and *modest*.

2. *You have to announce hymns and chapters.* Why announce them, unless you wish the congregation to follow you? But how can the congregation follow you, if you announce the numbers in a low or mumbling tone? or if you don't announce them at all, but simply gabble them? or if you give out the five-hundred-and-seventy-sixth hymn and three-hundred-and-

fifty-first hymn in the supplement, and get half way into the first verse before you take your breath? For my own part, I confess to a difficulty in giving out numbers, arising from the change of voice which should often be made, from the tone in which it is proper to announce the number, to the tone appropriate to the sentiment of the hymn. For example, in a large place of worship it may be necessary to say "five hundred and ninety-five" very loudly, but it might be shocking to say *as* loudly, "Alas! and did my Saviour bleed"; a subdued, tremulous tone best becomes the utterance of such words: on the other hand, the peal of a trumpet would be fitting for the line, "Praise ye the Lord, 'tis good to raise." I have found the best plan of overcoming this difficulty to be to *pause* for two or three seconds after announcing numbers; this plan has advantages for the hearer as well as for the speaker. In announcing hymns and chapters, you should be very careful to distribute the emphasis properly, or your effort will be a failure. In announcing, for instance, that you are about to read the second chapter of the first epistle of John, beginning at the tenth verse, great care is required: some persons (into whose secret may you never come!) would announce it thus, — "Let us read from the tenth verse of the second chapter of John's first epistle;" others, quite as bad, or perhaps even a shade worse, would say — "Second CHAPTER of the first EPISTLE of John, BEGINNING at the tenth VERSE": what a horrible perversion of plain common sense! The people do not wish to know that it is a *chapter*, but what *particular chapter* it is; they do not require so much to know that you are about to read from an *epistle*, as they require to know *whose* epistle it is. If I can represent emphasis by a variety of type, I will show you how, in my opinion, the announcement should be made: "The FIRST epistle of JOHN, — the SECOND chapter — beginning at the TENTH verse." Say this *twice* distinctly, and after a momentary pause proceed. While giving out numbers, don't hold down your head as if giving them out to the book, but speak straightforwardly as if you meant to be heard.

3. *You have to unite in the offering of worship.* How can you do so if you fumble in the Bible, spread out your manuscript, and make sundry arrangements which ought to have been made before you went into the pulpit? Have you no part in the song of praise? Are you a paid conductor, or a fellow-worshipper? In my opinion, the minister should enter heartily into the service of song, for even if he cannot sing, he can show by a reverent manner that his heart is engaged in Divine praise; he can sing with the spirit and with the understanding.

4. *You have to read the Scriptures.* Few men read them intelligently and expressively. Some ministers read the Bible in a tame and deadening tone, as if they had mistaken insipidity for veneration; others read it with a theatrical rant which is shockingly impious; others again read it in a slovenly manner, as if the exercise was hardly worth attending to, in comparison, as Mr. Binney truly says, with "their grand intellectual sermon." What is the remedy? We must, first of all, feel that the word of God itself is actually before us, and our elocution will then be dictated by our veneration. In the next place, we must by private study prepare ourselves for the public reading of the Scriptures. I doubt whether it is not profane to read in the pulpit a chapter to which no attention has been paid in private. How can the adventurer who does so know anything of the sentiment of the chapter? How can he remember the punctuation? How can he be prepared for change of subject, or for parenthetic modification? He cannot read the chapter; he can only pronounce the words, and flounder through the meaning. The indispensable requisite for good reading is an intelligent and sympathetic conception of the author's mean-

ing; I say not only intelligent but sympathetic, because appreciation always suggests the best expression. It is said of a celebrated novelist, who occasionally reads his own compositions in public, that in anticipation of a public reading, he will spend not less than six hours a day in studying the most appropriate accent, cadence, and force. If he does this for a corruptible crown, what shall *we* do for a crown that is incorruptible? Surely we should at least read over in secret the portion of Scripture which we intend to read in public. Whether the public reading of the Scriptures should be intermixed with explanatory remarks is still a controverted question; Mr. Binney objects to a running commentary "as spoiling the force of the simple reading by a crowd of trite commonplaces," and no doubt the objection can be sustained by many confirmatory illustrations; on the other hand, some ministers have a very happy way of interposing an explanatory word: looking at both sides of the question, I should strongly advise that least one portion be read without comment, and that the minister feel himself at liberty to read another with such interspersions of his own as may in his opinion elucidate its meaning. A universal rule cannot be laid down; each man must work according to his gift; where a man cannot express himself tersely, he ought not to attempt an intermixture of reading and comment; if he should be infatuated enough to do so, the inspired word will soon be lost in the uninspired garrulity.

5. *You have to pray.* If few men, even ministers, know how to read, fewer still, it would unhappily appear, know how to pray. I have known ministers of great reputation for pulpit eloquence, whose prayers were simply discreditable. The ministers in question have stumbled, and often done so incoherently, through a set of the merest commonplaces; they have seemed to be doing a work which was quite strange to them, and consequently to be ill at ease. The *poverty* of

their prayers was lamentable; take out the "O Lords," and the "We beseech Thee, O heavenly Fathers," and what would be left? In the confession of sin, the sins have been enumerated as if they were only mistakes; and in the supplication for pardon, forgiveness has been asked for as if it cost God's heart nothing, and was quite a matter of indifference, though common courtesy required that some notice should be taken of it. Who can doubt that preparation is as needful for prayer as for preaching? "The preparation of the heart in man, and the answer of the tongue, is from the Lord." That some men have what may be called the gift of prayer in larger measure than others is evident, and that consequently it is easier for some men to pray than others is indisputable; yet preparation will secure great advantage to the least gifted. But *how* to prepare? Is it by *writing?* Is it by committing to *memory?* No. First of all, read the devotional portions of the Bible largely; in addition to this exercise, read the devotional writings of the most spiritual divines; and thirdly, make earnest and unsparing inquest into your own heart. To this end be much alone; don't live in excitement; pray God to "search you with candles" (Zeph. i. 12), and to reveal you to yourself. After such preparation you will, so to speak, pray *from a spiritual and not an external centre;* your prayer will be dictated by the Holy Ghost, and not merely suggested by circumstances; you will be inspired rather than instructed; you will descend upon the wants of life with heavenly strength, — not struggle towards them in earthly weakness. You have heard some so-called prayers which were nothing better than catalogues of church institutions and advertisements of church work; such as "bless the ragged school," "bless the band of hope," "bless an institution lately formed in this place, having for its object," etc., "bless the elder scholars' prayer-meeting." When the devotional service in a large congregation is made up of such petitions, it cannot be wondered at that some persons do not care to be in attendance "until the prayer is over." Of course there are times when speciality is necessary; my remarks apply to the *general* conduct of public worship.

In seeking a definition of prayer, I have been led to the conclusion that prayer means different things to different people, — however strange they may seem. To the man of strong emotional temperament, prayer signifies the pouring out of the heart in grateful praise and passionate supplication; languid and contemplative devotion is abhorrent to him; he must exclaim, and sing, and shout for joy, in the course of his rapturous prayer. On the other hand, to a man of more practical mind this rhapsody is distressing; he must base his prayers upon facts; he prays according to the circumstances of the time; his thankfulness never overflows; he is often satisfied, but seldom joyous. Then there is the suppliant the constitution of whose mind makes it very difficult for him to avoid an argument in his prayer; he sees life as a long process in applied logic; he devoutly reasons upon the succession and inter-relation of events; he prays upon his feet, he never takes wing that he may pray just outside the gate of heaven; he never sings his praise, he only states it in accurate and sequential terms. In strong contrast is the contemplatist; he knows nothing of reasoning, takes no heed of common life, never individualizes, and seldom makes a request; to him God is a Being to be looked at, talked about, and adored; the contemplatist has wonderful visions of creation, — he sees God upon the wings of the wind, hears His going among the trees of the forest, beholds His shadow flitting over the stars, marks His hand rolling back the covering of the night, and sees the pillars of His throne in the foundations of the universe. His prayers are dictated by his visions; they are wide in range, reverent in tone, subdued in feeling; in hearing them we seem also to hear a solemn silence, as if all things had paused that his voice alone might be heard; he never touches the sin, the sorrow, and the poverty of common human life, — he makes us feel that we live in a temple, and that we are encircled by Divinity. Of this kind of devotion Theodore Parker presents a distinguished illustration; for example: —

"A greater revelation than this of Thyself hast Thou made in Thy still small voice, which whispers in our soul that all this magnificence is but a drop of Thee, yea a little sparklet that has fallen from Thy presence, Thou Central Fire and Radiant Light of all. We know that these outward *things* are but a sparkle of Thy power, a whisper of Thy wisdom, a faint breath of Thy loving-kindness." Once more: "Father, we thank Thee for the world about us, above, and beneath. We bless Thee for the austere loveliness of the winter heavens, for those fixed or wandering fires which lend their splendor to the night, for the fringe of beauty wherewith Thou borderest the morning and the evening sky, and for this daily sun sending his roseate flush of light across the white and wintry world." Again: "We thank Thee for the exceeding beauty of this wintry day, we bless Thee for the ever-welcome countenance of the sun, so sweetly looking down upon our northern land, and bidding winter flee. We thank Thee for the moon which scarfs with loveliness the retreating shoulders of the night, and for all the wondrous majesty of stars wherewith Thou hast spangled the raiment of darkness, giving beauty to the world when the sun withdraws his light." And finally: "Father, we thank Thee for this beautiful day which Thou hast given us, for the glory which walks over our heads through the sky, for the pleasing alternation of light and shade, and all the gorgeous beauty wherewith Thou clothest the summer in her strength, making her lovely to the eyes of men. Father, we thank Thee that Thou never failest to Thy world, but sheddest dew on meadows newly mown, and rainest down Thine inspiration from the clouds of heaven on every little grass and every mighty tree. Father, we thank Thee that Thou feedest and carest for all Thy creatures, the motes that people the sunbeams, and the sparrows which fall not to the ground but by Thy providence, protecting with Thy hand the wandering birds of summer and the wandering stars of heaven, holding them all in the golden leash of Thy love, and blessing everything which Thou hast made." Now all this is very beautiful; but is it devotional? Is it not rhetoric rather than religion, or religion which never gets above rhetoric? In my opinion, all this could have been more appropriately said in an essay than in a prayer: it is adapted to the human ear; and probably it could not have been heard without drawing men to praise and magnify the "Great King above all gods." Mr. Parker could be more simple in prayer, and more human in his petitions, as for example: "We remember before Thee the sorrows with which Thou triest us, how often we stoop us at the bitter waters and fill our mouths with sadness; and if we dare not thank Thee for these things, if we know not how to pray Thee about them as we ought, we yet thank Thee that we are sure that in all these things Thou meanest us good, and out of these seeming evils still producest good, making all things work together for the highest advantage of Thine every child, with whom Thou hast not a son of perdition and not a single castaway. We thank Thee for that home whereunto Thou gatherest the spirits of just men made perfect, and for our dear ones who have gone thither before us, and bless Thee that they are still not less near because they are transfigured with immortal glory, and have passed on in the road ourselves must also tread." This is the voice of the heart, — how much better than the song of the fancy! You will find much in the prayers of *Henry Ward Beecher* to suggest trains of devotional thought; as an example of his simplest and best method of prayer take the following: "If there are those in Thy presence that by ignorance or heedless mistakes, who by courses of folly and wickedness in times past, are suffering severe penalties and trouble, we pray that they may not spend their time in useless murmuring, that they may not rebel against the past, but rather may they take hope of Thee, and with all their heart turn to the living God, and find in a newness of life that peace which they cannot find in the present nor in the remembrances of the past; and may every one have hope in Thee! May none feel that they are in a state without hope; the most guilty, the most wicked, those that have sinned longest and deepest and darkest, may they remember that there is a grace of God in Christ Jesus even to them, to those afar off as well as to those that are near! Oh, make Thine atoning mercy and the glory of Thy forgiving goodness apparent unto every one; and may every one be able to see that in proportion as they are forgiven, according to the magnitude of their iniquity and the greatness of their transgression, will be the glory transcending which Thou wilt have if Thou showest mercy unto them; and while we doubt ourselves, and while we may distrust one another, and while at times all things seem unstable and unsatisfactory, oh save us from that last and worst disaster,—distrusting Thee. May our faith in God be immutable; and even when we are so guilty that we cannot look up, at least may we be able to bow the head, to smite upon our breast, and say, 'God, be merciful to us sinners.' And if we dare not sit by Thee in Thy throne, if we dare not come to Thee as children to the knees of their parents, and look up, at least may we sit down at Thy feet, and find there that we are sitting at the feet of a Redeemer, pitying, gentle, forgiving, all succoring. We pray that none may be discouraged; may every one accept his life-work; may every one, undismayed and undaunted, go forward from good to better, from strength to strength. We beseech of Thee that Thou wilt make us useful; while we are seeking for our own growth, may we not treasure up strength gained, or experiences, or joys, for our own selfish using; but as we receive so may we give. May our whole life be a life of seed-sowing; may our life be a work for God and for man."

The use of what is termed "free prayer" may easily degenerate into the most pitiable barrenness and even into the most shocking absurdity. It requires the utmost discipline, the coolest self-possession, and the highest spirituality both of perception and feeling. To express the wants of the multitude, to interpret the common condition of the human family, to condense within one brief petition all that is most urgent, and to do all this with appropriate reverence and simplicity, is not within the reach of indolence or insensibility. There must be forethought, preparation, and consequent steadiness of mind and fulness of heart. Among the faults which you should strive to avoid are the following: —

1. *Doctrinalism.* — In your public prayer you should not take occasion to state or argue your theological opinions. Why should you tell man, in language ostensibly intended for God, why you are a Calvinist rather than an Arminian? Or why should you set up in your prayers a Trinitarian argument in opposition to the Unitarian theology? In a few minutes you will have an opportunity of discussing your doctrines in your sermon; why be so eager to drag them into your prayer? Have you no sin to confess, no mercy to implore, no praise to render, no blessings to crave, that you should turn polemic on your knees, and defender of the faith with your eyes shut? Your heart will have forgotten itself when your tongue becomes controversial in prayer, and it will be no wonder if God turn away from you as if His ear were heavy that it could not hear. How unprofitable, too, is such an exercise to the poor, the sorrowing, and the contrite!

They feel that the prayer lies remote from their experience, and so it becomes to them an unknown and unprofitable tongue; they would recognize with instant thankfulness the voice which expressed feelings which they themselves could never put into language, and would feel as if God had sent an interpreter to their aid. The heart responds to the voice which takes its tone from the common experience of the world; but it is silent under the barren words of a sectarian argument.

2. *Personality.* — Your office-bearers may have outvoted you upon a debated question; one of the seatholders has offended your wife; a Sunday-school teacher has called your authority in question; under these circumstances what a temptation there is to *pray at* the miserable offenders! How sweet to remember them in one condemnatory sentence! How just to brand them with one fiery commination! Or there is another plan: you may make yourself a martyr in prayer; you can adopt a whining tone of resignation; you can show the unhealed wounds of your suffering heart, and refer to them as if they were received and endured in a very becoming spirit; you can pray for your enemies with such desperate magnanimity as to create the suspicion that you would behead every one of them if a fair opportunity ever occurred; and thus by the very excess of your saintliness you may show how far you are from the kingdom of heaven. Never, never *pray at* your congregation, — *that* would be profaning the altar. It is even worse to *pray* at a man than to *preach* at him: both are bad, — the first unpardonable. When we go before the Lord, let us go without bitterness or malice, — how otherwise shall God hear us? Amidst our remembrances of sin against Himself, have we time or desire to think resentfully of wrongs which men have committed against us? Are we ourselves quite unchargeable with social offences? Have we never aimed a dart that was intended to injure, if not to destroy,

our brother? Think of this, and never make profanity the medium of forgiveness. On this subject the words of the late Rev. Edward Parsons are worthy of your best consideration: "But what shall be said of that spirit of rancor which so grossly violates the spirit, and perverts the design, of prayer? I am ashamed to reflect upon the angry and vindictive tones in which some are apt to address the God of love, whenever they happen to be offended with man. Whatever you may suffer from the scourge of the tongue, or any other instrument of a persecuting malignity, never let your sufferings extort from you a word that would savor of a retaliatory disposition. If we ought not to hint at private disagreements, disputes, and discords in preaching the gospel of peace, how much more cautious we should be against this, when we publicly supplicate the throne of grace! The man who can be so overcome by an evil temper as to 'pray at' those who displease him, is guilty of contemptible meanness and disgusting impiety."

3. *Favoritism.* — There is a very subtle temptation in this direction. When we pray in a rich man's family, how affectionate we are apt to be! "Bless Thy *dear* and *honored* servant; we thank Thee for all Thou hast done *for* him and *by* him, and we *affectionately* and *earnestly* commend him to Thy blessing; spare his *valuable* life, and may he and Thy *dear handmaiden* enjoy much of Thy presence; we bless Thee that *their praise is in all the churches*, and that all who know them love them for *their Christian worth*." You have heard such words? So have I, and been disgusted with them. Our prayer for the *poor* man has often been much shorter; we have seldom thought of him as God's *dear* servant, we have named him as a stranger in God's household, and barely admitted that God might care for him. Oh, shameful partiality, — miserable truckling to gold! But it is not *prayer;* it is *talk* that never goes toward heaven, *hypocrisy* which

delights the bad angels. Sir, remember that God is a Spirit, that He searches the heart, and that His poorest child is as a prince in His sight; and if ever you are tempted to dismiss the poor man's case with one cold word, may you be convinced of sin before you rise from your knees! When you pray for rich or poor, be it without partiality and without hypocrisy!

4. *Secularity.* — Many prayers relate almost exclusively to daily blessings, religious institutions, political affairs, passing events, and works of charity. These are not to be forgotten, yet surely they should not occupy the foremost place in supplication. Study to give *spirituality* to your prayers; pray for enlightenment of mind, obedience of will, and sanctification of heart; send out your soul in quest of the living God, and cry mightily for Him, until He draw near and make Himself known by His brightness and inspiration. *Pray much for the Holy Ghost;* from some prayers one might question that the church had ever "so much as heard whether there be any Holy Ghost" (Acts xix. 2), so low are they in tone and so limited in request. We forget that this is the age of the Spirit; the visible Christ has ascended into the heavenly place to appear for us before God; miracle and marvellous sign have been withdrawn; and now we live in the Holy Ghost, and He lives in us as temples which Christ has built. The Holy Ghost is the all-inclusive blessing; to have Him is to have life and love and comfort: pray therefore for the Holy Ghost; with this great petition as a groundwork, you may traverse the whole circle of human need; without it your most elaborate prayer will be earthly, barren, and heathenish, — worthy of a pagan altar.

Some advisers would caution you against *length* in prayer; for my own part I hesitate to do so. What *are* long prayers? The length of a prayer ought not, in my opinion, to be measured by *time*. A prayer of a dozen sentences may be long, a prayer occupying an hour may be short. Everything depends upon the spirit, the range, the appropriateness, and the purpose of the prayer. I have heard some prayers which I could have wished to go on for ever,—so wise, so tender, so deeply experimental, and so earnest were they; under their influence one felt that God was nigh at hand, and longed that He might "abide with us." On the other hand, I have felt constrained more frequently to sympathize with Whitefield when he said to a tiresome man, "Sir, you prayed me into a good frame, and then you prayed me out of it." As a general rule, I should urge you to study brevity; but there are times of spiritual enlightenment and quickening when you must abandon all technical rules, and give yourself up to the inspiration of the Holy Ghost. Above all things be *earnest* in prayer; *mean* what you say, and God will not leave you without a token of love; remember the words of Brooks, spoken two hundred years ago, but true forever: "It is only fervent prayer that is effectual prayer; it is only the working prayer that works wonders in heaven, and that brings down wonderful assurance into the heart. Cold prayers shall never have any warm answers. God will suit His returns to our requests; lifeless services shall have lifeless answers. When men are dull, God will be dumb."

Something has been said about preparation for prayer. I never wrote a prayer for public use, and never committed a prayer or so much as a sentence of a prayer to memory, with a view to its being recited in the pulpit; at the same time I have enjoyed the exercise of writing prayers, and have derived spiritual advantage from it. Three of such prayers are now before me, and as they will illustrate my meaning better than any description I can give of them, I subjoin them for your perusal:—

Almighty God, our hearts have longed for Thee with unquenchable desire; even as the hart panteth for the waterbrook, have we panted for the living God. There is no fountain in all the earth which can cool our burning; Abana and Pharpar cannot cleanse us, nor can all the waters in Israel take away our leprosy. We only know ourselves as we know Thee; out of Thy presence all is darkness, but when Thou art shining upon us, every feature of our life is made beautiful. Thou wilt give us more life, so that we shall grow away from the littleness of our spiritual infancy, and come to great stature and power in Jesus Christ. Hast Thou not exhorted us to grow in grace? And as Thou dost send down the rain and the snow from heaven, and pour the light of the sun upon the earth, that it may be covered with fruitfulness, so Thou wilt give us all help in this growth to which Thou hast called us, until we attain Thine own idea of perfectness. We have trembled under our Saviour's command to be perfect as Thou art perfect; it seemed to us a hard word, which could only distress our weakness and lead us to bitter disappointment; it sounded to us as a challenge to make earth as large and beautiful as heaven, and when we so regarded it our hearts sank in great fear. Lord God, our Father, tell us how we can be holy as Thou art holy! Our foundation is in the dust, and we are crushed before the moth; how then can we reach the measure of Thy perfection? Thou art not only holy, but glorious in holiness; Thy name is holy and reverend, and there is no darkness in Thee. But now we know wherein we erred when we were made sad by our Saviour's word; we thought only of our own weakness, we forgot Thy strength; we looked in upon our own poor hearts instead of looking away to the unsearchable riches of Jesus Christ: it is not in Thee to be harsh with Thy children, Thou dost not strain their power; therefore do we trust Thee, that in this call to holiness Thou wilt work mightily in us by Thy Holy Spirit.

It is in our hearts to speak freely to Thee to-day, and to tarry long before Thee. Though we cannot tell

Thee anything, yet we are comforted exceedingly whilst we commune with our Father; and in speaking of our sin and ignorance and shame, we feel as if Thou wert taking away our old garments, and clothing us with all the beauty of king's children. Oh, the sweet mystery of prayer! Lord, teach us how to pray. Open our hearts, that of our own will nothing may be kept from Thee. Thou hast made our life Thy care, and brought our feet into a large place. We remember the littleness of our beginning; how the scorner contemned us, and the haughty man looked upon us with disdain, but our secret trust was in God, and Thou hast crowned our confidence with exceeding honor. Thou hast made a place for us near the head stone of the corner, and set us high above many who prophesied evil of us. Lord, hold Thou us up, and we shall be safe! Sometimes our feet have well-nigh slipped in secret places, and whilst men thought we were good our own spirits smote us with many a memory of distrust and inconstancy and hidden sin. We shudder as we recall the narrowness of our escapes; yet they were not narrow, for did not all Thy love stretch between us and the pit of the enemy? Were not all Thy angels near us, in overshadowing and protecting hosts? Wast Thou not our shield and buckler? Yet we have sinned, and our lips are not worthy to pronounce Thy name. We mourn over secret sins; in the depths of our hearts we have had thoughts which have afflicted us with much pain; our words have not always been sincere to our fellow-men; the importunity of our own interests has often put to silence the heavenly voice; we have sometimes secured ease at a heavy cost of conviction and duty; we have dallied with the tempter, and have borne a faltering testimony when we might have spoken the word of truth boldly. What is our hope? It is still in Jesus Christ; His blood cleanseth from all sin; wash us, and we shall be whiter than snow; hide Thy face from our sins, and blot out all our iniquities. O Lord, have mercy upon us!

We will speak aloud of our joys, for they are many and great. The world itself has become a new place to us since we knew Jesus Christ. Thou hast given us the spirit of interpretation, so that all things have meaning to us which aforetime seemed to have no place in Thy ministry. The earth has become to us our Father's house, and all the hosts of heaven speak to us in Thy name; we see all living creatures around Thy table, they all wait upon Thee, Thou givest them their meat in due season. We thank Thee for our own daily bread; when Thou dost break it for us it becomes more than equal to all our hunger. What shall we say then of Thine unspeakable Gift? Thou hast not withheld from us the Son of Thy love; Thou hast set the treasure of Thine heart before us. At first we did not know Him; we thought He was without form and comeliness, and there was no beauty in Him to awaken our desire; we regarded Him as an intrusion and an offence, and gave our consent that He should be put to death. But now our best praise is too poor for Him; our hearts leap for joy; and though we look at Him through the mingled tears of penitence and thankfulness, we see His heavenly beauty. We need not that men should tell us that He is God, for we have proved His Godhead by His work in our lives; we judge Him no more by the testimony of the letter; we know Him by our transfigured and sanctified love, and His claims are upheld by the joyful and never-silent witness of our hearts. We thank Thee, that being delivered from the bondage of the letter, we have yet come to see in the letter itself beauties which had long escaped us, so Thy testament in Christ Jesus is verily new to us day by day, and while the Godhead of Thy Son rises beyond all our thought and draws after it the wings of our prayer, yet His pure and gentle manhood covers the whole breadth of our lives with the sympathy and protection of loving brotherliness. We would that all men might know Jesus Christ as we know Him; that they might lay hold upon Him as their Saviour, and feel how good it is to begin their lives from His redeeming cross. Hear us on their behalf!

Look upon us as a congregation, and let Thy look be love. May the ministry of this house be baptized as with fire, and may its whole organization work out the highest ends. Bless all the churches round about us, by what name soever known amongst men; and through the united instrumentality of all Thy people, may Jesus Christ's kingdom be established speedily. As for our country, may Thy power be its defence. God save the Queen. We thank Thee for all the gentle womanliness which she has displayed, and we commend her to Thy blessing, O King of kings; may her children be Thy children; and may the God of the families of the earth be the portion of her household.

This is our prayer; Lord, answer us in peace.

Almighty God, though Thou art unsearchable, yet in Jesus Christ we have seen the brightness of Thy face. We have long sought for Thee, but Thou didst not come closely to us in all the works of Thy hands; we said, Surely we shall find God in the light, and His face will shine upon us through the congregation of the stars; we have gone forward but Thou wast not there, backward but we could not perceive Thee, on the left hand where Thou dost work, but we could not behold Thee, Thou didst hide Thyself on the right hand, so that our eye could not see Thee. We heard that Thy way was in the sea and Thy path in the great waters, but in all the floods we did not hear the voice for which our hearts longed in sadness. We have wandered wearily through the temple of Nature, but it was a chamber in which there was no light; we have watched all the seasons, yet they have been to us only as the beautiful garments of an unknown guest. All this has often made our heart ache, and destroyed the balance of our thoughts; we have felt very lonely, and sometimes in our sorrow we have wished to die. This morning we glorify Thee that Jesus Christ has satisfied all our hunger and thirst, and has given rest to eyes tired with long watching; Thine only-begotten Son, who dwelt from unbeginning time in the bosom of His Father, has risen upon us as the dayspring from on high; and our hearts are sufficed. We thank Thee for His human form, because it brings Him so near us; and we thank Thee for His great sorrows, because their recollection often lifts us above our own griefs. Truly Thou didst in Jesus Christ give us an unspeakable gift; we can sooner stretch a line upon the foundations of the earth, and comprehend the dust of the earth in a measure, than find out the length and breadth, the depth and height of Thy love which passeth understanding. Why didst Thou so enrich us with all this love? Surely we had destroyed our beauty and perverted all the comeliness of Thine image, and all our dignity had been thrown down into the dust and covered with shameful dishonor; yet Thou didst come after us as if Thy heart was troubled by our absence, and Thou didst call us with a voice that was made tremulous by anxiety, so tender and overflowing was Thy love. Feeling our own poverty and littleness, we have often wondered how Thou couldst love us so much; why didst Thou not throw us into a pit of forgetfulness, and call around Thee the unfallen children of light, and throne Thyself above their adoring praises? Surely Thou hast purposed a great destiny for us, and in ages to come we shall know somewhat of the meaning of our amazing redemption: we confine our view within the dying day, and are lost in troubled wonder; but when we lay hold of our immortality in Jesus Christ, and think of the revelations which Thou hast yet in store for us, we are made strong and glad by a great hope.

To-day we are once more sheltered in Thy holy house, and in our hearts there is a calm. We are as men who have escaped from sore toil, and come suddenly to a sweet resting-place; round about us there is a light above the brightness of the sun, and the air is rich with reviving odors; surely God is in this place, and His hand is opened to give us gifts. We bring but a poor presence to Thy throne, and we might feel out of place when we think how many and how pure are the suppliants now gathered around Thee; the marks of the ravenous beast are upon us, we are quite without strength or beauty, and all that we can speak of in ourselves is unworthy of the calling wherewith Thou hast called us; yet we lift up our heads hopefully towards Thee because at Thy right hand is seated Jesus Christ our great High-priest, who has borne wounds and death for us, and who carries us all in the pain of His crucifixion and in the triumphant power of His resurrection. Blessed Jesus, our hearts overflow with loving thankfulness when we do but touch the hem of Thy garment, what then shall be our rapture when we see all Thy beauty and serve forever under Thy rule in a universe where there is no sin! At present we have a twilight vision, but we shall yet see the full day; Thou hast thrown a few spring flowers, we know not all the riches of the summer that is above; we delight to think that we have seen only the beginning, that the sabbath and the sanctuary, the book and the altar, are only as entrances to the palace whose foundations are laid in infinitude and whose top stone is high beyond all measurement, the palace of the great King! We are thankful for any suggestion which enlarges the idea of our destiny, and so calls us to dignity of behavior in the present world: the serpent told us that we should be as gods, and we believed his lie; but Thou, blessed and mighty Saviour, hast called us to sit upon the throne which Thou dost share with Thy Father, and our heart's desire is that we may fulfil Thy will.

Make our present communion very sweet; may our hearts have rest, and let our minds be filled with the riches of our Lord: Thou hearest Him alway, and for His sake Thou wilt incline Thine ear to our prayer. Amen.

Almighty God, we are glad to be found again in Thy sanctuary, for our feet are weary and our hearts long for rest. We have been all the week in the cold world, and have sighed over its sinfulness and disquietude. Yet how poor is our estimate of its condition when compared with Thine! We see only the outside deformity and blemish; but Thine eye searches the recesses of the corrupt heart, and sees through all the dark and pestilent chambers of death. There is nothing hid from Thine eye. Our service in the world has quickened our desire to enter into the praises of Thy sanctuary, for we have felt as men who sigh in a far-off land for the sweetness and comfort of home. Now are we in Thine house, and a sense of safety makes us glad; we feel that we are in a city of refuge, into which no manslayer may enter, and where no ravenous beast may be found. This is our Father's house, and the enemy has no place in it. Thou dost shut the gate upon the foe, and he cannot elude Thy watchful eye. Come, then, and meet us, speak comfortably to our hearts, and by the infinite tenderness of Thy love rather than by the alarming thunder of Thy law do Thou bow down our hearts in the joyful sorrow of penitence. We do not claim to be better than our fellow-men, for we are by nature the children of wrath even as others; but if there is aught in us well-pleasing to Thy holiness and love, it has been wrought in us through the brotherliness and priesthood of our Lord Jesus Christ, to whom as unto Thyself we humbly desire to give the adoration and thankfulness due to His Godhead. Yet though we are in our Father's house, we are not altogether at ease, by reason of those whom we have left behind. Our love to Thee fills us with love to men ; and this divinely excited love goes out in sorrowing wonder and earnest yearning after the wandering and the lost. How much more does Thy heart go after them ! We are amazed at Thy lingering patience, for we know not all the depth and tenderness of God's unutterable love. Yet all our hope is in that long patience, which is patient above all womanly love and motherly care, and which would gladly weary out the devices and temptations of the great enemy. To Thy love and all the ministry which is centred in Jesus Christ Thou needest not that we commend all who are not with us this day. Yet it is in our hearts to pray much for them, that they may be recovered from the captivity of Satan.

What shall we say of our own sin? We cannot speak of it without shame and confusion of face, especially when we think of all the mercy which Thou hast shown towards us. Thou hast given us so much that it would appear as if our very sin could not quench the fountain of Thy blessing, yet surely this is a foolish imagining on our part, for we cannot tell how much Thou canst give if we had but spiritual capacity to receive it. Our iniquities have kept good things from us. God be merciful to us sinners ! We lay our hand upon the cross, and find all our hope in the blood of Thy Son, which cleanseth from all sin. Think of us in Jesus Christ's name, and even yet our sins shall not shut Thee out. Thou seekest to dwell in us as in a holy temple ; come and do so, and be the only Guest in the whole sanctuary of our love. Thou hast made us for Thyself, and we mourn that other gods have had dominion over us ; they were unclean and cruel gods, and we would cast out every sign of their awful presence. While we are yet speaking of our sin do Thou forgive it, and though we would not have our sense of its enormity diminished, we would see Thy love exceeding and overshadowing our great sinfulness. How much hast Thou already forgiven us! We know not of any hour in our whole life that did not need to be purified and brightened by Thy forgiveness, that it might be worthy of a place in the immortality which is given us in Jesus Christ. Even now, whilst we are in this Thy house, let us hear Thee saying that all our sin is cast behind Thee.

We know not how to tell Thee of our many wants; our joy is that Thou needest not to be told. As Thy great waters flood all the beds of the sea, and Thy rains fall even upon the desert and the rock, and the light of the sun shines upon all the earth, even more doth Thy love pour itself down upon the poverty of our needy and anxious hearts. We would be wise in Thy wisdom; we would love more according to the quality and measure of Thy love; we would be high above the world as Thou art, yet ever caring for it, and helping to make it good; we would partake of Thy riches, that other men might partake of our bounty. Thou hast given us all that has ever been for our good, every clear idea of truth, every tender emotion towards human suffering and want, and every aspiration which has raised us out of the benumbing influences of grovelling pursuits. Nor have we exhausted Thee; Thou art not a hireling serving an appointed time, Thou art the everlasting Father, full of all riches, which Thou offerest to the children of men; therefore we come again to the overflowing river of Thy loving-kindness.

We aspire very highly this morning, being encouraged to do so by Thy rich providential mercies. Thou hast given us the joy of early harvest; and just as men's hearts were failing them by reason of long-continued drought, wherein the watersprings did fail and the rivers shrink from their banks, Thou hast made a way for the lightning, and through the paths of the thunder Thou hast poured the cooling and freshening rain upon the parched fields. Thou hast also showers of blessing for Thy church, yea, even a blessing which the church has not room enough to contain. Excite in our hearts intense covetousness for this blessing, that we may give Thee no rest until Thou hast opened the windows of heaven. Give us firmer hold of Christ's truth, and a truer experience of His unspeakable peace; and may we prove that Thou hast heard us by living a holy and most heavenly life among men. Father, Son, and Holy Ghost, receive the praise and trust of our waiting hearts. Amen.

X.

PUBLISHED SERMONS.

You may not have heard that we have formed a kind of ministerial club, which we dignify with the name of the City Temple Council. I propose, therefore, to make you acquainted with some of our proceedings, that you may see with what audacity we sometimes talk of better men than ourselves, and with what consummate wisdom we dispose of vexed outstanding questions in the world of the pulpit. We claim exemption from every species and degree of obligation; we care nothing for missing links; we rather pride ourselves than otherwise upon informality and abruptness of speech; and it is our glory that we dare tell what we think, under the defiant flag of incorruptible independence. Our number is purposely small; four talkers and two dummies are all that we care to have, though scores of brethren would give almost half their goods to be allowed to sign their names on the list of the dauntless Six. The two dummies are excellent men; we keep them to save us from the least appearance of heterodoxy, and most admirably do they serve the purpose. They cannot truthfully be described as men of ideas, though we dare not so much as hint at such a thing in their solemn presence; they have nice, shiny, round heads, which would instantly make the reputation of any society; and as they never take their black kid gloves off at the council board, they throw a kind of other-world air over proceedings which often threaten to be much too earthly and boisterous. You must not imagine that they are literally dumb, — if they were, how could they be members of a Preachers' Council? All that is meant is, that they very seldom speak in the club: their nice bald heads shine at us; their well-gloved hands chasten the appearance of the board; now and again they make a joint rush at some unusual statement; and this is about all, with the exception of a few sonorous "hear, hears," that they do in their strictly official capacity as members of the Preachers' Council. Yet nothing could tempt us to part with these excellent dummies, so established and indisputable is their character as Orthodox theologians; it may be wondered, indeed, how they can meet with such freebooters as ourselves; but when I tell you that we give them more than three-fourths of their homiletic outlines, you will see that they do not serve the board for nought, and that they have peculiar reasons for not meddling with our reputation as sound divines. The talkers should rather be spoken of as three than four; because, for reasons best known to themselves, the brethren asked me to be chairman, and for the same conclusive reasons I granted their request. Mr. Washington (thickly bearded, with a gentle hazel eye, and a voice which says the boldest things in the most timid tone) is a prince of high intellectual and spiritual degree. A truer man never breathed. Often the shiny round heads are doubtfully wagged when he is talking some of his grandest things, yet his words are chosen in wisdom, and his thoughts are drawn from the well of life. When he says anything severe, he says it with reluctance and moderation, and thus actually doubles the force which he intended to restrain. Next to him usually sits a bright little brother, who is so prudent yet so sharp, so honest yet so pricking in his talk, that we have agreed, with his own genial consent, to know him and speak of him as the Safety-pin. He knows nothing of self-control; he first speaks, then thinks, and concludes the inverted and vexatious process by assuring the brethren that what he has said has been in the strictest confidence. I wonder if he fancies that a wound is any the less deep because it is inflicted behind a screen! One thing is certain, he never agrees with any of us if he can possibly contradict and defy us; and if ever he is in danger of thinking as we think, he seems to feel his condition acutely. This unamiability is a special qualification for membership in a controversial club, and in that light is regarded by his associates. The third of the speaking members is Mr. Dolson, — a brother who has a perfect mania for various readings; he can never be satisfied until he knows whether BDKLΔ agrees with CLM^2X, and whether C^3D confirms CHL. Mr. Dolson would be an excellent theologian, if he could so far get over the etymological difficulty as to convince himself that any one word in any one language has anything like a definite and sensible meaning. As to the chairman, nothing must be said; he *is* the chairman, and is not that enough? I shall now proceed to report one of our conversations, with the hope that you may light upon something which will be of use to you as a student for the ministry.

"Seen Binney's new volume of old sermons, any of you?" Safety-pin inquired.

"*You* have, evidently," one of the dummies actually said, to the amazement of every member, "or you could not have described it"; and the shiny round head beamed brightly.

Yes; we had all seen the volume, and had read most of it.

"A capital volume, too," said Mr. Washington, "and I am glad to have such a memorial of such a ministry."

"Can't see it," said Safety-pin; "I like Binney as well as any of you, but it seems to me — though of course what we say here is said in confidence, that's understood, I hope —"

"Thoroughly so," said I, with official promptitude and emphasis.

"It seems to me," Safety-pin continued, "that Binney's book might have been entitled 'Bewildering Essays, or the Gospel made dark, or the Gospel argued to death,'" — the shiny round heads moved rapidly in sign of contradiction. "Well, brethren may shake their heads if they please, but that is my opinion. I can understand the texts, but not the sermons; the sermons seem to me very much like the attempt of a wry-mouthed man to blow a candle out, the candle being the text."

Dolson. "Whatever do you mean? your figure is extraordinary."

Safety-pin. "But correct. I mean that the texts are lights, and that Binney blows them out in a very laborious manner." Mr. Washington said, "No, no," and the two shiny round heads confirmed his judgment by vigorous shaking. "But I say it *is* so," added the Pin, and the brethren laughed heartily at this unsophisticated assurance.

Mr. Dolson proceeded to attack the Safety-pin by urging upon him the duty of being critically correct in expounding a text, and of collating the various readings —

"Tut, man!" the Safety-pin interrupted, "bag o' moonshine! What do people want with such technical arguments and cumbrous judicial summaries as some of you deal in! They make me cry out, 'whenever will the man get done? we know all about that; do get on, and let us have something to bless our trembling and anxious life.'"

"Does Mr. Binney not give you the *gospel!*" Dolson boldly inquired, amid the repeated and sonorous "hear, hears" of the dummies, who spoke both at once.

"Certainly not," said Safety-pin, "that is exactly what he does *not* give us" — (the shiny round heads nearly shook themselves off); "he talks *about* the gospel, he goes round and round the gospel, he makes hard riddles and problems out of the gospel, but the gospel itself, in its simplicity and adaptation to human want, he seldom preaches in this volume."

We all protested warmly against this, and most justly. The two solid brethren both spoke together, and thus destroyed the individuality of their testimony, which seemed to be one of great indignation against the censorious critic. Mr. Washington strongly resented the opinion of the Safety-pin, and sharply demanded what was meant by so libellous a statement.

The Safety-pin was not only unabashed, but rather proud, for he detested the stagnation of unanimity. "Gentlemen," said he, vivaciously, "rage away, and when you have cooled yourselves I shall tell you what I mean. Now it so happens that I have the volume with me; and I shall, if you please, open it at random, and read a few of the long words and technical expressions which have led me to infer a want of fervent earnestness on the part of the preacher, and to fear that he has been, however unconsciously, trying to make an important figure of himself. Now I read at random, and you may read with me if you like: 'limits of human consciousness; piercing intuition; system of natural law; re-establish the harmony of things; passive impressions; subjective excitements; concentrate the action of the mysterious force in this subjective process; revealing the objective faith; would infallibly flow, by way of necessary effect, from an ever-operating cause; slender and superficial hypothesis; the hypothesis of such Divine Personality; stoppage of the actions of moral law; an acknowledged philosophical course of thought; the most perfectly philosophic and satisfactory solution of all the admitted phenomena; philosophical naturalism; revealing the objective—'"

We all cried *stop;* the two solid brethren went so far as to say that by this plan of picking out a word here and a word there they could make nonsense of any book in the world; Mr. Dolson said it was shocking; Mr. Washington, that as a method of criticism it was simply ridiculous, an opinion in which the chairman concurred.

"Very well, gentlemen," said Safety-pin, "you may misunderstand me if you like, but for your own sakes don't run away with the notion that I am setting this up as a method of criticism. I am not doing anything so insane: I mean to say that Mr. Binney has talked a kind of semi-philosophical jargon, and that he has chopped up Christian doctrine into little technicalities, instead of boldly proclaiming it to sinners as a way of salvation and to saints as a hope of final sanctity. He always seems to be talking to people who are either infidels or scoffers, for every sermon is just like a pitched battle with foes that are more imaginary than real."

The shiny round heads were shaken again, and the face of Mr. Dolson settled into the aspect of despair.

"I am not prepared to deny," said Mr. Washington, "that, in one view of the matter, there is force in what Safety-pin has said. There can be no doubt that there is a strong tendency in Mr. Binney's mind to get round to the purely intellectual side of every subject, and to discuss his texts as if in the hearing of captious men, who were mentally contradicting everything he said; he wants to give reasons for everything, and to ennoble common sense by assigning it a responsible function in the sanctuary; he is always anxious to marry Reason and Faith, and consequently he defies all comers justly to forbid the banns."

"And is that a commendable way of preaching the gospel?" Safety-pin inquired.

"As a general rule I should say *not*," Mr. Washington replied, "and probably Mr. Binney himself would agree with us; but you must bear in mind that we do require defenders of the faith, and that their work is second to none in importance. Now, Mr. Binney is distinctively, perhaps above all his brethren, a defender of the faith; to his own mind Christianity is so eminently *reasonable* that he becomes almost impatient with those who hesitate to accept it as such; to Mr. Binney's mind there seems to be hardly any space at all between common sense and Christian faith, and he himself has such a joyful satisfaction in receiving Christianity through his *reason*, that he wishes all that hear him to be as he is."

"But where is there a congregation made up of doubters and infidels?" said Safety-pin.

"True," Mr. Washington replied, "and therefore I say that as a general rule such preaching would very likely not be acceptable, because it would not be appropriate."

One of the dummies here interposed that "such preaching would make its own congregation."

"Precisely so," Mr. Washington continued; "and no doubt Mr. Binney has had a unique congregation; probably more sceptics have found their way to his chapel than to any other chapel in England. I should say that is very likely; and if so, it is very satisfactory."

"He takes nothing for granted, you see," said Mr. Dolson, "not one thing in the world."

"And there he 's wrong," said Safety-pin; "men don't want to hear a preacher who is eternally prove, prove, proving, and arguing their very hearts out of them; it 's absurd."

"But is it not better to argue than to declaim?" one of the dummies softly inquired, in a tone that sounded like "beg your pardon for speaking!" The Safety-pin took no notice of this exciting inquiry, but after looking quizzically at the questioner turned round and said, "Now, Mr. Chairman, let us have the pleasure of *your* opinion."

"Well, gentlemen," said I, "you have spoken very frankly on this matter, and I shall not commence the game of ambiguity. I have read Mr. Binney's volume carefully, and I am bound to say that there are three things which I could not honestly do with it: (1) I could not put it into the hands of a scoffer, and say *this* is Christianity; (2) I could not put it into the hands of an inquirer, and say *this* is the way of salvation; (3) I could not put it into the hands of a student, and say *this* is the method of sermonizing which I advise you to adopt. On the other hand, there are three things which I could most sincerely and cordially do with it: (1) I could put it into the hands of a scoffer, and say, see how the strongest-minded men adore what you deride; (2) I could put it into the hands of an inquirer, and say, Keep this book to read when your mind is in the best condition for studying Divine truth; and (3) I could put it into the hands of any student, and say, Learn from this how to labor in composing a sermon. I can't deny that in attempting to form an impartial judgment of this book I have considerable difficulty. This difficulty arises partly from my admiration of the man. I cannot keep Mr. Binney himself quite out of view; I see him and hear him, and instead of helping the reading, this rather spoils it, because Mr. Binney cannot be *printed;* all the way through I say, 'Where's the illuminating smile? Where is the bold, clear tone? Where is the explanatory shrug? Where is the keen steady glance?' And this kind of feeling damages the book. I feel, even when my fancy is most vivid, that after all I am only sitting *behind* the preacher, and I want to go round and look him in the face." I paused a moment.

"After all," said Mr. Washington, "what we want most is preaching that goes directly to the life of our hearers; we have but a short time to preach, and they but a short time to hear, so our words should aim always at the one point of saving the souls of them that hear us."

"But ought not our ministry to be colored by the times in which we live?"

"To some extent, Mr. Dolson; yet I confess if I had my ministry to begin again, I should not pay so much attention in the pulpit to passing controversies as I have done. I should preach with greater clearness and fulness the doctrine of the Cross, for that, I am persuaded, is the doctrine that best meets the whole difficulty of life, — it is the answer of *love* to the problem of *sin*, and when men get hold of it they are unspeakably glad; and as to our criticism upon brethren in the ministry, we should be very careful not to inflict the slightest injury on their reputation, and specially not to inflict the slightest injury on their feelings — "

"Fair criticism is quite allowable, you know," Safety-pin defensively interposed.

"I allow that; and so long as it is confined amongst brethren, it may do good. Even fault-finding may be educational; what I insist on is, that we should honor our brethren in our general conversation with the public, and so help to strengthen and extend their influence."

The two dummies openly applauded this view of the case; the Safety-pin was silent.

"Gentlemen," said I, "Mr. Washington has said for me all that I could have wished to say for myself. I do think that criticism may be made advantageous, as I trust in our own case it will prove to be. At the same time it may become an infinite vexation and nuisance, and when it becomes derisive of good men, it must be a grievous offence in the sight of God. We have been speaking to-day of brethren [we had spoken of others whose names are withheld] who have most conspicuous and influential talents, and whose work in the church is valuable beyond calculation; no doubt, they themselves would gladly increase their adaptation to services which some of us can render with comparative ease; and we, on the other hand, would be glad to possess qualities by which those brethren are so highly distinguished. We belong to one another, we cannot do without one another, and therefore we should magnify and honor one another. Gentlemen, with these just sentiments, allow me to dismiss you to your several engagements." So saying, I left the chair amid the subdued applause of my honest fellow-councillors.

In concluding this chapter, I cannot but feel that some good may be done by the interlocutory method of criticism. A reviewer may find it difficult to put all his objections and all his commendations in his own name; he may feel that some expression of adverse opinion is needful, and yet may shrink from the responsibility of giving that opinion as distinctively *his own;* it may be an opinion pretty widely entertained, and there may be considerable force in it; at the same time the reviewer may be unwilling to have it charged directly and exclusively upon himself personally. The interlocutory method may be so adapted as to give a very impartial and complete view of any book; there may be such a successful blending of animadversion and commendation as to secure for the reader a good general idea of the merits of the work under review. I think, too, that some advantage may be derived by authors from such remarks as are made by a man like Safety-pin: he is, indeed, often reckless, and generally destitute of regard for the feelings of any writer, yet his exaggeration will not deprive his criticisms of the value which undoubtedly belongs to them, whilst it will protect the feeling which would be lacerated by a cooler attack. Mr. Binney himself will smile at the manner in which Safety-pin lays hold of his noble volume, yet Mr. Binney will consider whether in the next edition he will not insert a sermon or two which will show that his genius in argument is fully equalled by his power of pathos. Better still, Mr. Binney may be led to see the necessity of preparing a second volume of discourses,—sympathetic, consolatory, and affirmatively (not controversially) evangelical. Mr. Binney's first volume will be prized in the college and in the study; Mr. Binney's second volume will be a favorite in the retreat of weakness, sorrow, and penitence. I cannot allow this chapter to leave my hands until I have expressed my sorrow that at length Mr. Binney has felt himself called upon to relinquish, to a very large extent, the great pastoral responsibilities which for more than forty years he has sustained in the city of London. He has done a work which can never be forgotten. I cannot but think it a happy coincidence that the *place* will be removed as well as the *man*. A feeble succession in the Weigh House pastorate would be intolerable; better that the pulpit and the preacher should go down together, leaving a memory which men will "never willingly let die."

XII.

SUBURBANISM.

A SUBURBAN pastorate! my friend Mr. Washington, though too robust to be unsettled by idle fancies, or seduced into self-indulgence by morbid sentiment, had sighed for such a pastorate as a happy release from the clouded and restless city in which he had ministered for twenty years. He longed to escape from the tumult and roar of crowded thoroughfares, and to enjoy the silence and contemplativeness of country life, — specially of country life on *Sundays*, when the quiet of rural scenery is hushed into a deeper calm, and made to harmonize with the peaceful joy which trembles in the good man's heart. I did not wonder at his passion for the country, because he had the trained ear which quickly hears the going of God in the paths of nature, and the penetrating eye which sees more than the mere letters which are written on the earth and sky. God had made him a deep interpreter of natural signs, and given him that enriching gift of amplification and ideal development by which poets are able to make for themselves new heavens and a new earth. He walked as a free man in the most charming haunts of nature; he knew the voices of the birds, and was familiar with the names of many trees and plants; like an ardent lover, he never tired of the sunny scene, and long after phlegmatic observers had exhausted its attractions some new blush caught his watchful eyes, or some winged minstrel detained him to listen to a wordless song. That such a man had a desire for a suburban pastorate is easily imaginable, and therefore, though too reverent to force the gate which separated him from the enchanting land, Mr. Washington would gladly have assisted a higher hand than his own in opening it. To a fancy so fertile as his, there were many urgent allurements: the church on the hill-side, happy families trooping from all directions to the house of the One Father; the book of revelation illustrated by the book of nature; opportunity for self-introversion; and that refinement of spiritual education which to some men is almost impossible amid scenes which incessantly strain their activities; — all these things charmed and tempted him, and at length brought him into bondage. Why not? Is it not hard for the poetic mind to dismiss the idea of an intermediate heaven, — a quiet and sunny place just on the border-land, lying between the great Shadow and the greater Light? To such a mind it seems a long way to heaven from the thronged streets through which Mammon drives its sweltering votaries, and but a step from the flowery and fragrant landscape to the City of peace. So it appeared to Matthew Washington, and he desired its realization, though he had not lost one impulse of his generous humanity; his pitying heart had not been chilled or shrivelled. So sure was I of this, that I had a deep conviction that he would carry with him all his city memories, and that they would very probably add a thorn or two to the tempting rose which he was so eager to pluck.

In talking over his experiences in a suburban pastorate, Mr. Washington gave me a little insight into that intermediate heaven of which he had been dreaming for many a day; and as it is quite lawful to utter everything I heard about that murky and deceitful sky, I shall take the public into my confidence, and interpret the vision of a few kindred dreamers.

Mr. Washington told me that he never knew what respectability was until he saw it in the suburbs. He had been accustomed to its presence in the city, doing its business, eating its public dinner, buying its pennyworth of literature, and pleasantly mixing with all the varieties of personality and costume which go to the making up of a city crowd. This was quite familiar to him. But when he saw respectability away from its mixed and softening surroundings, when its decorations were prominently displayed, and it seemed to have written out its claims after the manner of a bill of particulars, he told me that his first sensation was that of intense coldness, — he shivered as if a hand of ice had suddenly touched him, and looked round for the old kind friendships which had often made him glow with love to the whole world. When the broadcloth, the kid gloves, the jewelry, and fancy decorations are more prominent than the man; when the shell is exaggerated to a maximum, and the soul is confined to a small dark corner; it is not to be wondered at that guileless and earnest men are conscious of a change of climate which threatens their very existence. No respectability of culture, of nobleness, of benevolence, could have been too refined or too conspicuous for Matthew Washington; he would never have complained of this; he would rather have revelled and gloried in it with exceeding appreciation and thankfulness. But when respectability exhausted itself in cabinet-making, upholstery, and tailoring, he shrunk from it as from an effigy which he had mistaken for a living friend. In the suburb which Mr. Washington had chosen as the scene of his ministry, there were forests of mahogany, whole potteries of elegant ware, and nearly every house had a fancy bazaar of its own. To his unconventional mind it seemed that there must be quite a dearth of household articles in the rest of the world, and that his suburb had laid itself open to a just charge of voracious and heartless monopoly. The influence of this oppressive respectability was felt everywhere, — on the road, in the house, at school, but specially and cruelly in the sanctuary. Mr. Washington was very earnest in his manner of speaking about this; it was the chief difficulty of his pastorate, and he chafed under it without any attempt to conceal his pain. He felt that he was expected to determine his sermons by the local standard of respectability; he was to preach quite as much to the mahogany as to the men; he was to think of the Turkey carpets in his exposition, and to remember the porcelain in his peroration; the idol was constantly before him, clipping the wings of his fancy, cooling the fervor of his passion, and whispering with cold breath, "Sir, look at me, and mind your manners!" To a man of Washington's make, this was intolerable; he suffered patiently for a while, but at last the soul made a way for itself, and delivered a startling and burning testimony. The earnest witness had of course to reap the consequences of his temerity; several seat-holders protested, a few besought him to return to his "beautiful" sermons, and an indignant boarding-school abandoned the desecrated place forever. Were they not right? Is it a proper thing to let loose a whirlwind upon a genteel suburb? Is it becoming or agreeable to thunder the terrors of the Lord in the hearing of rate-payers who keep three servants each, and sneer at every house which has less than four rooms on the ground floor? Here was Mr. Washington's error, in not discriminating between the rough and worthless creatures who occupy the ungainly city, and the genteel and peerless lives that keep up the respectability of the nation. His hearers required doctrine without controversy, a lavish interspersion of rhyming couplets, and a loving assurance that, whatever became of the rest of the world, they themselves only wanted wings to become beautiful and happy as angels. This would have met their modest expectations, and secured their well-regulated applause. Instead of this, their bold and ardent pastor committed the unpardonable impertinence of metaphorically dismissing their coachmen, setting fire to their mahogany, sending back their ornaments to the goldsmith, and talking to their souls the pure and revolutionary language of the gospel. This "sort of thing" would have done admirably for the people who spend their Sundays under the city cloud, but was insufferable to the human nature that kept gigs, and formed intelligent opinions upon the prevailing fashions. When human nature keeps a gig, and is sufficiently refined to discriminate between one perfume and another, it is only proper that its theology should be at least abreast of its civilization. The ten commandments must subdue their tone, the sermon on the mount must be republished with emendations of every alternate sentence, and the New Testament must be bound in vellum, and so arranged that it opens most easily at the precious promises. Let this be done, and the world will enter into rest. The Dean of Canterbury, in the year of grace 1869, asked, "Why is not an attempt made to get rid of religion?" and the bold interrogator added, "Men of the world must find it a great plague. It robs them of one day in the week, as far as outward business is concerned. It obliges them to submit to, and bear part in, a great deal of what they must feel to be atrocious humbug." Let the Dean talk the matter over with Mr. Washington, and perhaps he will learn that in some suburbs "religion" has been most genteelly entombed, and that a guard has been set lest any of its fanatical believers should attempt to take it away. Men "get rid of religion" more respectably by chloroform than by a poleaxe.

Pedantic respectability was not the only difficulty with which Mr. Washington had to contend. Alongside of it, so to speak, there stood a grim opponent, properly called *Sciolism*. Every one in the congregation seemed to know a little about some out-of-the-way subject; not one had drunk deeply at the Pierian spring, but all had tasted its delicious waters. Mr. Washington's church became like an incipient university, wanting nothing but genius and learning to make it almost moderately respectable. Every household had its hobby, and every child felt himself at liberty to put Mr. Washington through "the larger catechism with proofs."

Mr. Washington thus came by some strange experiences, not without instruction to the rising ministry. One family, for example, proud of a garden thirteen feet by seven, had undertaken the study of botany, and had duly classified a guinea's worth of plants into Phanerogameæ and Cryptogameæ. Mr. Washington amiably admired the happy distribution, and thought he was coming off with flying colors, when a young lady, in her thirteenth year, utterly humbled him by asking whether the *Primula farinosa* belonged to the epiphytic or parasitic series of plants? Of course the young lady herself knew, and of course her heart struggled between pity and contempt as she looked upon her uncultivated and plebeian pastor. The famous "schoolboy" to whom Lord Macaulay so often and so flatteringly refers (unknown, however, to all the world except the omnivorous baron himself), would have instantly answered the trifling question off book, but the unmannerly Washington bluntly replied that he knew nothing about it. The blunder had serious consequences, — the young lady could never comfortably place herself under the guidance of so ignorant a pastor. Another family had taken up the science of geology with consuming ardor. The importance of a knowledge of the structure of the earth was paramount: no man was fit to live who was not deeply versed in palæontology and mineralogy, or who did not know the difference between an argillaceous rock and a mammaliferous crag. This was the noble creed of the amateur geologists; from morning till night their inspiring talk was about fossils, specimens, and remains; every mantelpiece in the house bore some sign of felspars, hornblendes, micas, and zeolites; every child who had escaped long clothes had heard something of lamination, interstratification, and lateral variation; the proud parents, blinded by the dazzling genius of their offspring, glowed with admiring and speechless love as they heard their youngest son expatiate upon the contemporaneity of beds, and the distinction between anticlinal and synclinal curves. Poor Mr. Washington was "nowhere" on this deep subject; but he little knew the blankness and culpability of his ignorance, until a youngster, in the act of finishing a muffin, asked him if he could tell when the Jurassic period ended and the Cretaceous period began. The union of such splendid intellect with so ordinary and useful an accomplishment, while it intoxicated the parents with delight, filled the pastor with humiliating dismay. Other families had their favorite pursuits,— astronomy, ethnology, history, chemistry, and even ontology in all its abysmal profundity and hazy amplitude; but the most conspicuous instance of scientific devotion was represented by a little company of three families, numbering on an average six members each, associated for the purpose of studying music. As the improvement of congregational psalmody was one of the subordinate objects of the association, Mr. Washington was occasionally invited to attend the meetings. My reverend friend was soon distracted by subtle discussions about dispersed harmony, dominant sevenths, and the percussion of dissonances, — the last being forcibly illustrated by two eloquent ladies. Mr. Washington was, of course, delighted with the rare accomplishments of his people. He said so; said so with hearty and generous emphasis; said so again and again, as if he had nothing else to say; his only wonder was that with eighteen such brilliant singers in his comparatively small congregation, the singing was not of a higher type; though he was bound to acknowledge, in common fairness, that since the association was founded, he had heard of several of its eighteen members singing a common metre tune or two in a genteelly mumbling sort of style so perfectly scientific and refined that not a soul could hear them at the distance of more than four inches.

With all this pedantic respectability, and still more pedantic sciolism, there was, of course, a good deal that was unnatural in the spirit and habits of the people. Everything was done by rule; everybody was secretly endeavoring to find out "the correct thing," and was determined to do it, whatever pain it might involve. To have made a morning call before three o'clock would have degraded the caste of the oldest inhabitant; to have shaken, with anything like cordiality, the hand of the most intimate friend, would have damaged the most established reputation; and to have laughed heartily, would have blighted the fairest prospects of life. It was of course forbidden that anything even remotely approaching surprise should be expressed; a comet was to be looked at in a most composed manner, a total eclipse of the sun was to be regarded as a commonplace affair, no notice was to be taken of so trifling an event as an earthquake; and as for shipwrecks, railway collisions, and colliery explosions, to have so much as named them, would have plunged the excited newsmonger into the depths of vulgarity. This frigidity chilled Mr. Washington to the core; it chilled his sermons; and, worst of all, it chilled his prayers,—those great prayers, so rich, so simple, so wise! He still had the solace of God's fair field of nature, and he enjoyed it to the full. Early in the morning he worshipped in the waving woods, and carried forward the sweet song of birds to a higher devotion; great nature was kind to him as a welcoming mother, opening many a hidden door to his appreciative eyes, and adding many a modest and pleasant acquaintance to the long list of his quiet friendships within the circle of the wood. As a thinker who worked rather from the spiritual centre than from the base of information, his field rambles were very helpful to him; his mind was quieted and toned by the most potent yet gentle influences, and he gathered in those lonely rambles the vivid and truthful images which give to his writings the living charm which allures the busiest reader to their close.

Yes; we owe Matthew Washington's writings very largely to his suburbanism. When he was in the city he wrote hurriedly, merely hinting at his subjects, and never doing himself justice either as a thinker or as a writer. It was enough for him to throw out an idea in its boldest form; he almost despised artistic garniture and studious elaboration, — there was the *idea*, what more could people possibly require? The consequence was, that a certain class of sectarian reviewers handled him very roughly; they described his style as jagged, abrupt, almost coarse, and one reviewer so far patronized him as to say "Mr. Washington is improving." How these words made me tingle and burn with anger! Washington himself merely smiled at them. "Why, sir," said I, "it were better to be cursed outright, than to have such dead praise!" I cannot forget the beaming of his face as he listened to this burst of youthful enthusiasm, — "It *is* being cursed outright," he answered, "if you did but understand it; the writer of these words means to sink me with a heavy compliment." I did not comprehend the sentiment then, but it has since come to have a clearer meaning. When Mr. Washington went into the suburbs he pleasantly said he would "try to spin better"; it was like him to speak thus modestly; there was resolution in the words, though they were so simple and unpretending; how far they were fulfilled is known only to those who were made acquainted with the extent of his anonymous writings. I never knew any man's style undergo a greater change; where it was short, edged, and rasping, it became flowing, persuasive, and conciliatory; and where once it would have but pointed a directing finger, it now revelled exultantly over the whole space which the writer's thought was intended to occupy. In addition to many essays upon some of the deepest problems in theology, he indulged in repeated excursions into more cheerful districts of literature, and enriched the serials of the day with many an airy dream and tuneful lyric, of whose authorship the noisy world never knew. He has listened to praises of his writings by men who never would have looked at them had they known their author, but not once did he yield to the pleasant temptation to say "*I* wrote them"; he heard the verdict, and his reward for years of hard schooling was enough to satisfy him. I wanted to publish his claims as an author, but he reminded me that silence is older than speech, and that fame is better for the dead than the living. I disputed this, and flattered myself that my logic was better than his.

"Why, sir," said I, "is not fame but another name for iufluence? and is not every one bound to increase his influence to the farthest possible extent?"

"Possibly so," he replied; "but where an author's discovered personality might substitute aversion for applause, he might diminish his influence by attempting to augment it."

"On the other hand," I ventured to rejoin, "is it not probable that in many instances the force of prejudice might be broken, and men be brought to own their mistake and repair it?"

"Now and again such a conversion would probably occur," he admitted; "but taking a wide view of life, I believe that it is better not to risk the influence of the thought by disclosing too early the personality of the thinker; that is, if his personality be in any way likely to excite prejudice. What does a moment's popularity amount to? Let a man give his name at last, if it so please him, for death is the best answer to prejudice; a stern and terrible answer I admit."

With these views Matthew Washington continued his literary vizor to the end. Never was workman more punctually at his post than was Washington at his desk; he wrote with his heart as well as with his hands; and though I was honored with his confidence for years, I never heard him say that any paragraph of his own fully satisfied his critical judgment. He could have improved a word, or strengthened a sentence, or burnished an image, or filed off an asperity, or done something which perhaps nobody else ever thought was in any degree necessary or desirable. My fear was that his suburbanism was making him too finical, and that for the old abrupt vigor he would substitute an insipid refinement. Happily my fear proved to be unfounded, for though the change in his style of expression was most marked, the pungency and strength of his thought escaped deterioration. His literary pursuits saved him from the melancholy which upon such a temperament as his would have been superinduced by suburbanism; he had a secret world all to himself, a world bright with stars and beautiful with many flowers, and in this world he found bread to eat of which his suburban friends did not know. Yet there was a grief darkening and depressing the good man's heart; and that grief arose from the fact that his people looked upon suburbanism as a providential exoneration from a good deal of the hard work which falls to the lot of what may be called city Christianity. The *poor*, being out of sight, were to a large extent also out of mind; Sunday-school service was unknown; tract distribution would have been an elaborate insult; open-air preaching would have brought eternal disgrace upon the whole suburb; and any other form of work would have ruined the reputation of its projector. Religion soon becomes a superstition when it ceases to be a practice; and in proportion as the second commandment is neglected, the first commandment becomes the occasion of the most corrupt selfishness, — necessarily so, for reverence without benevolence destroys the universality of relationship which stimulates and strengthens the best affections of human nature. To do the simplest work is to save religion from the most aggravated misanthropy. For a man to light his last candle, and set it in the window of his cot, with the hope that its ray may catch the eager eye of the struggling mariner, who would give the world for light, is to please God more than to perform the most stately ceremony, as if the earth were no longer the abode of suffering humanity. True, we must not forsake the temple; but, equally true, we must not neglect the disabled man who lies daily at its most beautiful gate. It is not denied that the picture of suburbanism now drawn is purposely exaggerated, but it is solemnly affirmed that there is enough of reality in it to demand the serious consideration of all who wish to do the work which Jesus Christ undertook throughout the whole of His ministry. No doubt the city is less pleasant than the green country; no doubt the elegant sanctuary is more agreeable than the great meeting-house which stands in the thoroughfare of an ill-kept town; no doubt there is a powerful charm in select society. All this is freely admitted. But when the whole case is viewed from the Cross of our Lord Jesus Christ, I cannot but hope that there will be a nearly complete inversion of the effects of suburbanism; surely the happy day will come when the members of Christian families will say to one another, as regularly as the dawning of the Sabbath, "We have enjoyed during the week many of the sweet and healthful blessings of the country; let us go to-day to visit in Christ's name and for Christ's good purposes the great city, that we may teach little children, that we may relieve and cheer the poor, and that we may support the ministers who witness for Christ under many discouragements." Such a holy resolution would add keener relish to the enjoyments of the whole week, it would gladden many cheerless lives, and give robustness to the finest graces of the soul. Would not such a course be *troublesome?* Not if lovingly pursued for Christ's sake. Would it not be *expensive?* A few less luxuries, a diamond ring or two, half a dozen gay parties fewer, would go a long way towards the annual cost; but what of the annual, the incessant *compensation?* What enlargement of mind, what satisfaction of heart, what thankfulness, what peaceful joy! Undoubtedly there would be trouble and expense; but are not these among the chief modern tests of our love for the Saviour? Aforetime men risked their liberties and even their lives for Christ's sake, and now we murmur if we have to endure the slightest inconvenience in His cause! We may have left our poor brother in the city, but he is our brother still, and we are his keeper! Parents have taken away their children from the sad sights of the great city, but their children may be weaker men as a consequence of this fancied privilege. Great men are trained by great discipline; the soul must have a great school; the conservatory may be full of beauty, but it is in the great storm-rocked forests that men find the timber for the temples of the land and the navies of the world.

XIII.

DR. JOHN CAMPBELL.

The circumstances under which I first met Dr. Campbell were likely to make a vivid impression upon the memory. By his invitation I went to London to assist him in his ministerial work, and on reaching my temporary home in Hackney was informed that the Doctor wished to see me precisely at seven o'clock the following evening in his own house. At that time (1852) he was the popular and influential editor of the *British Banner*, which was published at 69 Fleet Street. In order to graduate my approach to what was then, in my estimation, a formidable presence, I made it my business to spend part of the following morning in walking backward and forward in front of the *Banner* window, in the hope of catching a glimpse of the notorious denominational editor, — so little, alas, did I then know of editors and their windows! The window might have been opaque, for any good it did me; no editor, no publisher, no clerk, was to be seen, — nothing, in fact, was to be seen but the last number of the *British Banner* laid out at its full length, having, to my eye, quite a defiant aspect. I looked, and wondered, and looked again, and again wondered; what if the editor should come out and I should see him without his being aware of that circumstance! Very foolish, no doubt; yet such was my plight. To my rustic simplicity the second great fact in creation was Dr. Campbell, and my rustic timidity quite staggered under the probability that there might be only a sheet of plate glass between us. A youth who had been born within hearing of Bow-bells would probably have felt a contemptuous pity for such backwardness, for what could *he* know of life among the hills, where the proportions of supposed greatness were exaggerated partly by distance and partly by denominational pride? Be that as it may, my preliminary survey brought me nothing but disappointment. In the evening I set out for Dr. Campbell's residence; but, being a total stranger in London, I had the misfortune of getting on the wrong track, and landing, not at Tabernacle House, but at Tottenham Court Chapel,—something like three miles from my proper destination. While standing there, lost in such wonder as only a youth from the far-away hills can know anything about,—a half-stupid wonder which made me feel as if every cabman knew my mistake, and every policeman thought that I was meditating a deep and dangerous design,—a taunting clock pitilessly struck *seven*. There was a malevolent mockery in the deliberateness with which it struck, as if the whole metropolis were sneering maliciously at the provinces. In less than half an hour, however, by the aid of a cabman who seemed to know by cruel instinct that I had come from that barbaric region which the cockney knows as "the kentry," I stood, or rather trembled, on the steps of Tabernacle House. I am not sure whether the right hand had forgot its cunning, but I have a distinct recollection that my tongue would gladly have cleaved to the roof of my mouth. Bow-bells will say again that this was very silly, but Bow-bells cannot know the disadvantages of being born in "the kentry." On ringing Dr. Campbell's bell, I felt as if I had brought upon myself a storm which might end in my ruin; it *did* ring; I heard the tingling through the door and through the windows, and all round about me,—oh! how it rung. Poe must not have heard it when he wrote of the bells, for if he had heard it, another verse would certainly have suggested itself on the spot, In half a minute my hand was in Dr. Campbell's, and there was comfort in the warm grip! Commend me to a man who has a hearty way of shaking hands, and save me from cold bones and palms of steel. Dr. Campbell shook hands in a most welcoming manner, and so did much to recall my ease. Look at him! Broad, erect, with abundant gray hair standing up as if it had been suddenly startled into disorder, and with linen enough around his neck to dress half a denomination. What a collar! At the back of the head it rose as high as the organ of philoprogenitiveness, on the cheeks it stood up like a protest against the ears, and in front pointed itself against society with a desperation that would have been alarming if it had not been comical. I had seen collars like it in engravings, but until that moment had seen nothing like it in actual linen. Then the voice, — what nervous young man from the mountains could be quite easy under such gruff tones? Its very gentleness was a kind of muffled roar; what then must it have been when sounding in full compass! There was positively a sound of doom in it. Who could safely contradict what it declared? In the Doctor's hand there was a long strip of paper, such as I had never seen; I did not know what it was, but afterwards found that it was the proof of a newspaper article, — in other words, a long, thick, rough rope for the scourging of any man who ventured to have a will of his own. That was the beginning of my acquaintance with newspaper proof-sheets, — excellent material no doubt, provided always that they are in excellent hands. I could not but notice a peculiar habit of breathing in my reverend host; that operation seemed to be conducted entirely through the mouth, and appeared to have been reduced to a system of powerful gasping, by which he was constantly declaring that he was not in the least asthmatic, notwithstanding the plainest evidence to the contrary. Happily I soon forgot everything in the gentle smile, which quite enlightened and softened the rugged Roman face, and almost overflowed the snowy collar. Dr. Campbell's friends will often think of his characteristic smile, how it played upon his shaggy eyebrows, wreathed his Cæsar-like lips into dignified complacency, kindled a genial glow on his broad brow, and lost itself in the forest of his upright and redundant hair. Does not everybody's smile do pretty much the same thing? Grant that, if you please, and still there will remain a peculiarity of expression which distinguished Dr. Campbell's smile from every other which I have seen.

"What age are you, sir?" the Doctor inquired in his blandest manner, laying down the proof-sheet, and breathing in the way described.

"Twenty-two, sir."

"Ah!" (gasping and smiling) "You are very young, very young; and though, sir, this is not the day for boys," (smiling very kindly) "we must have youthful energy; yes, yes" (gasping as if punctuating). "Well, sir, and what texts have you for to-morrow?"

"In the morning, sir, I think of preaching from Heb. xii. 18: 'Ye are not come unto the mount that might be touched,' etc.; and in the evening from Luke ix. 9: 'John have I beheaded, but who is this of whom I hear such things?'"

"Just so, sir, just so," the Doctor replied, with an ominous gasp, "very good; but now let me see, to-morrow is Easter Sunday, and some reference should be made to the resurrection. I tell you therefore what we shall do. I shall read a portion of Scripture bearing upon it and offer a running comment; I shall then offer prayer, and leave you about forty minutes for your sermon." Having said so, he smiled, as if the brightest of ideas had been propounded.

The idea did not lay hold of me in the same happy manner, but there was doom in the voice! Secretly I wished that the running comment could be postponed until some other Easter Sunday, but dare not have said so for the world. My own sermon might, I thought as I returned to Hackney, pass muster if it went by itself, but it will utterly fail under the strain of contrast. My own dream was a running comment, in a sense that is not exegetical, and in fear and trembling I appeared on the following morning to undergo the culminating trial of my life. When we met in the vestry, the first time I had seen the Doctor in daylight, I thought I had never looked upon a more intensely masculine and powerful face. There was not one weak line in it, one soft and plastic spot to which a young man from "the kentry" might trust in the event of failure. All was solidity, massiveness, force; and in the daylight I thought I saw even in the smile itself a curious wrinkle which looked a good deal like a mark of interrogation. Certainly it did not look so credulous as it did the night before; there was evident inquiry in it, and, as it appeared to my terror, a touch of prophetic success in the matter of the running comment. The forehead did not convey to me a strongly favorable impression of the Doctor's benevolence; but the whole head, by its magnitude, its broad base line, and its firm *set*, showed that its owner was a man of no little intellectual capacity. The eye was small, deep-set, not piercing, but calmly observant. I never saw the faintest sign of fire in it; it seemed to be a merely receptive eye, taking minute and general surveys, but never telegraphing to others any hint of the surveyor's impressions and reflections. One can sometimes catch a revelation in other men's eyes, even when the men themselves are doing their best to keep their secret thoughts; but Dr. Campbell's eye never showed a sign that betrayed his feeling. The nose was of the boldest Roman type, extremely large and most clearly outlined, the nostrils being particularly well curved and expressive. Not one man in ten thousand has such a nose; if it was not really as good as ten talents, it was certainly an excellent fortune to begin the world with. Behind so vast and energetic a nose there might have been volumes of martial poetry, several military romances, and at least ten victorious battles. And such lips, — lips enough and to spare! They overhung, they revelled in strength, they shut like iron doors! As for the mouth, it was not a mouth, it was nothing short of a cavern; and when a laugh came out of it, the sound was not the most refined which has ever been heard among men. There he stood on that memorable Easter Sunday morning, primed with a running comment; and there was I, rustic, hesitant, wonder-struck, with a few sheets of paper in my pocket, which seemed to me to be the most unsatisfactory sheets that ever were written. Friends at home had seen them, or heard their words, and with too partial love had spoken well of them; but on that Easter Sunday morning the very ink had almost faded out, and the orthodoxy appeared to have got a heretical twist. To my great alarm, the Doctor decided that we should go into the pulpit together; and having taken several papers in his left hand, away he went, his right arm swinging energetically, and striking back his coat with regular blows. He might have been going to fight a battle instead of giving a running comment; his port evidently meant war to any one who might have come in his way. Having opened the service very solemnly, he gave his proposed comment very much to my satisfaction. Without any attempt at verbal criticism, there was an intelligent apprehension of the idea, and an evident desire to bring the hearers into sympathy with the historic spirit of the day of triumph. There was no attempt at style, no critical choice of words, no aim at rhetoric; but there was a very solemn and urgent earnestness which well befitted the occasion. Most of the sentences were short, some of them coldly glittering, all of them practical, and throughout the whole a reverence mingled with joy which became those who were in imagination standing beside the empty tomb of their Lord. Dr. Campbell did not strike me, either on that occasion or any other, as a pulpit orator in the ordinary sense of the term. In the pulpit he was very formal, quite stiff in fact, as if he had suddenly become all collar together; he never fell into ease, or conciliatory familiarity, but always stood aloof as an imperial, an unapproachable presence. What soul would ever dare to go to such a man in the night of its trouble and wonder and weakness? His pulpit, a very volcano in the days of Whitefield, seemed to be a mountain of ice, and his words like storms of hail. This was the impression which strangers would often take, but I am bound to say that such an impression did not do Dr. Campbell full justice. He could be tender and sympathetic; after the hail could come the dew; out of the terrible mouth could come the gentle and healing word. Probably he knew nothing of the agonies which torment many speculative and sensitive souls; very likely he thought the Assembly's Catechism furnished "a sovereign balm for every wound"; and possibly he did not know what to do with those adventurous spirits that prefer flying to walking; still, within the limits of technical theology, he was no unskilful physician. In the pulpit he was lofty and stern; in the house he was familiar and gracious. His platform appearances were often very effective. He had a happy word for everybody, and an agile way of escaping difficulties. Sometimes he half threatened to be humorous, and though he never could sharpen a sentence into wit, yet he could nod his gray plume in a manner which indicated that only the restraints of grace kept him from the dissipation of jocularity. There was not much coherence in his speeches; they were like baskets full of fragments,—a bit for everybody, not excepting his critics and opponents.

From the Easter Sunday in question Dr. Campbell and I worked a good deal together, and my association with him enables me to say something about his character and habits which no one else has the means of saying. His method of directing my own labors was highly characteristic, while the spirit in which he gave his advice was often that of a truly Christian father,

To pronounce him a perfect man would be to ignore many most distressing evidences of imperfection; to pronounce him always a just man would be to wink at some of the gravest and cruelest injustice which disfigures the honor of public life; yet at the particular time of which I write there was enough about him to inspire confidence and beget a very cordial love. His advice was too mature to be treated with levity, and his generous consideration disarmed a very rigorous criticism. The general impression which he made upon me was that, in all cases requiring sound judgment, he was capable of rendering very valuable service; though if any prejudice should be at work in his mind, he could never rise above it, and speak with the serenity and candor of impartiality.

A sketch of the Doctor's manner of directing my work as his assistant will show one view of his various life. Suppose it to be Saturday morning, and probably I shall receive a note to this effect: "My dear young friend, tea at five o'clock, after which the preachers will go about their business. Yours cordially, J. C." Half an hour is spent at the tea table in the pleasantest manner; everybody is happy; the Doctor addresses minute inquiries to each guest as to health and pursuits, and hits each case so exactly that the guest supposes himself to have been enjoying the Doctor's consideration for some time past, — a very innocent delusion on the part of the guest, yet showing to an observer the great advantage to a pastor if he can only remember every toothache, every cough, and every fever, which may have afflicted his congregation. This was the Doctor's forte. If there were twenty people at the table, he could have spoken to each some word indicative of strong individual interest, and left the impression upon unsuspecting minds that when all other friends failed, he would be their friend forever.

"Now, sir, let us leave the ladies and betake ourselves to the study," the Doctor would remark, smiling upon the ladies in a manner which made our exit very easy.

"Well, sir, read your morning's sermon, if you please, and let us see what can be done." I would then read the morning's sermon from beginning to end. On concluding it, the Doctor would offer his criticism.

"Too long, sir, I am afraid. Suppose you cut down the first division, say one half. Yes, do that." Or again, "Too many heads, sir, too many by far. I don't like to hear a sermon that is broken up into a thousand fragments. A good many of the heads may be given without formal specification."

"Did not many of the old preachers use a good many heads, sir?"

"They did, but then they *were* old preachers, and the manners of the people were different. We must study what will be most effective and useful."

On another occasion the Doctor would say: "The morning text is hardly suitable for you; come, now, suppose we try something else: let me see; yes; take so and so (naming another text), and let me hear what you can make of it in the morning."

"But there's no time, sir!"

"No time! So, so! Never say that, sir; time enough! Come, now, let me break the bones of the text for you; in the first place there is," etc. And so he would go through the leading ideas of the passage, and wish me to write according to his exposition, never for a moment allowing me to escape on the plea that there was not time to do what he proposed.

"Now, sir, will you proceed with the evening sermon."

The evening sermon was read accordingly. "I am not quite sure, sir, that you are right in your exegesis; let me see." The original would then be appealed to, and one or two of the best critical authorities consulted. On all occasions the grammar, the rhetoric, and the theology of the sermons which had been prepared were freely criticised, so that I received the benefit of a life-time's education and thirty years' varied ministerial experience.

The sermons having been disposed of, I was next called upon to read my literary diary. Every Saturday the Doctor gave me theological, critical, or biographical works which I was expected to read, and on the following week I had to present him with a careful analysis of their contents, with criticisms upon the argument and style of each author. The thing which struck me most was the Doctor's clear recollection of books which he had read twenty or thirty years ago, a recollection which was shown not only by precise reference, but occasionally by almost literal quotation. I was glad of this, as I had the advantage of it, not only as a moral check, but as an intellectual stimulus.

When the sermons and the diary had received due attention, a part of the evening's engagement came which I can seldom recall without tender emotion. We knelt together in the study, and the Doctor offered prayer, which was truly the "preparation before the Sabbath." I never heard any one so gifted in private prayer. The solemnity, the simplicity, the fervor, were deeply impressive. The special supplications which he never failed to offer for myself were most pathetic, and so powerfully did he plead for a blessing that often my heart was enlarged in holy and loving desire towards God, as if the answer had been given "whiles he was praying." However much business the Doctor had on hand, the prayer was never omitted; and each prayer was as new as if the spirit of devotion was never exhausted.

So ended the Saturday evening in Dr. Campbell's study, and I returned to my own to give effect as far as possible to his suggestions. On the Sabbath morning there was always a smile for me, and some word of encouragement in relation to the day. On Sabbath evenings we spent many a happy hour in the Tabernacle House, reviewing the public engagements, relating incidents which illustrated the doctrine which had been taught, or listening to the Doctor's reminiscences of pastoral life. The Doctor, though ever genial, never allowed us to sink into frivolity; in his most relaxed moods he was always so self-restrained as to be able, without violent transition, to advert to the most serious subjects; and even in his liveliest moments, when he was indulging his most humorous sallies, he was quoting poetry, epigrams, or biographic incidents, all of which gave his lightest conversation a rare and most graphic instructiveness.

On the Monday morning after my first Sunday at the Tabernacle, I went by invitation to the editorial office of the *British Banner*, — a dark, dirty room, literally crammed with books and papers of the most miscellaneous description. Near the window sat the editor at his desk, and before him lay a scrap of paper on which he had jotted what he called a few "catchwords." On the other side of the table sat one of the Doctor's short-hand writers. The process of *dictating* a leading article was about to begin, and the Doctor having warned me to be "as still as a mouse," the editorial steam was turned on. A look at the scrap of paper, and then a paragraph; another look, and another paragraph; the great voice sounding, and the gray plumage of the noble head nodding, in the most characteristic manner. Sentence after sentence, paragraph after paragraph, now very epigrammatic and anon bordering on the rhetorical; here very sensible, and there nearly bombastic; one sentence striking like a dart, and another stunning like the blow of a hammer. As soon as the first leading article was finished, the bell was tingled, and reporter No. two came to the desk. The process was repeated; with a Johnsonian copiousness and often with a Johnsonian precision, the editor proceeded. Was it a *personal* article? Then let the victim be pulled bone from bone, and limb from limb, and let him be pounded in a mortar, and let the pounded victim be thrown to the dogs. Was it a *church* article? Then let great principles be asserted, let "the law and the testimony" speak, and whoever opposes, let him fall. Was it a *favorable* article? Then let all superlatives be called to the front, and summon every word that can be pressed into the service of praise; then the delineation will stand thus — unrivalled, matchless, magnificent, stupendous, overwhelming. Was it a *condemnatory* article? Then reverse the process, and the case will stand thus — presumptuous, outrageous, mendacious, flagitious, infamous, and diabolical. It may easily be conceived that as a young man I listened to this literary Niagara with some alarm, and not until I had learned that the Doctor did not really mean all that he said did I feel in any measure composed as a listener. When I say that he did not really mean it, the expression must not be misunderstood. He himself was personally sincere, else he would not have braved and even defied public opinion as he did; but he did not accept the great words in the sense in which they would be generally understood. For example, where an ordinary man would express simple regret, Dr. Campbell would express the uttermost anguish and horror of soul; where such a man would say that he did not approve of a certain course, Dr. Campbell would characterize that course as one which outraged alike reason and propriety, and rose to the point of shameless and scandalous mendacity; where the said ordinary man would nod approbation, Dr. Campbell would pronounce the commended object as the most magnificent and illustrious display of genius on which he had ever fixed his admiring and enraptured attention. Both the ordinary man and Dr. Campbell would mean pretty much the same thing, only Dr. Campbell always carried a longer ladder than was necessary to reach the object he had in view. Dr. Johnson speaks of somebody laying a forty-pounder to the door of a pigsty, and certainly Dr. Campbell would not have hesitated to have turned an Armstrong gun upon a dove-cote or a dog-kennel. His weapons were very often out of proportion to the battle; he often overlaid himself with instruments and armor, and so came in many cases to have the appearance of defending a garden wicket with a park of artillery. There was nothing ordinary in Dr. Campbell's world. All the geese were swans, all the swans were eagles, all the eagles were seraphs in disguise. It was a very stupendous world. Some of the German horse-trainers are said to be in the habit of putting highly magnifying spectacles upon young horses, that they, being deceived as to the magnitude of the stones upon the street, may acquire a high step. By some means the same kind of spectacles had been put upon Dr. Campbell's nose; so pebbles became paving stones, and the paving stones were the hugest boulders. He believed it most sincerely, and all his public course was more or less affected by the strange infatuation. Hence we find that if any speculative brother broached a novel theory, we were, according to Dr. Campbell, about to be lost in German mysticism; if any man hinted that the Westminster Confession of Faith was strict, the spirit of scepticism was coming in like a flood; if the pope wrote an extra letter, England was about to be carried away as with a whirlwind!

The habit of dictating his articles, instead of patiently and critically writing them with his own hand, while it enabled the Doctor to get through an immense amount of work, exposed him to very great peril. He often became rhetorical when he should have been judicial, and in rounding a period he was apt to be more careful about the curvature of a sentence than the absolute justness of the sentiment. Had he done less he would have done more. There can be no doubt that while the works which were written without the aid of an amanuensis contain many most vigorous and even beautiful paragraphs, replete with intelligence and exact in expression, many of his dictated productions are little better than waste paper. Undoubtedly there are sentences, and not a few of them, even in these productions, which are as accurate as they are vigorous; yet the productions as a whole are unworthy of the occasionally eloquent and graphic style of "The Martyr of Erromanga." For correspondence and brief notices of unimportant books, dictation may serve every purpose; but close, correct, and polished composition demands most patient and critical elaboration. But how could such elaboration possibly be given to all the works which Dr. Campbell undertook? Think of one man editing two weekly newspapers and two monthly magazines, besides conducting a voluminous correspondence and occasionally preaching, and addressing public meetings! Nor was this all: in the midst of such engagements he wrote a commentary on the Bible! That all this could have been done by his own hand is simply a physical impossibility; hence the truth of a remark which he once made to me in his own house. Throwing himself into his arm-chair, he said, "I have done more work to-day than any six men could have done without the aid of short-hand." That he soon felt the limit of his merely manual power is pretty evident from a paragraph written in the *Christian Witness* eighteen months after he undertook the editorship. "Experience," he wrote, "has already taught us that most, if not all, our labors in connection with committees, public business, and public meetings appertaining to religion and humanity, with special services of all sorts both in town and country, must be abandoned. Nor is this all; regular courses of general study must henceforth subside into general excursions, and all further attempts at solid authorship be at an end." When these words were written, Dr. Campbell was doing the full work of the pastorate; yet even allowing for that, it is almost incredible that he could have added so much more literary work to the editorship of a magazine which taxed so heavily his time and strength, — indeed, it would have been absolutely impossible to have done it, apart from the assistance of short-hand. But with a free use of short-hand came the most of his public mistakes, which were neither few nor trivial. Of course it is an easy thing for a man who to strong feeling adds an ample command of language, to sit in his editorial chair and fulminate against men and things in general. There is a pleasant excitement about the exercise; the use of short-hand relieves the physical labor, and what is saved in fatigue of body is added to zest of mind; oratorical excitement, too, inflames the editorial mind, and gives a keen interest to all combative engagements. So long as the language is vigorous, who cares for the absolute equity of the sentiment? If the sentences fall rhythmically, it is of small consequence what may be thought of the doctrine. This is the peril of dictation; the dictator finds it difficult to stop, the short-hand writer is waiting, the printers are crowding round the door, and the article must be finished. Under such circumstances many an ill-selected word and many an ill-fashioned sentence are allowed, to meet the exigency of the moment. Beyond most men Dr. Campbell was in danger from literary dictation. His sensibilities were strong; his turn of expression was naturally exaggerated; his prejudices were often unreasoned and generally very obstinate; so that to be hurried where he ought to have been calm, to be compelled to produce where he ought to have had leisure for the most critical revision, was to be put in the way of a most urgent and flattering temptation. It must ever be much the same where any man has to write by quantity, where work is weighed by avoirdupois and not by troy, or where square yards of type are of more importance than literal exactness. In this way I find it less difficult, knowing Dr. Campbell as I did, to account for many of the extravagances which justly offended those who knew the man only by his fervid and often bombastic leaders.

One circumstance I remember well, as illustrating not only the perils of dictation, but the method of Dr. Campbell's reviewing. A book called "The Eclipse of Faith" was sent to the *Banner* for review; and the Doctor boldly began his dictation with the sentence, "Another dart from the quiver of the enemy!" That book, I need not say, is one of the ablest defences of Christianity which has appeared during the century, yet it was so described by the rhetorical dictator. When he came home on the evening of the day on which that review was published, I was in his parlor, and well I remember him throwing himself into his arm-chair, and exclaiming, "I have made the greatest mistake ever I made in my life! I would have recalled the whole edition of to-day's *Banner* if I could."

Others, however, must be left to offer judgment upon Dr. Campbell's public position and services; my object is rather to cite such of his opinions and exhortations as were addressed to myself as a young preacher. In my youthful devotion I found time to write nearly all that my Mentor ever said to me respecting the ministry; and as many of his remarks have more than a personal interest, they may be useful to other students and young ministers. Take a sample: —

When I was a young minister a wet Sunday was a terrible annoyance; I would mourn that, after having labored in preparation for a whole week, the chapel would be half filled. Age has taught me this lesson — to preach as willingly to two hundred as to two thousand, knowing that men are accountable as *individuals*, and not in their aggregate capacity. Pride is not entirely wanting, when a preacher can only minister to crowds. Always remember that one soul saved is enough to repay the most laborious preparation.

Be careful in rebuking *ill behavior* from the pulpit; it is difficult sometimes to restrain indignation, yet when an angry word has been spoken it cannot be recalled; there is therefore great necessity for exercising discretion. In some cases a rebuke has been effectively administered by aged ministers, — their seniority has been the best possible shield from retaliation; a word from their lips would be useful, when the very same expression from the mouth of a junior would be considered ill judged and worse than wasted. Private expostulation is more commendable than pulpit correction.

In the course of a lengthened ministry I have met with some mighty nuisances in the form of *one-eyed* men, *one-legged* individuals; for example, there are those who will liberally subscribe to local missions, who would not give a coin to the support of foreign missions; they will patronize the Bible Society, but have nothing to do with Sunday-schools; they will be superintendents or nothing. They have their own peculiar notions as to Christian duty and propriety, and to those they cling with unyielding tenacity. It is impossible for young ministers to work harmoniously with such one-armed men; and not only so, but they frequently prove sources of intense annoyance to all who are earnest-hearted and willing to do anything that goodness and truth may universally prevail.

All young ministers should abstain from occupying much of their time in political or other controversy. Their business is to *preach the gospel.* As a father, I would entreat you to devote the first ten years of your ministerial life to the *pulpit.* There will be numerous calls upon you to advocate this and the other good cause; but if you spend your energies to any considerable extent in platform work, your preparation for the pulpit will be scanty and unsatisfactory. Nothing great will be accomplished without *singleness* of aim; there are indeed men who appear equal to any amount of work, however diverse; yet the majority of preachers are not so: therefore, whatever may be the exceptions, the general rule should stand thus, — devote supreme attention to Sabbath duty, and if you have any leisure time you can devote it to other good purposes. After ten years' laborious study you will be surprised to find how comparatively easy your work will then become; much, however, depends on the *habits* you form in the early part of your public life.

Dr. Campbell's public prayers were unusually rich and impressive. On the subject of prayer in public, he said to me: —

My custom for many years has been to ponder on a Sabbath morning such facts concerning the fellowship as might have come to my knowledge during the course of the week. I have taken a slip of paper and jotted down the several items, *e. g.:* — Are any sick? Is any member suffering from sorrow, relative or personal? Has any death occurred? What is there in the Sabbath-school demanding special notice? Are there any inquiring the way of salvation? By asking those questions, you will be in a position to meet the wants of the people in an acceptable manner. Be assured that if you wish the congregation to follow the line of petition you must touch every heart, and as far as practicable allude to every case; in this way, the devotional exercise becomes thoroughly *congregational.* It is lamentable to observe how much of our petitionary agency is mere vapid formality, performed in so perfunctory a manner that the congregation feels quite relieved when the prayer is concluded. It has frequently happened that men have been brought to God in the act of public prayer, — their case has been so strikingly marked out, and mercy so fervently implored, that they have been brought to consideration and penitence. It must of necessity arouse attention, when a professed worshipper can say, "*that's my case,*" while the minister is leading the devotion; and having excited attention, there is every prospect of creating sympathy. Observe, we must have *prayer,* not *talk;* the difference is essential. True prayer is the language of the heart; it is simple, earnest, scriptural. To succeed in public petition I know nothing so useful as a previous reading of the devotional portions of the Bible. There is no liturgy equal to many parts of David's psalms, — there you have the man's heart poured out in the fulness of simplicity. In order to preserve *variety* in prayer, — for it is as necessary in prayer as in preaching, — endeavor to ground the main line on the Scripture just read; it will be easy to bring in congregational thanks and necessities on this as a basis. Never try to be eloquent, flowery, or fine in prayer; be lowly, reverent, and simple. Avoid all eccentric expression, all trite, smart sayings, as incompatible with the spirit of acceptable devotion. When man communes with God, he should be utterly abased and filled with self-distrust; for only as man sees himself as nothing, and God as everything, will he learn to worship "with reverence and godly fear." Some men have a peculiar habit of quoting scraps of hymns and even couplets from poems of another order, while engaged in prayer. Abjure this practice: it is unbecoming and unnatural for a beggar to ask an alms in rhyme; men would consider it so were the case their own. On every ground, therefore, *sing* your *hymns* and *pray* your *prayers*, for this is the path of nature and propriety.

In the course of a lengthened pastorate Dr. Campbell did a good deal of Bible-class work. His opinion as to the value and conduct of such service will be approved by many pastors:—

Some men are pre-eminently adapted to this kind of work. Men who could never occupy any distinguished pulpit position have made their way most effectively by devoting supreme attention to Bible-classes. The talent required in these separate departments is quite of a different nature; the eloquent and impassioned orator seldom makes a calm and judicious teacher. He is too rhetorical to meet the wants of inquiring minds on the fundamental outlines of Christian theology. The same remark is conversely true respecting the mere *teacher;* he can break the truth into pieces, so to speak, suited to the capacities of all, but in the pulpit is destitute of that synthetic power which is necessary for rapid combination, so as to produce forcible and lasting impression on the minds of a popular auditory. Supposing, however, that a minister is adapted for class instruction, much of his success will depend on the *manner* in which it is conducted. As a rule, all *controversial* subjects should be avoided, and attention entirely confined to standard doctrine. When once young men begin to dispute and cavil, there is no saying where the matter will end; let them therefore in the first instance be thoroughly grounded in the "faith once delivered to the saints," and afterwards they will be in a position to encounter the various forms of error everywhere so abundant. Free inquiry should by no means be discountenanced; at the same time, reason and experience concur in affirming that all men should be conversant with certain first principles before they venture to appear in the arena of intellectual or theological contest. To enunciate and develop those first principles is one of the leading objects of every well-conducted Bible-class. So far as the students are concerned, it is well to cause *them* to *speak* as much as the case may require; such a course will deepen *individual* interest, and facilitate correct and fluent expression. When a man feels that *he* is expected to do something, he is quickened into action, he thus begins to feel his own deficiencies and manifest anxiety for their supply. On the contrary; when he knows that the interest of the class depends *entirely* on the conductor, he sinks into a kind of intellectual passivity, assenting to everything and examining nothing. A portion of Scripture — say, one of the epistles — should be chosen; a given number of verses should be announced as the subject for the ensuing week; every member should then be separately interrogated as to the scope and design of the passage; it being understood that the verses are read in rotation, and that each reader has the priority of expression as to the signification of the verse read. In this manner an interest is excited and sustained, which would not attend any individual exposition, however apt or luminous. It is also an excellent practice for each student periodically to prepare an essay on some scriptural subject. By this means he is instructed in composition, and is affording to others an opportunity of exercising their critical skill. There is one difficulty attending this matter, viz., when the choice of a subject is left to the class, an amount of hesitation is felt which prevents definite action; to the end that this difficulty be obviated, it is well for the minister himself to announce a theme and request an essay or essays upon it. This plan has been found to work admirably in the higher class of biblical tuition.

There is another object never to be forgotten, viz., at the conclusion of the service the conductor should detain one or more of the attendants, for the purpose of holding private spiritual conversation. This may be easily done, by stating that he wishes a brief interview in the vestry; persons who would shrink from close religious scrutiny in the company of others will feel quite at liberty to converse on personal godliness under such circumstances as now defined. The conversion of the soul is the great end of all pastoral labor, therefore every possible means should be employed for realizing this momentous object. In the pulpit you can only speak in generalities, even in your most fervent and searching appeals; but when you are speaking to only *one* individual, there can be no mistake as to the identity. In the sanctuary men hear for others, but in this close address the individual is compelled to hear for himself. Never shrink from this duty; sometimes it calls for much fortitude and self-denial, but be assured the reward is most abundant. The person will feel that his soul is cared for; he will see that whatever may have been his own carelessness, there is at least *one* who has ventured in faith and love to introduce the most important of subjects. The most hardened have been subdued in this manner; the man who would charge a minister with *preaching* for money may be undeceived by that same minister daring to arrest his attention on the matter of his personal salvation.

No man values the pulpit more than I do as an instrumentality in the propagation of religious principle. At the same time there are certain *adjuncts* which are inconceivably important, if not absolutely essential. Among these the Bible-class is worthy of high rank. It affords opportunities for conversing upon subjects which could not be handled with equal advantage in the public ministry. The voice of inquiry may be heard, and the response of wisdom be returned. Wherever the exercises of the pulpit are sustained with vigor, the Bible-class will be found powerfully instrumental for good; and where pulpit duties are inefficiently discharged, something is requisite to supplement their deficiencies and compensate for their weakness. Devote, therefore, your best energies to the encouragement and instruction of the young. They are the hope of the church, and as such imperatively demand the attention and sympathy of all who love the Lord Jesus. Wherever practicable, it is well to encourage suitable reading among the members, by forming a library of select literature; financially, this could be easily accomplished by each individual contributing a given proportion towards a general fund.

The following advice upon church discipline commends itself alike on the ground of prudence and feeling: —

A meeting of the church should never be convened until there is sufficient business to warrant doing so. To act otherwise is simply to squander time. Church meetings are seldom conducted in a proper manner. Some men appear to be so entirely ignorant of public usage and decorum that they deport themselves on such occasions in the most unbecoming spirit. It is certain, however, that the wisest men are never the most forward to call attention to themselves. One of the most noted men of his day has been heard to say that, while a private member of a church, he never once opened his mouth in its meetings. Small fellowships are most likely to fall into mistakes on this particular; every man thinks he has something to say which will enlighten the brethren, and very frequently when he has told his tale it amounts to nothing. The best way of preventing the introduction of foreign subjects is to establish the rule that no business of immediate importance shall be transacted, except such as has been previously submitted in the form of notice. In pursuing such a course the pastor can never be taken by surprise; he will have time for reflection, and will be thereby enabled to take a comprehensive view of the question in its varied ramifications. Every minister should talk over the forthcoming business with his deacons, so that the whole official staff may be prepared to move in harmony. Never be *anxious* to find out cases for church discipline; some men have wrought their official ruin by making every little annoyance a subject for church interference. Be faithful in *private* remonstrance, but until every other means has failed, refrain from submitting the matter to the judgment of the fellowship A trifling sore may be healed by a little address, but if it is fretted it may enlarge and mortify. Remember, however, that when a case of known delinquency presents itself, it is at the peril of the church to connive thereat. If the church is to be *peaceable*, it must first be *pure;* the stillness which is caused by impurity is the ominous quietude which precedes the thunder shock and the earthquake! Care not about lessening the numerical strength of the body; be jealous for its *purity*, and labor patiently for its increase. It is well to call the church together for special prayer; this practice ever reminds the people of the Source of all their strength and mercy.

Another hint on preaching is worthy of recollection: —

In choosing a text, don't be anxious to find anything very peculiar. Some men indulge a kind of pride in preaching from mottoes; for example, such words as "if," "so," "now," "but," etc., have been adopted as texts. The ignorant and childish may be struck with admiration of the preacher's talent who can "make a sermon out of so little"; but the more steady and intelligent will be grieved that God's word is so little honored. Never disjoint the sentence, always have complete sense; take the whole idea, and then you will have some ground to work upon. Here again comes up the old plan of expository preaching. He who honors God's word may expect his people to grow in knowledge and in understanding; he who continually sets forth himself and introduces controversial subjects, which are of minor importance, can scarcely wonder if the people become dabblers in polemics, and captious to an inconvenient degree. Having chosen a suitable text, confine yourself to it entirely,— *make it speak:* there *is* music in it; pray that your fingers may touch the chords aright, so that melody may be evoked. You are not expected to preach a body of divinity in every discourse. Some pulpit ramblers range the whole field, *flying* everywhere, but *digging* nowhere. Be you a *digger;* sink the shaft fearlessly, the gold is embowelled in the deep places; go down, persevere and bring it up. There is water even in the rock; smite it with a heaven-directed hand, and it will gush most freely: there is poetry in the old historic page; breathe on it with prayer, and the song will be heard: whatever your text be, it is capable of turning out plenty of material to sustain a separate discourse; *honor it so*, and you will never lack scope and variety

Dr. Campbell would have spared himself many a battle if he had acted upon his own advice, as given in the following extract: —

Be careful to form and maintain a *character;* as to reputation, that must be left to take its own course. Character is what a man really *is;* reputation is what people *say* he is. A man may have a good character and a bad reputation. You cannot fail to enjoy esteem if you truly deserve it and thoroughly work for it. It will not come in a day; it may be a slow growth, but none the less certain on that account. Be firm in your principles, modest in their avowal, straightforward in your dealing, and men will value you at a proper price. A man's character will be formed by his thought, reading, society; his reputation will be the estimate which observers place upon his objective developments. Character applies to spirit, feeling, desire; hence, when these are brought to bear upon daily life, we profess to see what a man's character is by the actions which he performs. Be careful how you enter into any *public* defence of character; if you are called upon to sustain charges, your course will be to acknowledge them if *true,* and to leave them to a natural death if *false.* There are doubtless circumstances in which a minister may be imperatively called upon to refute charges and "answer fools according to their folly," but generally speaking it is best to "live" your enemies "liars." Whatever you do in this particular, be careful how you *write,* either privately or for the press. Never write in a passion; the document may remain a perpetual monument of your folly; a hasty *word* may be forgotten or modified in its meaning, a *written* statement will be judged by a different standard. Never think of going to the press with any "Appeal," "Statement," or "Defence," except you be placed in such circumstances as no minister ever was before you; and even then pause — pause! The public have nothing to do with church annoyances. A vitiated taste is ever craving for such disclosures, but men of wisdom and piety will be very slow to gratify such a morbid propensity. *Speak* with caution — fast and pray before you *write!*

Such is a sample of a rather large stock. It is not my present business to offer any detailed criticism upon Dr. Campbell's public life, as such criticism would be out of place in a paper devoted to personal recollections. There cannot be any doubt that the severest charges against many of Dr. Campbell's opinions and public practices could be sustained, as there cannot be any doubt that in innumerable cases he proved himself to be wise, generous, and just. One thing is pretty certain, the Congregational body will happily never have a second Dr. Campbell; it will have many men who can do the same kind of rough and ready public work, but if they presume to touch *his* hammer, they will soon be compelled to lay it down again. The reign of the hammer has gone, and as civilization pursues an ascending course, there is happily no prospect of the return of so rude a sovereignty. Honoring the memory of Dr. Campbell in one or two of its aspects, I cannot but feel that he outlived the time in which his peculiar influence could have any value, and that increasing life would have meant decreasing power. For patience, perseverance, and self-expenditure in hard work, probably the most industrious man amongst us would yield the palm to Dr. Campbell; for vigor, sententiousness, and fervor of hurried composition, high praise is undoubtedly due to the most voluminous of denominational editors and authors; and if his defences of orthodoxy were often the severest blows that could be aimed at the object which he sought to serve, he was not the only man whose services would have been improved by moderation.

XIV.

A CHAPTER ON PASTORAL THEOLOGY.

A GOOD many most gifted and scholarly young men have failed rather in the administration of affairs than in the discharge of their pulpit duties. This circumstance has chafed them, has rendered them impatient, and in the long run has occasionally wrecked their public usefulness and honor. I have known a few marked instances of this unhappy experience; and have seen how strong is the temptation to fasten upon the supposed imperfections of a system the faults which are distinctly traceable to want of practical discipline on the part of unsuccessful men. Believe me, it will be of small service to you as a pastor if you know how to parse a chapter in the Greek Testament, but do not know how to accost an unfriendly critic or give the turn to a disagreeable debate. Not a few young men who have been able to discuss Aristophanes have been utterly routed by a third-rate shopkeeper as to the order in which resolutions and amendments should be put to a meeting. No doubt this is very humiliating: the third-rate shopkeeper was utterly ignorant of "The Clouds" and "The Frogs," yet he had a grain of common sense, and with that he was able to overthrow the Goliath of scholarship. Too often the said Goliath has abused the church system which gave such men an opportunity of displaying their tiny abilities, never dreaming that he himself might have been qualified to beat such opponents on their own ground. Now, I wish you to be a sensible man in all practical affairs, to have a knowledge of men and things, and in all departments of your work to be a workman who needeth not to be ashamed. Happily in your case there is no occasion to reply to the senseless conceit that business is vulgar. Some dazzling geniuses of the clerical order solace themselves with the comfortable falsehood that men of their rich culture need not stoop to the engagements and distractions of common mortals. It is enough that they discuss various readings, that they bestow a languid patronage upon the literary club, and that they dream of their own overshadowing greatness and destined immortality. It is amazing how many of those gigantic men manage to slip out of the world's sight into total oblivion! They began so blazingly, their programme was so polished, their tone so elevated in unearthly refinement; and yet in less than two years people hardly care to inquire whether they are yet in the world: this, I say, is very amazing, and yet perhaps after all it is not so very wonderful, when we remember in what a crooked, hard-grained, vulgar world our lot has fallen. Do you remember Mr. Washington's story of the truly learned and thriftless snob who astounded a ferryman by a display of his attainments? "My good man," said he, "do you understand mathematics?" The boatman ingenuously answered that he had never heard of them, whereupon the man of learning assured him that one-fourth of his life was lost. "Do you, then," continued the refined inquirer, "understand astronomy?" The boatman shook his head. "Then," said the mighty man, "another fourth of your life is lost." After a pause, the sage put a further question: "Do you know anything of the science of chemistry?" The ferryman replied that he knew nothing about it, and instantly the scholar assured him that three-fourths of his life was lost. The boatman looked uneasy; he turned to the right hand and to the left with the air of a frightened man; a powerful steamer was bearing rapidly down the river. Addressing the intellectual fare, he said, "Did you ever learn to swim?" And when the illustrious scholar said "No," the boatman replied, "Then all your life is lost together!" The man of genius went down into that dreary cemetery where no marble is allowed to mark the pillow of the sleepers. The story is its own moral, whether applied to common people or to manufacturing and machine-made scholars, — beware of knowing everything except the one thing needful!

It would be easy to show you that in practical life common sense is better than genius. Of course, if you can have both common sense and genius, by all means have them, for it must be an advantage to have wings as well as feet. My object is to guard you against the genius that has no sense, and to save you from the colored bottles that carry nothing but labels. It would not be difficult for a minister of twenty years' standing to name half a hundred of his brethren who by common sense, without brilliance or scholarship, have preached the gospel and administered the affairs of the church with the most marked efficiency and success; brethren, too, who have been sneered at by clerical fledglings, who have sought to make their way through the ministry into gentlemanhood. You need not trouble yourself with the sneers of such men; they cannot injure you; you have time as your vindicator, and in seven years the sneerers will have been "buried with the burial of an ass." It is no doubt troublesome to the flesh to be exposed to the small remarks of small men; but if you live in your work, and never lose sight of your Master, you will soon be inaccessible to the influence of critics who work from the point of personal mortification. What you have to do, then, is to make yourself master of the affairs which must necessarily engage your attention; for a time they may be irksome; for a time you may long to escape to more congenial pursuits: but you must resolutely fight out the battle, and in your chief difficulty find your chief joy. Some of your people may mistake sciolism for scholarship, and others may not be able to distinguish between noise and music; but the majority of them will not be long in forming a just opinion of your business capabilities, nor need it be matter of wonder if you gain their respect and confidence by showing yourself their equal in departments with which they are most familiar. On the other hand, a sensible man will be careful not to be fussy and meddlesome in the discharge of his duties; he will not force himself into everything as if nothing could be done without him, but by timely withdrawment, by seeing as if he were not looking, by leading as if he were following, he will double his influence and multiply his friends. I know a good man who has never been out of hot water simply on account of his self-importance in the matter of church business; his only fault is his omniscience; he knows everything better than anybody else; he writes all the resolutions, nominates all the officers, dictates all the programmes, dismisses his helpers without notice or reason, and so keeps himself in about as hot a bath as flesh and blood can bear. He is quite a *terrible* man of business; he strikes the business with a steam hammer; he thunders and lightens at the business; fire and brimstone cannot keep him back from business. And what a business he makes of it! He knows the trust-deed off by heart; he can quote all the acts of parliament which relate to public meetings for political and religious purposes; he can beard revising barristers and claim his vote as the minister of the few mouldering bricks which he calls his chapel; he knows about magistrates, summonses, subpœnas, and affidavits; and all this knowledge he has so far turned to account in his ecclesiastical arrangements as to make his church into nothing better than a baptized police court. And such a man he is for technicalities! If a member of his church has a simple and inoffensive resolution to propose, he must give three weeks' notice thereof to the pastor; a copy of it must be sent to a preliminary committee; the name and address of the seconder must be duly entered in a book kept for that purpose; and the unfortunate speaker must be thrice assured that if he say one word contrary to the trust-deed (of which he never had an opportunity of reading a sentence), he may be ecclesiastically dismembered on the spot. You will readily believe that the wretched man is a martyr to his insane devotion to business, and that he no sooner gets a respectable seat-holder than he loses him. He does not know the mystery of artlessness; he cannot preside unless he is in the chair; he is so burdened with rules as to be utterly without law; in a word, he is so orderly as to necessitate his living in a state of chronic disorder. If the *light* that is in thee be darkness, how great is that darkness!

A few nights since we held another council meeting, and as the subject is immediately related to the topic now before us, I will give you a rough note of our proceedings. The Safety-pin was in full force, and as is usual under such conditions, he boldly plunged into the first subject that occurred to him.

"As to church meetings," said he, "I should like to know the opinion of the brethren; I confess they are my *bête noir*."

The dummies were shocked, for they are both managing men; their idolatry of prudence has kept them at a long distance from everything that looked like a lion's den. "For thirty years," said the elder of them, "I have never had a divided church meeting, nor even the appearance of divided sentiment": this he said in a tone which nearly meant something.

"You must have been an awfully dead set of fogies, then," Safety-pin replied; "why, in one-tenth of that time, two of my officers prayed at me because I had not candidates enough to propose, and one old sinner hinted that he would like a little less theology and a little more Christianity in the sermons of 'Thy dear servant our esteemed pastor'—a prayer unanswered to this day."

The dummies looked uneasy, for they had patiently listened to the same solid devotions regularly once a week for many years, and had never ventured to dream of the possibility of one sentence being changed, or one new petition being conceived.

"A very wicked thing is that of lecturing people in prayer," our critical friend observed.

"A little prudence on the part of the minister —" one of the dummies was saying, when Safety-pin cut him short with a malediction on prudence which I will not repeat.

"Still," said Mr. Washington, "we should not forget that sometimes courage is concealed under prudence, and it has often been shown that wisdom is better than defiance; in fact, as to all these questions of management, I may give it as my opinion, founded on considerable experience, that in nine cases out of ten a minister may have his own way if he will only manage things properly."

"That is," said Safety-pin, "a man may live as long as he likes, if he will only keep out of the way of death."

"Well, not exactly so," Mr. Washington answered; "at the same time a man should not expect to live long if he indulges pretty frequently in poisonous doses, and amuses himself by trying the effect of edged instruments on his throat."

The dummies were satisfied: the nearest approach to pleasure which they ever made in our meetings was when a keen word was said to Safety-pin; they dared not attack him themselves, but they warmly cheered the brother who laid a heavy hand upon him. We think ourselves courageous when we applaud courage in others.

As chairman of the council, I requested Mr. Washington to give us his idea of managing things properly; for, though secretly, I had a suspicion that there was room enough in that elastic expression to admit the meaning which Safety-pin intended to convey by his blunt remark.

"I cannot do better," he courteously replied, "than refer you to a few points which my old pastor wrote out for me. He said they had saved him from a good many mistakes in a long public life."

"Who was your old pastor, by the way?" Safety-pin interposed.

Mr. Washington would have answered, but it was ruled from the chair that we must have the points. Accordingly we set ourselves (with the exception of Safety-pin, who lay back in his seat and surveyed the ceiling with the air of an injured man) in an attentive posture, and Mr. Washington read the instructions of his venerable pastor: —

1. When a poker falls out of the fire, never take it up by the hot end.

2. When a man has anything to say in opposition, insist upon his having the fullest opportunity of being heard, and when he is approaching a conclusion, beg him not to think of giving over.

3. Never water a weed.

4. Never allow an opposition motion to be put to the meeting on its first proposition. Express your interest in the novelty of the suggestion, and tell the proposer that it is *due to him* that a resolution so important and so far reaching in its bearings should have the advantage of careful study in private, and that you will feel obliged to him if he will politely allow you to take it home for critical reflection. (Few men can resist the pleasure of being publicly strangled in the noose of a compliment.)

[Safety-pin groaned, as he thus saw prudence degenerating into deceit.]

5. If you want to have the *pulpit* lowered a little, begin by asking to have the *spire* taken down.

6. If you suspect opposition in any quarter, privately request the suspected opponent to take charge

of the very resolution which he is expected to oppose; tell him you feel the *importance* of his doing so (which is perfectly true); say that such resolutions ought to be introduced by the ablest men in the church; if he hesitate, ask him to dinner.

["What an old ras—" Safety-pin said, but the chairman called "silence" peremptorily.]

7. If a man oppose your preaching, instantly request him to supply the pulpit.

8. If the deacons suggest that "a change is desirable," say that is exactly your opinion, "*mutatis mutandis.*" The Latin will save you.

When Mr. Washington ceased, the Safety-pin sprang to his feet, and declared that the old pastor was neither more nor less than a crafty old fox, and he was glad that no name had been given.

"Wait awhile," said Mr. Washington, anxious for his pastor's honor; "calm yourself for a moment, and be good enough to answer one question,—are we not commanded to be wise as serpents?"

Both the dummies instantly showed, by rapid motions of their shiny heads, that they had a lively recollection of the command.

"I say," Safety-pin boldly replied, "that the honesty of a minister should be immaculate."

"And has anybody in this council said anything to the contrary?" the elder dummy inquired.

"That paper is full of deceit," was Safety-pin's curt reply.

"I must claim a hearing on this point, Mr. Chairman," Mr. Washington exclaimed, with more than ordinary resolution in his voice, "because my old pastor has been misunderstood. Of course, his words are to be taken in an accommodated sense; he did not know what it was to truckle to any man, or to conceal an opinion where any great principle was involved: at the same time he did not voluntarily run his head against a wall, nor jump into a ditch just to see how deep it was. He was a consummate tactician, so that he did by skill what others attempted by force ; and if you will read his paper in the light of this fact, you will find nothing objectionable in it."

"A man's morality should not require a glossary to explain it," Safety-pin persisted.

"Nor should it need a flaming sword to defend it, amongst brethren," Mr. Washington sharply rejoined.

"Brethren," said I, "I agree with you both —"

"Nay, nay," said Safety-pin ; "be honest, and fight one of us."

"I can be honest, and agree with both of you," I firmly continued. "The paper which Mr. Washington has read was never intended as a lesson in Loyola-ism ; it was evidently meant to be humorous, rather than serious, and to take the study of human nature out of the list of hard subjects. The very fact that the bright old man allowed the paper to be copied, and to pass from hand to hand, is to me evidence enough of his candor and simplicity. If he meant it as a lesson in snare-making or man-trapping, he certainly outwitted himself, and put the collar round his own neck as a public deceiver."

This view of the case had a happy effect upon the council ; and here I may note that the most successful reasoning in such circumstances is to show that no man would willingly make such a fool of himself as your opponent is anxious to prove. For a few moments our conversation was suspended ; we were looking for that most useful and much-worn old bridge by which unskilled interlocutors cross to a new subject. Bridge or no bridge, we soon found ourselves discussing the question of pastoral visitation, which we did in a tone of general dissatisfaction and complaint.

"An infinite nuisance!" said Safety-pin, "at least so far as I am concerned. Talk about old pastors," he continued, with recovered good humor, "I'll match my own against any of yours for pastoral visitation. I never saw such a man in all my life. No sooner was one of his people ill than the old boy was down upon him twice a day the first week, and once a day ever after, until the poor patient was glad to get better in order to escape him, I can assure you. And as for a memory, it was perfectly astounding; if you met him after an interval of a month, he would say, 'Good morning, Mr. So-and-so; is your toothache quite gone?' Of course you would look half stupid, as if you had no recollection of what he was talking about, and then he would remind you that when he saw you last you were crazy with toothache, not having slept for a week, and so on; and then you would suddenly remember your old torture and laugh at it, and thank the old man, and say how kind he was, and all that sort of thing."

"I know the style of man," Mr. Washington replied, "and have often coveted the memory you speak of, for it is really marvellous. For my own part, I should be thankful to remember people's names, whatever might come of their ailments: it is very humiliating to be talking to one of your members, and yet to be unable to mention his name, and that kind of thing is after all set down to a man's disadvantage."

"I am rather fortunate in that way, so far as adults are concerned," I replied; "but when I go into a family where there are from six to ten children, I am often at a loss to recollect their names."

"Legitimately so," the younger dummy interposed, with his usual simplicity of speech.

"Yet, as necessity is the mother of invention," I continued, "I have hit upon a plan which serves me very well. When an unknown youngster runs up to me I hail him with the challenge, 'Now you can't spell your first name?" Then he begins: 'Tho—,' 'Jose—,' 'Hen—,' and he is mine safe enough. You will find that to remember a child's name will cover a multitude of sins in a sermon."

"But, after all," said Mr. Washington, "ought not the preacher and the pastor to be two different men? You have men who devote their whole time to the study of the human eye, and others who devote their whole time to the study of the human ear; why should it be thought unreasonable that another class of men should give their days and nights to the study of preaching, and others spend their lives in the equally important work of comforting and directing the disconsolate and perplexed?"

"You overlook a point, I think," the Safety-pin suggested. "You will find that sympathy on the part of the people is established in connection with what they hear from the pulpit; the preacher excites their admiration, satisfies their judgment, and so secures their confidence; the natural, and, I must confess, happy consequence is, that when they come into circumstances requiring special solace or counsel, they wish to see the man whom they love and trust as their public teacher. Send a stranger to them; and however wise and excellent he may be, there is no point of sympathy to begin with, they do not know his voice, they can make no references to his teaching, they have no cause of thankfulness in relation to him, and the consequence is a prevention of hearty communication."

Mr. Washington instantly allowed the soundness of the doctrine. "I only contend," said he, "that it is to be regretted that men who have a marked gift of preaching, should be under the necessity of attempting a kind of work for which they are quite unfit; where a man has the double gift of the preacher and pastor, his service must be the source of the purest joy which the heart can experience upon earth: my remarks must be understood to refer solely to ministers whose one gift is the gift of preaching, and yet who have to undertake engagements for which they have no fitness."

"An unavoidable necessity though, I am afraid," said I, "especially considering what has now been said about the sympathy which comes naturally from gratitude for pulpit services. There are men in our ministry who ought never to leave the pulpit; they should be chained to it if ever they are to do any good; they seem to have a knack of getting into blunders; by levity, by love of eating and drinking, by a fatal habit of always saying the wrong word and never hitting the right time, they somehow bring themselves into contempt. On the other hand, there are men in our ministry who ought never to be allowed to enter the pulpit: in the parlor they are charming men; they can set their voice at the right key, they have nice little sentences for nice little occasions, they can make inquiries about a headache in a tone which exquisitely combines sympathy and hopefulness, and they can ask for the children in a manner which wins the parental heart most entirely. In higher matters, too, they are quite as successful; they know what passages of Scripture to read under any given domestic circumstances, and with most consummate tact can throw into a supplicatory form the most secret desires of the heart. I know two or three such men, most admirable and useful men in their own way, yet when they get into the pulpit they are stiff, cold, pointless preachers, always drivelling upon the brevity of time, the uncertainty of life, and a place which they refer to as 'yon bright world above.' The consequence is that the young (unless they happily escape to a livelier ministry) become prematurely old, the old fall asleep, and the lackadaisical report to them that they 'have had such a *beautiful* sermon.' Still, in the face of all these things, I see no prospect of separating the pastoral from the ministerial, so far as Congregationalism is concerned."

"There is one point you have omitted," said one of the brethren with the shining heads, "in making out the list of qualifications possessed by some ministers who are not preachers; I mean their qualification for

Bible-class teaching, — an important department of our work, you will allow."

Safety-pin anticipated me. He said that he had no opinion of men who had young ladies' Bible-classes, young men's Bible-classes, and children's Bible-classes; he always thought there was a screw loose when men had to get up so much collateral machinery to keep their ministry going. My note of our proceedings on the occasion in question ends here; yet I must, in the absence of Safety-pin, give it as my opinion that he was wrong in his judgment of his brethren, and I can give this opinion the more freely that I have no claim to the high title of a Bible-class teacher. I question whether you can get at the deepest veins of biblical wealth in the pulpit; the process, besides exposing you to the charge of pedantry, is too minute and (for want of a better word) scientific to be followed by a miscellaneous congregation; not only so, there are portions of Scripture best developed by cross-examination on the part of the class, and that, so to speak, will show their brilliance only after prolonged and careful friction. You will find, when you come to this department of work, one thing requiring special attention: many of your pupils will seek to engage you in useless speculation, they will start unprofitable inquiries, and try to detain you upon all the points which are in debate among Christian thinkers. I have always found it best to acknowledge at once that there are unsettled questions which it would be presumptuous for any but the ripest scholars and theologians to attempt to discuss, and to decline on that honest ground to intermeddle with such subjects in an ordinary Bible-class. At the beginning of the second period of my ministry, a few conceited sciolists made a determined attempt to force such difficulties on my attention; but happily, though perhaps at the expense of their self-complacency, I was enabled to escape their importunity, and ultimately to drive them from the field. A remembrance of that fact causes me to put you on your guard against a very powerful temptation to vindicate yourself from a charge of incapacity or cowardice, by "rushing in where angels fear to tread." In the Bible you will find scope enough for the exhaustion of all your ability and resources without frittering away your time on things too high for you. I have found it very convenient and profitable to follow up in a Bible-class a course of expository preaching: say, for example, you are expounding one of the gospels in a series of Sunday morning lectures; get the members of your Bible-class to take notes of your exposition, and to give the criticism or argument in their own words. This will supply an excellent basis for further discussion in class; and if your experience correspond with my own, you will often receive suggestions enough to enable you to prepare a second and better lecture on your last Sunday morning's subject. You will probably find a difficulty in getting some of your members to adopt the habit of taking notes and making abstracts or paraphrases, but a little gentle persuasion in private will often secure the object you have in view. In conducting processes of this kind, I have received many a hint as to the best method of preaching. You find out the ignorance of your hearers; you see how they mistake the meaning of words which to the preacher are quite simple; you feel how slow they are to comprehend any process of reasoning, and how little account they can give of arguments on which you set great store. These facts will often clip the wings of your soaring rhetoric, and force you, if you are an honest steward, to preach not to *yourself*, but to *others*. This is the condescension which comes of being crucified with the Saviour, and this the holy desire which is intent on the one infinitely blessed object of saving the souls of them that hear the holy word from your lips.

XV.

UNSUCCESSFUL MEN.

As a matter of fact there are several scores of educated men who have not been able to secure pulpits in which to exercise their ministry; there are also hundreds of pastors who would be heartily glad to see a way of escape from their present position to more congenial spheres of usefulness. I cannot pretend to exhaust the reason of this unsettledness; probably it would be safe to say that "there are faults on both sides," and so leave the matter without going into detail. There are, however, a few things which have been made so clear to my own mind, that a candid statement may be of use to you, either in directing your personal ministry, or giving you a hint as to the best method of meeting some difficulties in your pastoral relations. It may be prudent to premise that there are several proper though differing interpretations of the word *success*. One minister may succeed in overcrowding his chapel; another may have a very limited congregation, and yet may succeed in exerting a most stimulating and healthful influence upon special classes of Christian thinkers and workers. One minister may succeed in doing a most useful pioneer-work; another may succeed in organizing and edifying undisciplined and uninstructed beginners: so, also, one minister may succeed in binding to him the affections of the young, and another may have a special adaptation to teach and comfort the busy, the afflicted, the speculative, or the indifferent. I think it well to point out this difference in the bearings of the word success, and thereby assist to remove the mischievous impression that all success is to be measured by one arbitrary sign or standard. Success is a question of individual adaptation.

1. The first place on the list of unsuccessful men is, of course, occupied by those who, in seeking admission into the ministry, have evidently mistaken their calling. In such cases it is not a question of a distinct call or an indistinct call; there is simply no call at all. A youth, on becoming conscious of living in Jesus Christ, on seeing heaven opened and the angels of God ascending and descending as ministers of the church, feels a most pure and urgent desire to preach the gospel: with this end in view he appeals to his pastor for the requisite introduction to college. The pastor hesitates, suggests further consideration of the important subject; by and by the appeal is renewed, the parents of the youth express a strong opinion in favor of his request, and sanguine friends join in the ill-advised opportunity. At length the minister yields, with a reluctance which is met by exclamations of angry surprise, and the youth is admitted into college. In a short time the most favorable reports are received; in a few months more, the youth passes an examination in a highly creditable manner; at the end of the first year he takes a prize, and at the end of the second he gains a scholarship; thus the opinion of friends is abundantly confirmed, and the hesitation of the minister is openly ascribed to an unworthy motive. Ask the minister himself what his opinion is in the face of this rapid and flattering success; he will probably reply, "My opinion is the same now that it ever was; I never doubted the young man's conscientiousness; I never questioned the young man's ability to read books and get off lessons; but I say now, what I said at the beginning, you may cover him with gold medals and give him an armful of certificates, but he will never persuade a congregation that he is called of God to preach the gospel." This reply is perfectly sound; the great error is that *fitness for literary pur-*

suits is not distinguished from *fitness for public speaking.* We need not go far for proofs that literature and eloquence are not interchangeable terms: in the houses of parliament you will find the most learned and polished men, who are quite unable to express themselves with perspicuity and effect; yet, if as Christian youths they had applied for admission to one of our colleges, they would have been instantly admitted, and would have passed their curriculum with the unanimous and cordial applause of the professors. The minister, whose case we have been supposing, awaits the justification of time. The young man leaves the college well supplied with the most commendatory credentials, and in the flush of academic success indulges an innocent sneer at the expense of men who know more about preaching than they know about the differential calculus. The parents and friends of the young man perhaps triumph over what they consider must be the disappointment and mortification of the minister whose judgment has been so signally dishonored. Still the minister bides his time, and what is the upshot? For two years the young man carries his credentials round the churches, but the churches never give him a chance of settlement. The young man then discovers that deacons are vulgar and selfish, and quite unfit to guide the opinion of Christian communities; for another year he continues his melancholy round of applications, but nothing in the way of a settlement is offered. People say they have "no doubt he is a clever man in his own way," or that "his sermons have been elaborately prepared," or that "he is more fit to be a professor than a preacher"; the young man, however, cannot live upon these compliments, and therefore, under stress of various kinds, he cannot resist the impression that "the system is all wrong together," and so he settles down into shopkeeping and churlishness. Or if he succeed in getting a settlement he soon becomes uneasy; he says that his people don't appreciate him, that he cannot stoop to their low habits of thinking, and that he is open to an invitation to another pulpit. He thinks if he were in a large town he could do better, he would draw his own class around him, literary people would flock around his pulpit, and he would lead the highest sentiment of the community. But, no! It won't do! He stumbles, falls, lies down, grumbles, and then perishes out of the way. Now it was a cruel kindness to urge such a man to seek admission into the ministry. He was a man of ability, and as a private Christian might have been of much service in the church; but his friends sacrificed him to an unreasoning if not an ungodly ambition. Let me at this point strongly advise you to keep back as many men as possible from the ministry. Of course, where you have a distinct persuasion of a young man's fitness for the pulpit, you will encourage him most earnestly to give himself to needful preparation; but be doubly sure of the fitness before you offer him the least assistance. Where there is most fitness, there will often be most self-distrust.

2. Another class of unsuccessful men may be ironically described as *hyper-super-intellectualists*, — something, in spite of the ugly word, very aerial and sublime. These magnificent and unapproachable royalties, throned among the stars, and clothed with clouds of many colors, expend their lives in one desperate determination to say something that is not in the New Testament. The moment they are about to put one word of gospel into their sermons, they recoil from the vulgarity as from a temptation to be profane. As a consequence, they excel in *not* preaching the gospel. They delight to prove to their pew-holders that they "are abreast with the foremost thinking of the day" they refer with great familiarity to "a certain modern school of thought," and with infinite skill gibbet neo-Platonists, transcendentalists, pantheists, and positivists, before a wondering if not applauding audience.

But their chief joy — O their sweet, precious, transporting joy, their joy of joys, their dancing, screaming, delirious joy! — is to discourse upon a most mysteriously dangerous individual called *Comte*. When a reverend snob of the hyper-super class can bring in the name of *Comte*, he is sure that it will instantly show the greatness, and the might, and the majesty, and the glorious glory of the learned minister. He would not for the world refer to Baxter, or Henry, or Doddridge, or Watts; Owen, and Bates, and Charnock, and Howe, he does not deign to know; — he knows *Comte* (as far at least as translations can reveal that personage), and is not *that* the last reach of culture, the crowning-point of attainment? M. Comte himself would wonder if he could know how many magnificent nobodies conjure with his name. It is no consequence that not a soul in the awe-struck congregation knows whether *Comte* is the French for devil or the Italian for an angel; the one thing to be sure of is that the minister is "abreast with the foremost thinking of the day"; as to saving the souls of them that hear him, is it not better to extinguish an absent speculator than to save an unlettered man? Cultivated reason can have but one answer to the impertinent inquiry. The congregation of the hyper-super is a curious medley, the chief feature being the advanced young man who belongs to the new Lyceum, and who simpers over the top of the penny newspaper that in *his* opinion the day of the pulpit is over forever. This is a very formidable young man; from the serene heights of his noble culture he could not think of descending to consult so ancient a personage as his father, and all filial duty is exhausted when he languidly smiles at the practical suggestions of his mother. The young man loves to hear of *Comte*, Comte is so bold a fellow and so very common-sense; he dotes on Comte, he dreams about Comte, and if anybody should innocently suggest in a tremulous and deprecatory tone that he "is becoming quite a Comtist," his manly bosom heaves, his flashing eyes blaze with double brightness, and his towering head stoops lest he should injure the ceiling, which is not more than seven feet higher than himself. The reverend snob glories in the youth; he looks on him with pride; and in grateful recollection of his intellectual presence comforts himself that he will draw around his pulpit the genius and the culture of the neighborhood. How much genius and culture there may be gathered around his Comtean pulpit, it is impossible, in consequence of their invisibility, to say. But, as a matter of fact, weary, troubled, sorrowing men do not gather round it; people who are tempted, overborne, crushed in heart, do not gather round it; and in about twelve months the reverend lecturer on *Comtism* gathers his neat little essays together and looks out wistfully for another charge. The common opinion of such a man is that he is "fit for a college"; alas, how many distinguished geniuses there are at this moment waiting for the shoes of honored professors! You will observe that in all this description of a certain class of unsuccessful men, I do not say one word against learning, culture, or mental ability; my remarks are directed against the chilling pedantry which works at so remote a distance from the sin and sorrow and hunger of the soul. In view of this shocking mockery of all that is honest and effective in Christian preaching, let me pray you to be ever on your guard against the temptation to preach what are mistakenly called "great sermons"; don't preach for the gratification of your own vanity, but for the salvation of all who hear you; don't preach, I once more entreat you, to the two or three most intelligent or most pretentious men in your congregation, but speak to the common heart of humanity with the pathos of unaffected sympathy; and the blessings of many will cause the cup of your reward to overflow. You may preach with such ostentation of learning as to excite wonder in the vulgar, and disgust in the devout; you may win the reputation of being a clever man, who is not afraid of hard texts and difficult subjects; but no heart will ever own you as a messenger from God. What do we want with all this so-called *great* preaching? Do you say we are obliged to occupy a certain time, and that to do so we must avail ourselves of references and quotations for which we ourselves care nothing? I have an instant and, to my own mind, a sufficient answer to this suggestion: it *ought not* to be necessary slavishly to occupy exactly so much time; we should take our time, not from the clock, but from the heart, and, according to the inspiration which may have been granted to earnest prayer, speak to those who trust us as God's servants. How good it is, when the heart is weary and the sight of the soul fails through long watching, to hear a preacher who speaks simply and lovingly the word of the Saviour! How tuneful, how soothing! But when a man is aiming at something that lies far from the trouble which darkens upon us, when he meets us with sentences artistically turned, in which he proclaims nothing but his own vanity, we shrink with mortification and anger from his sapless, mocking ministry. Nor is it we that shrink, but the dishonored Spirit of Christ that is in us; the voice of "the stranger" torments and insults the heart. Be you a man who reveals and exalts the mystery of the Cross!

3. A third class of unsuccessful men may be described as consisting of ministers who regard *preaching* as quite a secondary consideration; ministers they may be, but preachers certainly not. You will express surprise at the statement that men so devoid of common-sense can be found in the Christian ministry; but your surprise will decline as your observation extends. As the class is somewhat diversified, it may be necessary to particularize a little. One of its representative men figures conspicuously at the public library, and is generally seen with a new book and a bundle of news-

papers under his arm. He lives on pew-rents, but certainly not among pews; he has a neat little world of his own, well stocked with heretical books and other delicacies; occasionally he may so far condescend to acknowledge his pastoral relations, so called, as to turn a telescope on that dim speck of distant matter which he mistakenly denominates his chapel; otherwise, except on well known quarter-days, he is grandly independent of his people. His people, in fact, are very much like a necessary and remunerative nuisance; they read nothing, they go nowhere, they are commonplace and vexatiously uninteresting, — a very sore trial, in short, to any man with a taste for reading. Another representative man of this class is known for his appreciation of good society, and a strong liking for fine scenery. When he left college he said he would not settle except amongst a refined people, a delicate people, who call hell *hades*, and dilute damnation into condemnation; he could never do with vulgar people, who bluntly call a spade a spade; he could only do with shoemakers when they described their places of business as boot-halls, and he always referred to the butter-merchant as one who was in "the provision line." As to saving the souls of those to whom he preached, he would have recoiled from the suggestion, except the said souls could be saved by distant references to moral intuitions and innate ideas; if they chose to be saved from hades, Gehenna, or *sheol* by *that* way, he had no strong objection, for their religion might then become a suitable frame for the picture of their social graces. When he settled in the pastorate, his boast was that all his people belonged to the uppermost stratum of the middle class; and this he said with the air of one who had made great sacrifices for his principles, intimating thereby that but for conscientious scruples he might have been surrounded by the aristocracy of position and genius. This very refined brother seldom spoke above a subdued whisper, and when in a forgetful moment he shook his forefinger, in sign of earnestness, he received with thankfulness the solaces of those who were sure that he must have exhausted himself. He heard with shuddering disgust of preachers who spoke in a loud, clear tone, and occasionally lifted up both hands in the pulpit; they were wanting in taste, they were pandering to the wishes of the ignorant mob, they were lowering the dignity of the pulpit; in short, they had proved themselves to be very despicable persons. The career of this dear brother was short and not merry; he was so very super-refined that even his most longsuffering friends lost patience with him, and those who clipped their own words most gradually grew into the conviction that he was a heartless snob. This made it very difficult for the dear gentleman; he knew that he was a first-class traveller, who could afford only a third-class ticket; and the look of annihilating contempt with which he took his seat in a third-class carraiage, confounded the ticket collectors, and sobered several of his fellow-travellers. A cruel providence seemed to dog his elegant footsteps, and but for one consolation he would have fallen into despair, — the consolation that all his mischance befell him because he would not stoop to the habits of the common herd! He persuaded himself that if he would only throw off the gentleman, and do as other people did, success would flow upon him like a river, and he would be the first man of his day. But the sacrifice was too great, — to the last he remained by far too refined for so disorderly a world as this. You will not ask whether it is impossible for refinement to succeed in the ministry; you know perfectly well that I am not condemning or ridiculing refinement, but rather its detestable simulation. There is no necessary discrepancy between refinement and strength; on the contrary, true refinement is power, as certainly as pedantry is feebleness. Of course, we must be particular as to the relation between the fineness of the weapon and the special quality of the work which it is intended to do. A razor, for example, has a keen edge and a polished surface, but no razor will ever fell a tree or dress a beam; on the other hand, an axe may be sharp and strong, yet it might be inconvenient to use it for shaving. So with men, and so specially with ministers. We must not be too fine for our work. We must so far go away from our own little preferences, as to live for the advantage of others; we must, in effect, say to our hearers, "this is not for my own gratification, but for your benefit," and by so much as the spirit of the Cross regulates our ministry, will the blessing of reward crown our labors.

In thus endeavoring to describe some of the unsuccessful men whom I have known more or less, my object is to point you to the unchangeable conditions of a permanently successful ministry. If in your heart of hearts, you do not love the work of preaching the gospel infinitely above all other work, you must fail; for this work must be either the most thrilling joy or the most unendurable torment which any man can experience. I shall assume, then, that you love it; that you love it supremely; that without it you would be wretched and hopeless. The instant inference from this all-absorbing love is, that you will study the best methods of bringing the gospel to bear upon the sin, the sorrow, and the aspirations of the human heart. The Gospel will not be to you an abstract science, or a recondite theory; it will be God's messsage to the disquiet and need of sinful and hungering souls, and your constant anxiety will be to interpret and apply it accordingly. Under such a hallowed and constraining inspiration you will not allow yourself to be driven to a position that is remote from the most pressing need of your hearers; you will rather suffer the imputation of being an unlearned and ignorant man. than run the risk of concealing any truth that tells immediately upon spiritual character and destiny. You will give men to feel that you *know* them, that you *live* for them, that your sympathy flows along the whole course of their experience; and you will show that all this knowledge and devotion on your part arises entirely from your incessant and adoring communion with Jesus Christ. To know Jesus Christ is to know man; to be as Jesus was, will be to draw all men unto you. There will undoubtedly arise temptations to discuss speculative subjects, to show off your own talent, and to gratify your own tastes; but you must break such temptations upon the cross, and out of your own crucifixion bring a richer tenderness to bear upon the spiritual condition of your hearers. Believe me, in proportion as a sermon is a mere effort of the intellect will it be a failure, and in proportion as a sermon is an expression of the heart will it succeed in doing good. This leads me to repeat that, to be truly effective, a sermon must be *part of the preacher himself;* when it is so it will be delivered naturally, with unaffected pathos, and with a nobler earnestness than can be secured by the most artful preparation. Better not to preach, than not to preach from the heart; better to stand before your congregation dumb and confounded, than to talk merely for talking's sake; when you are true enough to do this, you will be strong enough to put to flight most of the difficulties that interpose between you and the highest success.

You will of course remind me that many ministers, known to be most spiritually minded and devoted to their work, zealously pursuing what may be called the most intensely *moral* purpose of the ministry, have failed to secure anything like distinguished success. You can name such godly men in quick succession, and prove how far short their ministry has fallen. All this I allow, as a simple matter of fact, and yet the ground of my exhortation is untouched. You must remember that I have never insisted upon goodness as the sole condition of a successful ministry. The goodness must be vitalized; goodness must, in a word, become *virtue*,

— strength, force, activity; goodness must have manly faculty, an eye that brightens and melts, a heart that rejoices and saddens, with all the sudden changefulness of the world's daily drama. There is a goodness that is negative rather than positive, contemplative rather than active; a goodness that must be inquired into, before its existence can be distinctly recognized: on the other hand, there is a goodness modestly self-affirming, full of life, revealing itself in a thousand delicate insinuations, and in many public proofs of power; a goodness that becomes genial, tender, severe, judicial, pitiful, with a rapidity of alternation that may easily be mistaken by the superficial for inconsistency; a goodness that rules the intellect, by first correctly determining its province and compass, and that rules the life by a gentleness that is mightier than the most studied austerity. No amount of training can impart this living goodness to any man; it cannot be taught in the schools; it cannot be assumed by an artist; it is the holy and sublime individuality wrought in the soul by the Holy Ghost; and where it is absent there can be no true, far-reaching, and long-continuing service for Jesus Christ. I will not allow that a man is good, simply because he prays, reads the Bible, and engages in regular religious exercises; he must have life, — not life in his bookshelves, his outlines, his sermon book, or his professional desk, but *life in his soul* — the very life of life, the very eternity of God. When a man is delivered from himself, with all the petty considerations and tyrannies that torment the ill-kept soul, and centred in Christ; when his supreme passion is love of his Master, he is good, and his goodness is pungent as salt, purifying as fire. Brother, are we thus deeply and lovingly good? Not ascetics, not churls, not scorners, but saintly, gentle, heavenly-minded? O Holy Spirit, bring us evermore under Thy great power; work in us all the mystery of Thy holy purpose; deliver us from the harsh exactions of the mere letter, and prostrate us under the better dominion of the living Spirit. So enlighten us, so enrich us, so inspire us, that we may be amongst the simplest, the wisest, the strongest, of our blessed Master's servants.

XVI.

BEWARE OF MEN.

Take this advice, and your steps will be ordered wisely. As a young man, you will naturally take a hopeful view of everybody, and be disposed to give your confidence without asking much in the way of idemnification. It is not pleasant to me to awaken suspicion in an unsophisticated mind; yet as every man's experience should be regarded as a fund for the benefit of society, I must force myself to point out a few traits of character which you may expect to meet in the course of your ministry, and which will invariably signify what is bad. I have sometimes thought that the Christian ministry developed human character in a way strictly peculiar to itself. The feeling subsisting between pastor and people differs from almost every other feeling. The minister enjoys the freedom of his people's hearts, if they be true to him; where other counsellors would be treated with stubbornness, he is met in a spirit of conciliation; himself the representative of the Cross, he is regarded as bringing with him all the calming and rectifying considerations which attach to the highest form of self-crucifixion: hence men will often yield to his word, through veneration for the blessed Master, whose interests he is supposed ever to represent. Under such circumstances they will either show the very best aspects of their character, or they will cloak themselves under the most detestable simulation. As I have undertaken to deal with some of the darker shades of character that will surprise you in the course of your ministry, I think it right to claim your attention to a preliminary word on the other side. After a course of pastoral service extending over more than seventeen years, it would be unjust on my part if I did not most gratefully and cordially acknowledge that there are in nonconformist churches many most noble-minded men. I have been made their deep debtor in many instances; on occasions without number I have witnessed their steadfastness in the faith, their self-denying and zealous perseverance in Christian service, and their high-minded honor in cases in which by dexterous temporizing they could have escaped difficulty and loss. Were I to commit myself to a portrayal of the excellencies which have come directly under my own observation, I know not when the sunny picture would be completed; you will not understand me, therefore, as writing in a cynical or unthankful spirit, but in a spirit of honest criticism, without fear and without malice. It is with deep reluctance that I put aside for a moment the happy memories which form by far the largest part of the ministerial scenes through which I have passed; it pains me to ask even one friend to stand aside until I point out the blemishes which disfigure this character or that, yet I must, as your guide, be faithful, and lead you through shaded valleys when I would gladly linger with you where the light is brightest.

In the course of my ministry I have met with *men who have concealed their true dispositions under a thick coating of false amiability*. In my early ministerial course, I was much victimized by smiling men. The young heart refused to disbelieve the sincerity of a pleasant voice or a cheerful countenance. I remember one man, a minister too, who concealed the heart of a wolf under the wool of a lamb; and as his characteristics were so broad, I may remark upon him as the type of the men whom I have now more particularly in view. His great weapon was flattery, and his most successful flatteries were lies. He sought to open his way in society by the key of indiscriminate praise. Hard-working men were cheered by his commendations, unsuspecting women were won to confidence by his beguiling attentions, poor men were flattered by his patronage, and rich men were occasionally befooled by his compliments. His face was always putting on a smile which he intended to be fascinating, and his voice was artistically softened to suit the ear of his devoted prey. In fact, he called himself "an artist," and prided himself on successes which honest men instinctively regarded as crimes. With him, to fail in self-promotion was an unpardonable sin.

"Man," he would say to me with a feigned and mocking laugh, the recollection of which makes me shudder, "you should not speak out so boldly; you should do as I do, if you would get influence in the denomination."

When I repelled the proposition with indignant disdain, he would repeat his horrid laugh, and say, —

"That is all very well, but I have a cunning way of getting behind fellows, and warming them up into my notions. I go in for the artistic side of life, — I never offend a man as long as I can get anything out of him."

"Then I hate your policy," said I; "there's nothing I would not do to get at the truth."

"Don't mistake me," he would add, in an altered voice. "I know what I am about with these fine fellows: don't you see how I do? I smile upon them and get everything out of them; but if they turn awkward in my hand, I soon let them feel the poleaxe. Men tell me things in confidence, and I assure you it is a fine thing to have a sting in your box for every man; it keeps him quiet, you know."

"You wretch!" said I; "that is the creed of a murderer"; and from that day I abhorred and disowned him.

Yet you will be surprised how that man holds on his crooked course to this day, and how many honest men he holds in his well-arranged but most cruel coils. His deluded victims have told me he "shows such a Christian spirit," that "he never says an unkind word against me," that he "holds out the white flag of truce"; and I suffer under the imputation of being less magnanimous than he! I glory in the imputation, knowing the falseness of the man; God has given me power to look into the deep den of the wretched heart, and truly it is full of unclean and venomous reptiles. This is the language of the most dispassionate charity. I write it in the interests of truth and of social honor, and with the sobriety and self-restraint of a man who appeals to the judgment seat of Christ. I am aware how difficult it is to maintain a position like this by mere argument; you can hardly believe in the possibility of such dissimulation; you feel that my statement must be, perhaps unconsciously, exaggerated by resentment; your love of truth, your honor, your charity, will not allow you to believe that any professedly Christian man could act in the way described. I do not complain of your incredulity; it is natural, and it is creditable. Meet me ten years hence, and we shall talk on more equal terms. In the meantime do be careful not to commit yourself to men on the mere ground of their amiability. I have suffered more from simulated amiability than from any other cause; it has betrayed my confidence, it has lured me into dangerous paths, it has disappointed my best expectations, it has wounded and exasperated my most generous sensibilities. Think of a man calling you his "dear pastor," and then condemning you to your friends or to strangers; or think of him praying for you as "Thy dear and honored servant our beloved pastor," and then complaining that your salary is too large; or think of him pledging the most cordial friendship, and avowing the most entire disinterestedness in a trade transaction, and all the while having ten per cent upon all that he does for you; or think of him involving you in deep obligations by making you the most solemn promises, and when you ask him to redeem his promises, telling you that now your friendship must cease. Can you bear any more? Then think of office-bearers wishing you a happy holiday, and immediately summoning your hearers to take counsel as to the best way of getting rid of your ministry. But I forbear. Such things have happened in the experience of ministers whom I have known, and for that reason I feel that it is quite within my duty to put you on your guard against the amiability which may conceal the worst degrees of evil-mindedness. You will not misunderstand me as saying anything against amiability. Amiability is a Christian grace, and as such should be cultivated and displayed in all the intercourse of life: but in proportion to its value is the temptation to its perversion; were it less Divine, it would be less enlisted in the service of the devil.

In the course of my ministry I have met with *men who have wished to enjoy the good-will of all parties.* Such men ought not to be spoken of indiscriminately, yet it is not easy to classify them. One section may be described as simply timid, — another as selfish time-servers. The timid man is very difficult to understand. In the sunshine he will be as bold as a lion; he will even venture to talk about "nailing his colors to the mast"; and in private, where no one but the minister hears him, he will go any length in committing himself to the ministerial cause. Nor do I think him insincere in doing so; he is faithful to his mood; his full intention is to take the very next lion by the beard and to slay the beast with a stroke, yet when the said lion puts in an unexpected appearance, the timid man prudently gets out of the way with all despatch. I have known some men who really could not fight; men of distinguished excellence of character, willing to give any amount of money and to render any extent of service, provided there be no controversy; they would hardly contend even for the right, — they would give for it, *work* for it, *pray* for it, but never *fight* for it. If the minister came into collision with any of the people, his timid supporters would quietly move off to the seaside until the result was known; if the minister felt himself called upon to engage in unpopular controversy, the said friends would never be found at his side; but if he succeeded in turning the popular current into his favor, they would boldly acknowledge that controversy has its uses, and that Christian ministers are bound to contend earnestly for the faith once delivered unto the saints. They will go even fruther: if public excitement be turned in favor of the minister, if he become the hero of the hour, if newspapers extend his reputation, and if great men give honor to his name, the timid friends who deeply felt the necessity for sea air at the beginning of the fight, will courageously suggest in a very private meeting whether a testimonial ought not to be presented to the champion of great principles. And in both cases the timid friends will be quite sincere. The simple fact is, they cannot overcome their natural timidity; they cannot bring their moral courage abreast of their moral impulses; to *will* is present with them, but how to *perform* they find not. I have often had occasion to hear of the unhappy consequences of defective courage, especially in the working out of the most republican forms of ecclesiastical life. Take the case of an Independent church, in which there is some division of opinion upon an important question, and the course of events will probably be as follows: a few talkative, self-confident, and pertinacious individuals will lead the opposition; around them will be gathered half-a-dozen youths (apprentices, clerks, and errand-boys), who have studied the art of impertinence in what are called "mutual improvement societies," and who are just eloquent enough to cry out "hear, hear," and "fair play," when the elder opponents are being hard driven. When such a state of affairs arises, nearly every man of intelligence and good feeling will absent himself from the church meeting; men and women who are desirous to cultivate spiritual-mindedness, and who wish the church to be the centre of their happiest associations, will not subject themselves to the annoyance and exasperation of carping and malicious criticism; — hence it may be perfectly possible to pass a resolution at a church meeting, and to pass it unanimously, from which all the educated, refined, and earnest members of the church most strongly and determinedly dissent. You will say this is a most anomalous state of affairs, and I allow it; yet it is matter of fact, and admits, I think, of easy explanation. In proportion as any man lives a deeply spiritual life will he shrink from frivolous debate, and especially from offering opposition to the Christian ministry: he will have no taste for resolutions and counter-resolutions, for committees and sub-committees, for amendments and riders; he has a nobler and diviner idea of church life, and nothing will tempt him from his high eminence to mingle in the dusty frays which occasionally disgrace the working out of ecclesiastical republicanism. This is, on some grounds, to be regretted; the minister often suffers most painful injury by it; he is left in the hands of a few men who are quite capable of driving roughly over all the sensibilities that have been refined by high education and deep communion with the Spirit of truth; and whilst he may have the sympathy of the largest and best portion of his people, he is left to smart under an official resolution which may have all the effect of a virtual falsehood. You will say that the men who could pass such a resolution ought not to be in the church; this is true, but unfortunately we have to suffer from facts, and not to discuss opinions. With all the supposed care with which the gates of church membership are guarded, low-minded and worthless men do secure public standing; and as they are men who have nothing to lose, they are often reckless in their opposition. They regard the church as a kind of debating club; their piety is limited to impious discussions; they think the church is dead if a stirring controversy is not proceeding, and that the world is in mortal danger of damnation if the ballot-box and the sub-committee are not in constant requisition. Rely upon it, these are *not timid* men; they are rather what the apostle Peter describes as "natural brute beasts made to be taken and destroyed." I refer to them, though with infinite repugnance, merely to show how little the minister has to hope for from *timid* supporters. The coarse men will always be foremost; to them a fight is a revival, a secession is a means of grace, and a change of ministry is a gracious device of Providence. Now, between the very boisterous and the very timid men, there is a class that attempts to please all parties; the members of this class are often very clever; by a nod they can encourage the opposition, by a smile they can cheer the timid, by a shake of the hand they can strengthen the minister, and by a shake of the head they can aid those who are seeking to drive the minister away. There is undoubtedly great versatility of power in all this, and the most perfect security too; for who can publish a nod? who can report a smile as an item of denominational intelligence? what is the practical value of a shake of the hand? and how many contradictory ways are there of shaking a head that has nothing in it? The all-pleasers do not commit themselves by speech or writing, they express themselves with a significance which admits of no repetition, and defend themselves by a look of surprise which may be made to mean anything the observer pleases. This manifestation of character will often distress you. As a man of God, you will demand truth, honor, courage, and individuality of conviction, in those who claim you as their pastor; but I forewarn you, in the recollection of many a bitter disappointment, that there are staves that look strong and trusty that will break when you lean upon them, and pierce your hands!

In the course of my ministry I have met with *men who, without intending it, have put hindrances in the way of my work.* Chief among these have been *over-zealous defenders.* I don't know how it is with other men, but to me it is an infinite nuisance to be defended. Some kind-hearted people have told me with an air of intense self-satisfaction that they have "defended me through thick and thin," — whatever height of insanity that expression may be intended to signify. Over-zealous defenders don't appear to see that they actually provoke opposition. Men like to torment them; reports are taken to them by men who have a comical vein in their nature, and are with mock solemnity submitted for confirmation or denial; dull hours are enlivened by quizzical comments upon the ministry, and harmless inquiries are put with well-simulated anxiety to know the truth. Instantly the over-zealous defender takes fire, and soon puts himself by extravagant statements into the hands of his friendly tormentors. I advise you to ask your friends never to defend you; beg them to let you alone; assure them that when you need defence you need to be put an end to. I do not know whether your friends might not occasionally be permitted a disdainful retort upon your critics, for I believe in disdain as the best answer to some evil questions. I know a boy who defended his father in the best possible manner; said boy was in the habit of expressing himself somewhat quaintly on things in general, so much so that he had quite a local reputation as a budding genius. On one occasion, whilst visiting the boys in a neighbor's house, the head of the family (a very stiff and important personage) took opportunity of putting the young philosopher to the test. "So," said he, in a grave and dignified manner, "they tell me, my boy, that your father drinks?" The youth (whose upper lip is singularly expressive of scorn) turned upon him with the utmost quietness, and said, "You great daft thing!" Not a word more; it was enough. In that way I should like ever to be defended: first, so to live as to be like the boy's father, above suspicion; and then to be so trusted and beloved as to expose all slanderers to the just charge of being "great daft things." I prefer abuse to defence. Undeserved abuse always does a man good; defence is almost sure to do him unintended injury. Count it a blessed day in your ministerial history when low-minded men write against you in the newspapers, and speak against you in the social circles; the time for doing good has then come: but when the devil is quiet, when he is treating you with indifference, when he does not think it worth while to set his very least imp upon you, be sure there is something wanting in the energy with which you strike him. The probability is that the over-zealous defender will also be the over-zealous reporter; this you will find to your cost when he comes to you with tale after tale, not one of which is worthy of a moment's attention, but all of which, taken together, may irritate and unsettle you. The officious though well-disposed reporter will say, "You know, sir, one can't help hearing those things"; "the other day I was compelled to hear so and so"; "of course, having a place of business in the very middle of the town, a good many people drop in and tell me things I should not otherwise hear"; "of course you know, sir, I don't tell you these things to trouble you; it is only to put you on your guard that I venture to name them"; and in this self-excusing, yet self-deluding manner the poor man constitutes himself into the very sewer of the church, and imagines that he is doing service to his minister! I have known not a few good men pestered in this way. Things they ought never to have heard have been carefully told them by indiscreet sympathizers, and in moments of despondency such things have been exaggerated by nervous apprehensions, and so a thoughtless friendship has given them more pain than open enmity. On this matter I have two simple pieces of advice to offer you, — first of all, *never believe a word you hear*. Be sure a tone has been altered or missed, a circumstance has been altogether forgotten or mistaken, so that the meaning of the original speaker has been lost, and that consequently if he were to hear the tale to which his own name is attached, he would be amazed at his own cleverness or knavery. It is next to impossible to relate anything exactly as it was first told. Every word may be carefully repeated, yet the savor may be lost; the bottle may have been steadily carried, yet as the glass stopper has been exchanged for a common cork, the spirit of the contents has exhaled. To this recommendation of universal disbelief let me add a second piece of advice — *never defend yourself.* I know what the ardent young minister is apt to do. Immediately that he hears of some unlucky man who has been criticising his sermons, he makes it his business to wait on the unhappy critic and to pommel him well by a high-wrought defence of himself and his method of preaching, he turns on the great wheel for the purpose of killing a fly, and the probability is that he cannot stop the wheel when the magnificent slaughter has been accomplished. Or there is another way in which the young enthusiast may attempt self-vindication, — he may *stand upon his dignity* when he meets offenders. He may speak to them coldly, he may hold them at arm's length; he may assume the most chilling airs of haughty self-reliance; and a hundred other foolish things he may do. Now, my dear sir, hear me; *don't* stand on your dignity; *please* don't stand on your dignity; forget your dignity; leave your dignity at home, and be a Christian gentleman. A Christian gentleman never stands on his dignity, and therefore he is never undignified. Suppose *you* stand on your dignity, what then? Why, of course, Mrs. Tallow-chandler will stand on *her* dignity, so will Mrs. Laundress, so will Mrs. Charwoman; you will all stand on your dignity, and your fall into the ditch will be all the greater for your elevation. There is yet a third way in which a fiery youth may put in a word for himself; he *may rush into print*. In a blaze of indignation he declares his intention not to be put down. "No," says he, "I shall appeal to a discriminating public!" The excited youth forgets that the public is *not* discriminating; the public is an overgrown fussy baby, so busy weaving cotton and selling potatoes as not to care one iota who is right and who is wrong in an ecclesiastical brawl. Never print whilst you are angry; and whether you are angry or not, never print anything in your own defence. Print poetry, because nobody will read it; print sermons, for that is the most decent form of burial; but never print personal defences, because every gossip in the neighborhood will buy your hot preparations, and scald you with them some other day. May you know the blessedness of those who have neither pens nor ink, who never condescend to write a letter, and who hold original composition in contempt. 'Twill save you from a thousand snares, to throw your pens away.

I shall take my own advice, at least for the present; so let my final word be upon the desirableness of not committing yourself to anybody. Never tell all you know. Never mix yourself with the petty confidences of cliques. Dine as seldom as possible in company, especially in company with the members of your own congregation. Select your friends with the most critical care, and when you find a really true man give him your heart, let him feel the influence of a strong, deep love, and he will prize your confidence when he knows that it is not indiscriminately bestowed. I am afraid you will think me somewhat severe, yet I make my appeal to *time*. I have trusted many, I have found a few chosen men in whose keeping my very life would be perfectly safe; yet looking at the breadth of a lifetime, I feel constrained to repeat the Saviour's words, "*Beware of men.*"

XVII.

DIRECTORIES.

You are not to suppose an intention on my part to review all the Helps, Guides, and Aids to the power of public speaking which have appeared from the time of St. Augustine. My modest wish is to say a word or two upon books which are of recent production, and which, as will be seen, deserve notice both as warnings and examples. The other day I laid out a small sum in the purchase of the most magnificent work ever penned upon the subject to which it is devoted,—nothing less than "a complete guide to the attainment of purity and elegance of style in speaking and writing." The sum expended was "two and eleven,"—how far the investment was such as to tempt you to follow my example you shall presently see. Please to remember that the book in question is not merely a guide, but a *complete* guide, and not a complete guide to rudimentary writing, but to the attainment of *purity and elegance of style*. What is said on the title-page is repeated on page 33,—"our treatise being designed for the advanced student," etc. Notwithstanding this high design, the condescending author gives on his 16th page "Preliminary Hints to Juvenile Readers," the originality and value of which do not admit of two opinions. Here they are:—

"Be careful to pronounce each word deliberately, with a clear and distinct utterance of every syllable, and with due attention to the vowels, diphthongs, and final consonants. Read as if conversing in polite society, not as a task, not thinking of your voice and how you impress your listeners, but, as far as you can, forgetting yourself, and entering into the feelings and sentiments of the author: and a caution to youthful readers may here not be ill-timed, viz., that they especially guard against an over-serious and formal tone and manner. The object of reading is to give pleasure, while imparting information; therefore the voice, as well as the expression of the countenance, should indicate cheerfulness, making it apparent that the reader takes an interest in the subject, and is gratified by the exercise. There is a natural charm in a lively and unaffected tone; and, to conclude, we recommend the old-fashioned couplet as a very good rule for beginners, viz., —

> 'Learn to speak slow, all other graces
> Will follow in their proper places.'

"A variety in exercises gives mastery, and for this it is advisable to practise alternately the different styles of composition, from the light and humorous, to the more grave and dignified."

The comprehensive advice to be careful about vowels and diphthongs, yet not to think of the voice; to forget yourself, and yet to let the countenance indicate cheerfulness; not to think of the voice, and yet to aim at a lively and unaffected tone, is most charming, enabling the author to come in at the front door and go out at the back, and to say contradictory things in such a manner as to be bound to neither of them. The youthful reader is not to think of how he impresses his listeners, yet he is to show that he is gratified by the exercise; he is to be indifferent to his hearers, and yet to remember that his object is to give them pleasure and impart to them information. They must be *very* juvenile readers for whom such lucid hints are designed. You will be pleased to observe that the countenance is to indicate cheerfulness, as a proof that the reader takes an interest in the subject, whether the subject be "light and humorous," or "the more grave and dignified": the great object with our pleasant author is to be *cheerful*, in whatever direction the rhetorical wind may blow.

So much for juvenile readers. Coming to "advanced students," the author "doubts whether the strict formality of methodical systems may not often prove rather a hindrance than a help to minds of a superior cast." Keeping his eye upon "minds of a superior cast," the author sublimely says: "Had the early genius of Shakspeare been thus cramped and rigidly tied down to precise modes and details of study, we much doubt whether his imagination would have expanded with the noble freedom, and bold and graphic originality, which constitutes the great charm of his dramatic compositions. We admit that, so trained, he might have been eminently shrewd and clever, but he would not have been Shakspeare as he has come down to us, and as we delight to know him." This is, of course, a most satisfactory explanation of Shakspeare. We now see clearly all about him. Avoid precise modes and details of study, and you will probably be a Shakspeare; keep clear of "hints to juvenile readers," or you will never write "Hamlet." The judicial mind of the author admits that had Shakspeare read such hints, and been foolish enough to take them seriously to heart, he would have been a tolerably shrewd man on the whole, — nay, more, "eminently shrewd and clever," which is a poor encouragement to the public to buy our author's "complete guide." How any man can have brought himself to imagine that Shakspeare could have been "cramped and rigidly tied down to precise modes and details of study" is not to be satisfactorily accounted for, except on the principle that he himself was "rigidly tied down" in his youth, and has never been able to shake off his bonds.

Having thus explained the majesty of Shakspeare, the author adds with wonderful simplicity: "We have therefore purposely omitted much of the introductory matter commonly found in school treatises," etc. This is one of the collateral blessings which Shakspeare has conferred upon the world. Because Shakspeare *might* have been spoiled by modes and details, our author shrinks from the possibility of nipping some young Shakspeare in the bud, and *therefore* avoids "precise modes and details of study." This was very daring on the part of the author, yet he recovered himself by the aid of a great name. "Nor," says he, "are we without support in this our view. It was the advice of Dr. Johnson," etc.; clearly showing how impossible it is even for the strongest minds to proceed far in original thinking without coming upon unexpected and illustrious companionship. Dr. Johnson advised a young man to give his days and nights to Addison, and our author adds this important remark, "We hold the counsel advisable, for his writings exhibit a faultless style and classic purity, while breathing a cheerful spirit, enlivened with a rich vein of humor and a playful but harmless satire, and as a moral essayist he has rarely been excelled." After this, no one will be at liberty to question the "advisableness" of Dr. Johnson's advice: in the first instance, Dr. Johnson supports our author's opinion, and in the next, our author supports Dr. Johnson's opinion, and thus the whole question is settled. Still, remembering that "by some this celebrated essayist is regarded as out of date," the author judiciously adds: "We deem it well, then, to begin with Addison, but by no means to end with him." Certainly not! *Begin* with an author of "faultless style and classic purity," but "by no means *end* with him." Give your days and nights to Addison, and the remainder of your time to somebody else!

One brief division of this "complete guide" is entitled "The Suggestive Faculty," and in giving "Hints for its Exercise," the author says: "In order to be fluent in speech, we must be fertile in thought, for words being but the signs of our ideas, to have a copious command of the former we must multiply the latter. Whatever, therefore, sets our thoughts actively at work, will serve our turn, and claims our first attention. For this, formal rules are not needful, a single suggestion may suffice. We will then at once commence." Prepare yourself, my friend, for one of the most pathetic illustrations ever addressed to your heart, and please to remember that it forms part of a book intended for "advanced students," — not for tyros, but for men of capacity and strength. The author's object is to teach his advanced students how to "multiply ideas"; and how admirably the illustration is fitted to serve this useful purpose you will see without the aid of a commentator: "You have received, we will suppose, two invitations, each being to spend a month, one with friends in town, the other in the country; you must choose between them, and perhaps are puzzled in so doing. Ere you decide, you will think and turn over in your mind the pleasure and advantage you may expect from either. On the one hand, the country tempts you with its freshness and beauty, its rural scenes, its walks and rides, and healthful recreations. On the other hand, the town attracts with its gayeties, its social pleasures, and diversified entertainments; in either case, not omitting the companionship you may prefer, and the society you will enter into. Here is no lack of matter for thinking, if you would choose discreetly; and it will be helpful to note down separately the *pros* and *cons*, and then weigh and consider. We have merely thrown out the hint for the youthful composer."

"Here is no lack of matter for thinking"!! You will observe that the town attracts you *with* its gayeties; you will also observe that you are not only to *think*, but to *turn over in your mind*, and the difficult part of your work is to think and turn over "the pleasure and advantage" which exist only in expectation, and therefore don't exist at all. It is very prettily said that the *country* tempts you with its *rural* scenes. Observe the intellectual process through which you have to pass before going out for a month's holiday: "think — turn over in your mind — note down separately — then weigh and consider"; *that 's all!* Why, you could not do more if you had to choose between life and death! I am afraid that if anything could have enfeebled the wings of Shakspeare, this process of "thinking" would have succeeded in doing so. If you should ever avail yourself of this absurd advice, pray don't tell the friend whose hospitality you accept that you have made your way to his house through the briers of such sharp logic, and especially keep the secret from his wife, or she will not ask you whether you will take tea or coffee, for fear you should retire for an hour to "note down separately the *pros* and *cons*." It is, however, a great relief to find our author saying, "We have merely thrown out the hint for the youthful composer"; if the youthful composer will do the same thing, the hint will be treated exactly as it deserves. No, no; we must have something better than this, worse is impossible: why, this is infinitely better — a minister, whose command of words was positively alarming, was asked by what method he had acquired such amazing fluency, and he frankly owned it was the result of practice; said he, "when I go out to walk, I say to my stick 'long stick, hard stick, strong stick, smooth stick, thick stick, light stick, nice stick,'" whereupon his waggish listener added "*dry* stick," and left him.

You are not to be deterred from the practice recommended by our author by its difficulty, because "such a process constitutes the element of solid improvement," and, besides this, "the task becomes easier with practice, one thought begets another, till at length we master the difficulty, and become conscious of our power · we then begin to take a pleasure in duly ordering our ideas, and in giving a becoming expression to them." This word of encouragement is needed, considering the painfulness of the task appointed by the exacting author. Some of us have great difficulty in "commanding our thoughts"; judge therefore of my delight in coming upon this luminous passage: —

"It is most desirable to acquire betimes a habit of fixing the attention, and concentrating the thoughts, which are ever prone to wander, especially with the unpractised; a watchful guard is therefore requisite to counteract this propensity; and it is no less needful to be able to control our ideas than to have formed them aright. In the choice of words, also, to give a judicious expression to our sentiments, due care and discretion are indispensable."

That settles the question, by putting you up to the art and mystery of mental concentration. You see now exactly how it is, don't you? Appoint a watchful guard, and give due expression to your sentiments, — that's all, nothing easier, my dear sir, if you know how, which is not the business of the "*complete*" guide to tell, especially for the trifling sum of two and elevenpence. Still, our author must have felt that in putting the case in this clear manner, he had made a considerable contribution to that form of authorship which, as George Eliot says, "is called suggestion, and consists in telling another man that he might do a great deal with a given subject by bringing a sufficient amount of knowledge, reasoning, and wit to bear upon it."

You will admit, I am sure, the importance of "variety in forms of expression"; on this subject our author is conspicuously great, as you will see by the following: —

"This is effected by changing the position of the component parts of a paragraph, or compound sentence, without altering the words.

"EXAMPLE.

1. When a good man dies he leaves all his bad behind, and carries all his good with him. When a sinner dies he leaves all his good, and carries all his bad.
2. When a good man dies he carries all his good, etc.
3. A good man when he dies leaves, etc.
4. A good man when he dies carries, etc.
5. When he dies, a good man, etc.
6. A sinner when he dies — When a sinner dies, etc.

N. B. — This sentence admits of twelve variations."

Now, sir, no more talk of want of variety in preaching! By a skilful use of this novel permutation, one sermon will last you a lifetime. When I reflect on this it is impossible to begrudge the two and eleven-pence for so complete a guide. Query: if one sentence admits of twelve variations, of how many variations will two sermons admit? Then the *text* may be varied; begin one inch from the beginning, then begin in the middle, then read it backwards, and then try it from the beginning. If the order of words may be varied, why may not the *emphasis* of the words be varied too? See how rich a field is opened by this simple plan! Take the text, "Go thou and do likewise"; and the results are truly wonderful. Thus: —

Go thou and do likewise; that is, don't do it *here*, but go out and do it.

Go *thou* and do likewise; don't work by deputy, do your own work.

Go thou *and* do likewise; it is not enough to go, you must also *do*.

Go thou and *do* likewise; don't merely think or approve, but *act*.

Go thou and do *likewise:* don't be original; copy and reflect, but don't originate.

N. B.—This emphasis is adapted to all subjects and occasions."

The native delicacy of the author's taste is strikingly shown in his remarks upon "Qualified or Softened Expression." Some of us have an unfeeling way of calling a spade a spade, and a shameful habit of calling a liar a liar. To all this rudeness there may now be a happy end. Speaking upon "Qualified or Softened Expression," the author says: "This serves to mitigate the severity of rude and harsh sounding words, by avoiding all such as are highly offensive. Thus, instead of branding the individual with the odious epithet of liar, we may accuse him of misrepresentation. Instead of the stigma, sot, sluggard, or idler, we say, deficient in energy, the reverse of diligent, prone to inaction. Insufferable pride will be exaggerated self-esteem; for madness, alienation of mind; and instead of brutal folly, a lamentable want of prudence."

This rule would considerably change (not improve) the method of putting things in some parts of the New Testament. For example: "If any man say he love God, and hateth his brotherhood, he is a liar," would be—he is guilty of misrepresentation: a much gentler method of dealing with the case. Even Solomon, wisest of men, might be amended; when he says, "Go to the ant, thou sluggard," he should be read as saying, "Go to the ant, thou who art prone to inaction!" When Jesus Christ calls Herod a "fox," He should be understood as calling him "that animal of the genus *Canis*, with a straight tail, yellowish hair, and erect ears,"—decidedly more polite, and considerate of human feeling.

It is with much relief that I turn to an eighteen-penny book, by Mr. Holyoake, called "Rudiments of Public Speaking and Debate." Get this book if you can; I am afraid it is out of print. It is full of wise and practical counsel, and rich with allusion and quotation of the best kind. An extract from the chapter on *Effectiveness* will show what I mean. "Young men, poetical from ardor, and enthusiastic from passion rather than principle, will often rush from libraries crammed with lore with which nobody else is familiar, and pour out before an audience what the speaker believes to be both sublime and impressive, but which his hearers cannot understand. They grow listless and restless, and he retires overwhelmed with a sense of failure. A B, a young friend of considerable promise, thus failed in my presence. I endeavored thus to divert his despondency.

"Failures, I urged, are with heroic minds the stepping-stones to success.

"'Why have I not succeeded?' he asked. 'I can never hope to say better things of my own than I said to-night of others.'

"The cause of your non-success is obvious. You commenced by addressing your auditors as men, and you left them as children. A young preacher who had ascended the pulpit with great confidence, but who broke down in the middle of his sermon, was met by Rowland Hill as he was rushing from the pulpit. 'Young man, said Rowland, 'had you ascended the pulpit in the spirit in which you descended, you would have descended in the spirit in which you ascended.' Something of this kind will explain your case. In your exordium you should address your auditors as though they were children, state your arguments as though they were learners, and in your peroration only assume them to be men. On the threshold of a new subject men are as children; during its unfoldment they are learners; only when the subject is mastered are they as men, with manhood's power to execute their convictions. Had it struck you that probably no man of your audience was familiar with the habits of society in the days of Spenser's 'Faery Queene,' or of the high and mystic imaginings of the solitary Paracelsus, would not the thought have caused you to recast your whole lecture? Take care that you do not render yourself amenable to the sarcasm of Swift, who, when Burnet said, speaking of the Scotch preachers in the time of the civil war, 'The crowds were far beyond the capacity of their churches or the reach of their voices,' Swift added, 'And the preaching beyond the capacity of the crowd; I believe the church had as much capacity as the minister.'"

An extract relating to debate will show you Mr. Holyoake's spirit and somewhat of his method: "The object of discussion is not the vexatious chase of an opponent, but the contrastive and current statement of opinion. Therefore endeavor to select leading opinions, to state them strongly and clearly, and when your opponent replies, be content to leave his arguments side by side with your own, for the judgment of the auditors. In no case disparage an opponent, misstate his views, or torture his words, and thus, for the sake of a verbal triumph, produce lasting ill feelings. Your sole business is with *what* he says, not *how* he says it, nor *why* he says it. Your aim should be that the audience should lose sight of the speakers, and be possessed with the subject, and that those who come the partisans of persons shall depart the partisans of principles. The victory in a debate lies not in lowering an opponent, but in raising the subject in public estimation. Controversial wisdom lies not in destroying an opponent, but in destroying his error; not in making him ridiculous, so much as in making the audience wise." The wisdom of these counsels may be turned to advantage even in the pulpit, for though you do not there enter into debate in the ordinary sense of the term, yet you have to reply to objections, to anticipate difficulties, and to commend your cause to the judgment of all who hear you. It is specially needful in a minister who has the entire conduct of a service, that he should be noble in his treatment of all supposed objectors. Their arguments should be stated with all possible clearness and force, and courtesy should never be sacrificed to victory.

Have you seen Paxton Hood's book, with the singular title, "Lamps, Pitchers, and Trumpets"? Get it, by all means. The mere arrangement of the subjects might be considerably improved; but the matter, the spirit, the enthusiasm, and the poetry leave nothing to be desired. The book has called me out of many a gloomy fit, and helped me to begin again after I thought the end of my work had come. There is not a tame sentence in all the book; if there is, I have not seen it. Wisdom, anecdote, individuality, illustration, parable — plenty; insipidity, monotony, cold exhortation — none. Mr. Hood gives his reader to feel how sublime a thing it is to be a preacher. We are not allowed to drop the preacher into a secondary rank; he is called of God, he is inspired by the Holy Ghost, he is the interpreter and revealer of the Redeeming Heart. Read this book if ever you be tempted to give up the exercise of your ministry.

Vinet, Baxter, Bridges, Greswell, Porter, Cotton Mather, and others will have a good deal to say that is "profitable for doctrine, for reproof, for correction, and for instruction" in homiletics. Remember that no preacher was ever made by rules. You may have a bag full of excellent tools, but if your fingers be unskilled, your instruments are of little use. Does the *spade* make the gardener? Does the *easel* make the painter? A man may read guide-boards and finger-posts all the days of his life, and yet never take a walk; or he may be profound in Bradshaw, and yet never enter a train. It is possible, too, to be a critic without being an artist, and to be able to find fault, without being able to do better. Many of your hearers will complain of your sermons, who could not write a sermon if they were to be rewarded with heaven for doing so. Don't upbraid them for their inability. Faultfinding is a distinct and special talent. What would you have thought, if, when you told your shoemaker that your shoes did n't fit, he had challenged you to make a better pair? Remember this, and be humble!

XVIII.

THE GUARANTEES OF A SUCCESSFUL MINISTRY.

To-day I feel as if I would much rather *speak* to you than address you in writing, as my heart is full of a subject which requires to be explained in the tenderest and most urgent manner, and in secrecy, as between friend and friend who are both conscious of the presence and looking forward to the judgment of God. I do you no injustice assuredly in presuming that you are most anxious that your ministry should be successful. Success, when applied to Christian work, is a term which requires to be carefully explained. Already I have given you my views pretty fully upon this point; but as the subject is one of extraordinary importance, you will excuse me repeating that success in ministerial service is not to be confounded with success in any other engagement of life. Naturally you think of success in connection with crowded chapels, ample pecuniary resources, and a sounding reputation: far be it from me to say that these things are not to be desired in a proper measure; at the same time I hold distinctly that it is perfectly possible to fall short of them, and yet to be realizing a very high degree of success in the Christian ministry. I think it exceedingly unreasonable on the part of any person to ridicule large congregations, or to attempt to undervalue outward and visible signs of a powerful ministry. It is certain that if people do not come to hear you, you cannot do them any good; on the other hand, it is probable that if they do come to hear you, the word which you preach may touch their hearts; on this ground I hold it to be unreasonable to say one word against able ministers of the gospel whose ministry secures an overflowing attendance of hearers. Success, in fact, is a term which has different meanings according to the different circumstances under which it is employed. One man is a successful preacher,— his style of thought and his manner of expression are such as to constitute him a master of great assemblies: Another man has a style of thinking and a manner of expression which give him a quieter, but not less useful influence. One man is qualified to direct a crowd; another is capable of exerting a most beneficent influence on a few select minds; in both cases there may be the highest ministerial success, though the outward signs differ so much. I hold that no ministry is successful that does not work in men a profound conviction of the sinfulness of sin, and an earnest desire to know Jesus Christ and His blessed salvation. Assuming that we are equally earnest in endeavoring to reach the highest point of success in our holy vocation, allow me to put before you a point or two which will show you my own view of the case, and may lead your own mind into still further pursuit of the conditions which are essential to the highest service for Christ.

It is perfectly clear to me that our first business is to keep diligently our own heart. For a moment let us exclude the idea that we are called to any special office in Christ's kingdom; forgetting that we are ministers, let us think of ourselves as individual *Christians.* As sinners recovered by the grace of God, we are never to lose sight of the fact that our salvation is derived entirely from the cross of Jesus Christ, and not at all from the exercise of our ministerial gifts. We are not first ministers, and then Christians; we are first Christians, and then, by the grace of God, we are called to minister in Jesus Christ's name. What, then, is our spiritual condition before God? Is our heart really alive to the grandeur of the redemption of which we profess to have been made partakers? Do we find rest in the blessed fact that we ourselves have cast our souls entirely upon the Saviour, and given up our destiny to His keeping? There is, as you will come to know, a dread possibility of our sinking the Christian in the minister, and of our seeing even God's own book rather for ministerial than for strictly personal and spiritual uses. Holding, as I do most tenaciously, that the ministry of the gospel is not a profession, but a vocation, I am yet well aware how powerful is the temptation to regard all things appertaining to our ministry in a professional light, to turn Christian meditation into a kind of professional study, and to discharge our obligations as hirelings rather than sons of God. Retirement, self-examination, devout study of the Holy Scriptures, are entirely indispensable to any man who would grow in grace and qualify himself for public usefulness in the church. Are we much alone with God? Do we turn away from the world with all its distractions and allurements, and enjoy the secrecy in which God is our only companion? Rely upon it, we shall be mighty only in proportion as we are devout; and only as we walk with God, and enjoy deep and constant fellowship with Him through His Son, shall we be able to speak in a manner which will commend our ministry to every man's conscience. I know the difficulties which lie in the direction of profound spiritual culture in the individual heart: there is so much excitement, there is so much to be read and to be heard, there are so many conflicting opinions to consider and balance, so many inroads are made upon privacy by the demands of custom, that it is next to impossible, apart from the severest economy of time, to secure opportunity for deep and loving intercourse with the Father, the Son, and the Holy Ghost. I don't know why I should hesitate to say that there is great danger, in the multiplicity of claims which are constantly made upon our attention, of overlooking the distinctive claims of God's own book. I do not know how far your observation and my own may coincide, but to me it is a very painful and humiliating fact that few books seem to be less known, even by ministers themselves, than the book of inspiration. I have known men of very limited culture, whose ministry has yet been signally owned, through a devotion to the Scriptures, which has enabled them to meet the necessities of the people with an appropriateness and sufficiency even which no man of general reading could ever have secured. Truly in us who are called to preach Jesus Christ, the word of God ought to dwell richly and abound. We ought not to stumble in our quotation of the Divine word; that word ought to be hidden in our heart, and ought to be so precious to us as to be within instant call of our memory whenever occasion arises for its application to our own spiritual condition or the interests of those to whom we minister. Do not imagine that I am in any degree enforcing my own example upon you, when I venture to say again and again that unless you be shut up as it were with the Father, the Son, and the Holy Ghost, in secret retirement, no unction will rest upon your ministry, however eloquent your language, or splendid your illustrations, or vehement your public appeals. It is impossible to disguise the spirit which comes of profound contemplation of religious subjects; it is impossible to conceal the fact which is produced by prolonged and loving intercourse with the Saviour. If the countenance itself do not shine with unearthly lustre, there will be in the whole manner an influence which will proclaim itself to have been originated by the highest intercourse. Let us, then, seek to deepen our Christian conviction and Christian feeling. Let us live very near the cross; let Jesus Christ be the one all-commanding Object of our attention and our love. If such be the case, we shall know what it is to long with unspeakable desire for the presence and guidance of the Holy Ghost. Some of us, indeed, are in danger of forgetting that this is the dispensation of the Holy Spirit, and that all Christian usefulness is now to be conducted and directed by Him alone. The Holy Ghost is to be given in answer to fervent and unceasing prayer; let us wait diligently at the throne, until we receive this most blessed and inspiring Gift.

Our work in the ministry will be a failure unless we seek to discharge our obligations in the spirit of Jesus Christ. We must work as He worked, and for the purposes which formed the great object of His ministry. The spirit of Jesus Christ was a spirit of true sincerity, courage, unselfishness; Jesus Christ was always seeking the redemption of men. We shall grow cold in our work, if the fires of our heart be not renewed by the love of the Saviour. We must seek to obtain his view of human life, alike in the individual and in society. Jesus Christ did not work on great occasions only, He sought to make every occasion great. He devoted Himself as entirely to the service of one sinner, as to the teaching of the greatest multitude that thronged upon His ministry. The spirit of Jesus Christ was the spirit of hope; He did not discourage the worst persons who sought His counsel and His sympathy. His delight was to seek and to save the lost. Are we not in danger of attending almost exclusively to the sections of society which are distinctly denominated *respectable?* We think it a great thing to see a respectable congregation; we speak applaudingly of the men who gather around them the rich and the learned. I fear that in doing so we may miss the influence of the spirit which inspired Jesus Christ. Jesus Christ sought the lost, the lowest, the vilest, the outcast, and the despised. You will no doubt remind me that in connection with most ecclesiastical organizations there are agencies for the recovery of the lowest class of the population. I am quite aware of this, yet I feel a danger even here, because some of us may be seeking to do by deputy what we ought to be doing in our own proper person. Believe me, it does not appear to me to be sufficient to delegate to others the work of informing ourselves of the condition of the most ruined people; there is not a minister amongst us, how remarkable soever his gifts or exalted his position, who would not be stimulated and encouraged in his work by spending a little time now and again in visiting the darkest haunts of our incomplete civilization. I cannot but think that Jesus Christ Himself would not always be found on the busy thoroughfares of our cities or in their attractive suburbs; I cannot but feel that oftentimes He would be found in the lowest places, speaking to men, women, and children out of whom all that is human has almost perished. Ought not the spirit of our Saviour to constrain us to make some personal sacrifice in this direction? Of course, there must be adaptation on our part to meet such as those now specially referred to; at the same time it is quite possible that when we put ourselves into the right circumstances, adaptation on our part may be unexpectedly developed. The highest talent is often required to meet extremities. It appears to me to be quite a mistake to imagine that inferior talent is good enough to meet the requirements of the outcast masses; on the contrary, my conviction is that the highest gifts may be most profitably employed in meeting the difficulties, the objections, the hardships, and the perplexities of men whose case has too often been regarded as utterly hopeless. Now nothing can enable us to undertake with spirit and determination work of this kind, but deep sympathy with Jesus Christ. We cannot engage in such service with any personal satisfaction; our taste will be disgusted, our energies will be impaired, our whole nature will recoil, unless we go into this work animated by the self-sacrificing and all-loving spirit of the Redeemer. Not only so, our own morality will be corrupted if we take with us anything less than the protection of the holiness of Jesus Christ. We ourselves are but men; if we touch pitch, we shall be defiled; but if we seek Christ's companionship, and defend ourselves by Christ's righteousness, we shall be enabled to pass through the most revolting scenes without loss of virtue, and not only so, but with a positive gain of moral strength in our hearts. I do not ask you to undertake work of this kind as a man of letters, or as a mere philanthropist, or as a political or a social reformer; I ask you to undertake it because of the cross of Jesus Christ, which is the symbol of all that is Divine and blessed in sacrifice.

The great object of our ministry is the salvation of souls. The term salvation, as I here employ it, is the most inclusive term which occurs to me to describe the whole service of our holy vocation. It includes not only the persuasion of men to go as penitents and believers to the footstool of mercy and the cross of Christ, but the teaching, the enlightenment, and strengthening of all Christian principle in the hearts of those who have avowedly given themselves to the Lord. It will be of poor value to us, on the great day of final judgment, that we have been applauded for preaching great sermons, if we have not brought sinners to a knowledge of the way of salvation. I know of no bitterer irony, or more humiliating satire, than to be told that we have delivered splendid discourses, and yet to know that not one soul has ever been led to Jesus Christ by a ministry so flatteringly described. I do not despise the uses of criticism, nor do I say one word against the charms of speech; but I do increasingly feel, as my experience of men extends, that there is nothing worth living for compared with the grand object of winning souls, working in them, by the aid of the Holy Ghost, those Christian convictions which save men from death. To be told by any poor creature that you have been the means of turning his attention from things that are earthly to things that are heavenly, is to receive the highest reward which is possible to Christian labor in the present scene of life. It is a hint of what will be said to you on another day and in higher circumstances. Let us seek for this applause, — the applause which testifies to the rousing and converting power of an inspired ministry. I know you will be tempted to engage in controversies; you may also be tempted to show off in some degree your many acquirements and your distinguished abilities; but let me entreat you, as I would in the fear of God entreat myself, to pray, study, and preach more distinctly for the conversion of men. "He that winneth souls is wise." If we convert a sinner from the error of his way, we shall save a soul from death, and hide a multitude of sins. "They that turn many to righteousness shall shine as stars for ever and ever." I see not why we should not enter into a vow, to give our souls no rest until we have used every endeavor to bring men to a knowledge of the truth as it is in Jesus. We cannot indeed command success; we cannot say that this and that result shall assuredly accrue from our ministry; but if we work as if we were determined to command success, the grace of God is such that we shall surely not go without the highest reward. For your encouragement, as well as for my own, I would remind you that no minister ever knows the extent of his usefulness. We see again and again instances which save us from despondency; but we cannot tell what may be the indirect influence of our Christian service. Strangers hear us; we never know their names or their circumstances; yet some word of ours may have been to them as unexpected and precious light, and they may go on their way rejoicing; words of which we thought but little at the time may have sunk into the hearts of some who have been burdened with secret grief; a cheerful tone may have animated others who had not courage enough to lay before us the circumstances which gave them pain. I think we do right to remind ourselves of these possibilities, lest we be cast down for want of evidence of a more distinct and public nature.

When you enter upon your sphere of service, let me advise you to confine as far as possible the energies of your first years to that sphere. You are to be a pastor, a shepherd, a man who loves men, and desires their salvation and Christian instruction and refinement. It must be a poor sphere which is not large enough to exhaust all the energies of a young minister. Let me implore you to work for your own church as if it were all the world to you. I know there is a supposed magnanimity which looks beyond details, localities, and individual claims, and luxuriates in large ideas and boundless enterprises. Without saying one word against this, I venture to appeal to you on every ground that you consider sacred, to keep diligently the vineyard to which you have been appointed in the providence of God. I am afraid that some of us will have occasion to say at last, "other vineyards have I kept, but mine own vineyard have I not kept." When in the fear of God you can truthfully say you have exhausted the sphere to which you were appointed, when you have taxed every power, when you have carried light into every home that is accessible, when you have taught every child who is willing to be instructed, when you have carried the inspiration of Christian conviction and stimulus into every household belonging to your church, then it will be time enough for you to consider whether you cannot do something beyond the limits of your particular appointment. You will consider that I am warning you against public work, and I do not hesitate to say that my advice is intended to operate to a large extent in that direction. You will tell me that you are a patriot as well as a Christian; that you are a citizen as well as a minister, and therefore you have rights of this kind or of that kind, which are not distinctly ministerial. I know, my dear sir, all that can be said upon this point. I am not speaking to you as to a man who has had twenty years' experience in the ministry, but to a youth who is just putting on the ministerial harness; and I say again and again, with most urgent importunity, let me entreat you to devote the first of your years and the best of your powers to the interests of your own church and congregation. After you have been seven years with your people, and become accustomed to the work which is expected at your hands, I do not say that you will not feel yourself at liberty to help in services which lie somewhat remote from your ministerial and pastoral engagements. You may be able to serve your day and generation by authorship; you may have a useful word to say on the passing topics of the time; you may be able to teach on the platform, and stimulate useful courses of thinking; you may increase your influence by several kinds of collateral engagements; but let the strength of your life, the richest power of your nature, be still devoted to the exposition and enforcement of Divine truth. You are a minister, not an author; you are a minister, not a lecturer; you are a minister, as was Paul; be as devoted as he was to the Cross and the kingdom of Jesus Christ. How noble and glowing was the enthusiasm which said, "God forbid that I should glory, save in the cross of our Lord Jesus Christ"; how resolute was the will which declared, "I determine to know nothing among men but Jesus Christ, and Him crucified." Believe me, there is scope enough in the Christian ministry to exhaust the fullest resources of any man; no man who gives himself entirely to the work of the ministry has occasion to complain of having too little to do. Let us then, giving our days to study and our nights to prayer, endeavor to show ourselves "able ministers of the New Testament."

You will observe that in this letter I have changed my usual style, and sought to express myself with the utmost simplicity and earnestness. I feel the need of doing so more and more. The work of the ministry becomes to me daily more exacting in its demands.

I know not that I ever had so high an idea of what a Christian preacher should be, and of what Christian preaching may be, as I have to-day. The pulpit will go down if the preacher goes down; the preacher will go down if the Christian goes down; but if there be due service at the sacred altar, if there be profound and earnest meditation upon the Divine oracles, if there be earnest searching of heart and continual desire to live as before the judgment seat of Christ, if there be anxious study and preparation for public appeals and for pastoral services, the Christian pulpit will retain its hold upon the sanctified judgment and affections of all men.

XVIII.

FIGURES, PARABLES, AND ANECDOTES.

It is easy to tell a preacher to adopt a figurative style of preaching; but what if he have no figures? This difficulty is not provided for by the rhetoricians who lay down rules, and illustrate them by borrowed examples. Most unquestionably the use of figures is to be highly commended, and it is because of a strong belief that a good deal can be done to improve what I may (for want of a better name) call the metaphorical faculty, that I urge you to insist upon your mind giving you something in the way of illustration. Look for figures; work for them; take them in their rudest outline, and improve them. It is hardly necessary to remind you that figures are not to be expected to meet all the points of a subject; let it suffice to have one main line of application, and to shed light on one particular point. I may confess to you in this confidential correspondence, that I cannot do much in the way of metaphor; yet this confession, coupled with the fact that I use all diligence to turn my fraction of talent to account, does not deter me from urging you to glean even where you cannot reap. To provoke your criticism, to encourage the feeblest of your efforts, and to awaken your emulation, I venture to send you a sample of figures and illustrations which my poor fancy has yielded with infinite reluctance.

What do you do when, in reading the massive folios of ancient English authors, you meet passages written in an unknown tongue? Paragraph after paragraph you read with all possible fluency, instantly apprehending the author's purpose; but suddenly the writer throws before you a handful of Latin or a handful of Greek:

what then? If you are absorbed by the interest of the book, you eagerly look out for the next paragraph in English, and continue your pursuit of the leading thought. Do likewise with God's wondrous providence-book. Much of it is written in your own tongue, — in large-lettered English, so to speak. Read that; master its deep significance, and leave the passages of unknown language until you are farther advanced in the rugged literature of life, until you are older and better scholars in God's probationary school. The day of interpretation will assuredly come.

You have seen an old man tottering with the gathered infirmities of a weary lifetime, and wandering in darkness on which no summer sun could shed the light of morning: blind! blind from his birth! never saw God's outer robe of many colors; never saw God's shadowed outline,— his own mother's face! You have seen such a man, led along the thronged highway by a little child, to whose young, bright eyes he committed himself in hope and faith. *I* am that poor blind wanderer through the way of God's mysteries, and that little guide represents the benevolence, the mercy, the tenderness, with which God leads me from horizon to horizon, until I stand amid the encircling glories of the perfect revelation. The commonest mercy of the daytime flames up into a fire-guide, that lights men through the gloom and trouble of the night.

I am afraid that many of us are defective in moral symmetry. Some men are great Christians upon one point, and some are great Christians upon another. One man is a great Christian in the matter of Sabbath-school teaching, and another a stupendous Christian in the matter of total abstinence from all strong drink. We may be too much in the habit of singling out special virtues, to feed them up to a high pitch, in order to carry off the prize at the ecclesiastical show. This would give but a poor idea of the roundness, the completeness, and the inclusiveness of the Christian life. Suppose that next summer should grow little but sunflowers, and the following mainly abound in roses, and the third be chiefly distinguished for violets: however rich might be the product of each, the summer, as a whole, would be accounted poor and ill clad. Summer develops all the growing power of the soil, and so moral summer does not bring forth an isolated excellency, but clothes the human tree with "all manner of fruit."

Mysteries! What are they but as the earth at night-time, speeding on with swift wing to the all-revealing brightness of morning!

We say of some men: "They are not altogether bad; every now and then they come pretty right; so much so that it is hard to distinguish between them and Christians." It is much the same as if we should say of a clock that is not going: "Really, that clock is not so bad after all; every now and then, twice in the twenty-four hours, it is perfectly right; it may be right all day by and by." No; not until the mechanism is put in order, and the pendulum is started. So with man: the *heart* must be right before the life can be true.

Every man must bear his testimony in his own way. Standing in a watchmaker's shop near noonday, I was surprised to find how many different ways there are of announcing twelve o'clock. One bell tolled it out in most solemn tones, leaving a considerable space between the resounding notes; another rattled off the hour in a most flippant manner, and seemed to say to the first, "Get on with you; put some spirit into your work, don't stand droning there!" One clock spoke with a silvery voice; another gave its message with a shivering clang; a third repeated the hours as if burdened with the effort; a fourth, having struck twelve very cheerfully, began to chime most sweetly. Every man, like every clock, has his own way; the one important thing is to keep true time, and not to be ashamed to tell it.

Some clocks don't strike. You must *look* at them if you would know the time. Some men don't *talk* their Christianity; you must look at their lives if you would know what the gospel can do for human nature. A clock need not be incorrect because it strikes; a man need not be inconsistent because he *speaks* as well as acts.

I dream: far out on the waste of waters there moves a pirate vessel; day by day it preys upon the lawful commerce of all countries; its decks are wet with human blood, and its coffers laden with plundered gold. It is the terror of all navigators. Its every pursuit is destruction to the pursued. It fights no losing battles; the mightiest quail, the stoutest surrender.

I dream still: over the yielding billows there rides in proud majesty another vessel, — vaster, stronger, quicker; on board is a captain surpassing all in genius, in courage, in resources. Against his assaults all artillery is but as the rattle of a child's toy against the eternal granite. He strikes the pirate ark once, and again he strikes, and once more; until the timbers rend, and the enemy is engulfed in the great deep.

What is the interpretation of my vision? What but that death is the great enemy coursing ever on the seas of human life, slaying the strong, blighting the beautiful, plucking away the young, and striking dread everywhere? And that great counteracting force, what is that but Christ, who came to "abolish death," and give His saints full triumph? And ages upon ages hence, if men should inquire "Where is death?" they shall be answered as with the voice of many waters,—SWALLOWED UP IN VICTORY!

Preachers and teachers of all degrees may know the way to heaven, yet never walk in it, just as a man may know every detail of the railway time-table, and yet never take a journey. Men who spend their lives in preparing other people for heaven, but never advance themselves towards it, may be likened to the inspectors, porters, and other railway servants, who are occupied in setting out travellers, but who themselves never see the ocean or the landscape.

It is right for you, young men, to enrich yourselves with the spoils of all pure literature: but he who would make a favorite of a bad book, simply because it contained a few beautiful passages, might as well caress the hand of an assassin because of the jewelry which sparkles on its fingers.

A great deal of misery would be prevented, if ministers would endeavor to form an honest estimate of their qualifications, and, as a consequence, seek appointments for which they are specially qualified. If one might teach unpleasant doctrines through the medium of figure, one can imagine how inconvenient it would be, in the event of a great cathedral clock wearing out, for a neat Geneva watch to put itself forward as a candidate for the vacancy. The Geneva might be a beautiful little thing, and might keep the most exact time, and might be called endearing names by the ladies and little children; yet, to speak the language of charity, it might hardly be adapted to be set a hundred and fifty feet above the ground, in a circular vacancy at least ten feet in diameter. In such a case its very elevation would become its obscurity. On the other hand, it would be quite as inconvenient if a great cathedral clock, weary of city work, should ask to be carried about as a private timekeeper. There is a moral in the figure. That moral points towards the law of proportion and adaptation. One can imagine the petted Geneva looking up from a lady's hand, and calling the cathedral clock a great coarse thing, with a loud and vulgar voice, which indicated the most offensive presumption; and we can imagine the cathedral clock looking down, with somewhat of disdain, upon the little timekeeping toy. Oh, that some sensible chronometer would say to the rivals, — "Cease your contention; you are both useful in your places." The one as a private chaplain, the other as a city orator, may tell the world to redeem its flying time.

Though mysteries culminate in the Cross, yet there is enough revealed in the Cross for man's present pardon, and his final enfranchisement in heavenly immortality. The secret things are not ours, — the revealed things are. We have not so much to do with the top of the ladder, which is lost in the effulgence of the heavens, as with the foot of it, which rests on the earth; nor have we so much to do with the bright angel ministrants who throng it, as with the messages of mercy and hymns of hope which escape their tuneful lips. Fool is he who, in running from a town in flames, will not cross the river until he speculates concerning the architecture of the bridge, and makes inquiry into the origin and the date of its building. "Speed away from the pursuing flame," say you; "tarry not until you are far beyond its range, and afterwards, if you please, discuss your speculations concerning the bridge." The illustration may be applied to the sinner who wishes to escape from his sin. His first business is to reduce to practice all that he does understand, to manifest a disposition to accept all the arrangements of Divine wisdom, and in chidlike trust to give himself up to God. The Cross has a side that is "secret," and a side that is "revealed," — a side that shines towards God, and a side that shines towards a sinning world. It lights the heavens as well as the earth, but man's whole business now is to accept the beam which falls upon himself, and in its light to penetrate his way to the higher and better spheres. . . . Do not anticipate the course of study. The volumes will be given by the great Librarian, one by one. Understand what you can, and in doing it you will increase in knowledge; understand that in all the wastes of folly there can be no greater fool than he who will not believe his Father's telegram, because he cannot understand the mystery of the telegraph.

Circumstances have much to do with the formation of opinions. I overlook from my window a field which in April looks like a desert; it is flat, sterile, and most dreary in aspect; not a green thing visible in all the breadth of its twenty acres; it looks like a plague spot on the landscape, and the eye turns from it as from a repulsive spectacle. In August that same field is the richest, the grandest in the whole prospect, for *then* it is laden with golden wheat. It is the same field, yet how different the appearance! So I have observed that young men who modestly begin life with little or no demonstrativeness, often have a very luxuriant and substantial maturity. It is well to defer our judgments until August.

The gospel of Christ may be either the savor of life unto life to a hearer, or a savor of death unto death. How so? All depends upon the man himself. The sun brings life to some branches, and death to others. If a branch is on the tree, and the tree is properly rooted in the soil, the sun will bring life to it; but if the branch be amputated, the sun will wither it to death. It is the same sun, and the branches have grown in the same forest, or even on the same tree; and yet the shining of the sun means life to the one and death to the other.

It is precisely so with the gospel: if a man will not put himself in a right relation to it, it will be his utter destruction.

All men cannot work in the same way; "there are diversities of operation." Upon the face of a watch you may see an illustration of my meaning. On that small space you have three workers: there is the second-pointer, performing rapid revolutions; there is the minute-pointer, going at a greatly reduced speed; and there is the hour-pointer, tardier still. Now any one unacquainted with the mechanism of a watch would conclude that the busy little second-pointer was doing all the work, — it is clicking away at sixty times the speed of the minute-pointer; and as for the hour-hand, *that* seems to be doing no work at all. You can see in a moment that the first is busy, and in a short time you will see the second stir; but you must wait still longer to assure yourself of the motion of the third. So is it in the church. There are active, fussy men, who appear to be doing the work of the whole community, and others who are slower. But can we do without the minute and the hour pointers? The noisy second-hand might go round its little circle forever without telling the world the true time. We should be thankful for all kinds of workers. The silent, steady hour-hand need not envy its noisy little colleague. Each man must fill the measure of his capacity. Your business is to do your allotted work so as to meet the approbation of the Master.

I saw a man watering the roads this morning. He was very careful where he began and where he ended. Three hours afterwards a heavy shower of rain fell, and it blessed the whole neighborhood with its impartial benediction. Thus it is with law and grace; and thus, too, it is with people who work from the point of duty, and the nobler people who work from the point of love.

From figure to parable is not a difficult transition. I have found in the course of my own ministry that parabolical representations of truth have excited a most healthful and profitable interest. All men have somewhat of the dramatic element in them; hence they watch with eagerness the development and consummation of a plot, or a plan, if you like that word better in this connection. *How will it end?* is the anxious inquiry. If you keep your eyes open, you will see the working of this dramatic element in many of the common concerns of daily life. Dispute with a cabman about his fare, and the baker, the milkman, and the lamplighter will soon gather round you to see how the controversy will end; offer to put a hundred pieces of curiously shaped wood together, so as to make a complete figure of them, and all the children in the house will give up their lessons, and press upon you to see how the mystery is solved; tell a child that it is his duty to be honest, and he will infallibly pronounce you a bore; but give him a hint that you can tell a wonderful story about the hair-breadth escapes of a thief, and he will tease you to relate the tale, and will perhaps beg you to go over parts of it again and again. What of it — and especially what of it in relation to the ministry? We must seek the readiest entrance to the human mind, and through that entrance must convey Christian instruction. I know that you will ask, whether this, that, or the other is legitimate, or is in keeping with the dignity of the pulpit. Enough for me to know that Jesus Christ dramatized truth: all the elements of a most exciting romance are to be found in the parable of the prodigal son; why therefore should we hesitate to follow, with such power as God may give us, the example of the Master? Everywhere there is keen interest in life, character, destiny; little children feel it, and old men are not superior to it. This interest has undoubtedly been debased by vicious novels and corrupt dramas, but this is no argument whatever against novels and dramas that are good. You can convey just as much solid truth through the medium of a drama as through the medium of an exposition or exhortation, with this most valuable advantage, — you carry the attention of your hearers with you from beginning to end, and are likely to give the subject an abiding-place in their recollection. Of course, if you construct a clumsy or inconsistent parable, you must bear the mockery which you deserve. I am speaking of parables that recommend themselves by a basis of strong common sense and a fair share of fancy and eloquence; such parables, delivered with a simplicity which is at the farthest possible distance from theatrical affectation, will never fail to secure the best results.

In writing thus, a great fear comes upon me lest you should be indiscreet enough to ask me to show you how such parables may be written. Perhaps I do you injustice in supposing that you would condescend to ask such a question; yet I feel some relief in being permitted to indulge a supposition so dishonoring to your proud powers. It would display sound judgment ou my part, were I to try to bring the requisite fancy, wit, and wisdom to bear upon the outline and execution of your task; but I am afraid the advice would not be of much service to you. Frankly, then, I own that the power of writing parables is not so freely distributed as the power of reading them. If you have not the power, don't waste your time in parable grinding. A poor sermon is bad enough, but a poor parable is intolerable. A parable that is cumbrous, mechanical, labored, will offend and weary the unhappy victims on whose patience it is inflicted, and their maledictions will be the fit reward of the foolish speaker. There must be no display of mere cleverness in the construction of the parable; the moment the hearers are so far released from the grasp of the thought as to think anything about the forms, the highest object of teaching is lost. This being so, the Christian parabolist cannot allow himself to dally over points on which the mere artist may lawfully linger; the preacher is more than an artist, and is therefore bound to watch himself jealously lest art become a temptation to him. The preacher is an architect, it is true; but he is especially a *builder*. His plans may be good, what if he build nothing? He must build, and he must build *completely*. Each parable must have its own distinct lesson; if it be fragmentary, it will be distracting and useless, and truth will be dishonored. The execution may not be polished, but the conception must be complete. The parable of the prodigal son is complete, though there is no attempt at literary embellishment. You must have an object, and towards that you must move steadily and fervently. Before beginning your parable, put to yourself the question, What end have I in view? Suppose the answer be, to prove that the way of transgressors is hard; or, to show that the paths of wisdom are pleasant; or, to point out what may be done by faith, — you have then to outline a narrative which will most graphically illustrate your meaning: you have the main point, and it remains to gather around it elucidatory material. This is perhaps an infelicitous way of insisting that your teaching must be *distinct;* it must not be simply allusive; people must not be thrown upon their skill in drawing inferences; the doctrine must be clear, the lesson must be emphatic.

I confess to some difficulty in giving advice about the use of anecdotes, as, in my opinion, nearly everything depends upon the taste and skill of the relater. The same anecdote told by two different men may produce two contrary effects, — it may disgust, and it may please. When there is drawling over unimportant points, or heaviness in the expression, or a long preamble before the story, the effect is sure to be bad. As soon as I hear a preacher say, — "My beloved brethren, let us illustrate this by one of the most beautiful and affecting anecdotes which it was ever my privilege to hear," I make up my mind to endure a dreary recital of very painful nonsense. Anecdotes should not be prefaced. Anecdotes should not be long. Anecdotes should be true. I have heard of a preacher who in one discourse related twenty-seven anecdotes, yet they were so skilfully introduced and so pithily told as to be quite enjoyed by educated and critical hearers. This is an exceptional case; don't set set it up as a model, or I shall never hear a good account of you. If you can now and again put a simple and telling anecdote into your sermon, do so; but be very careful not to go anecdote mad. People will believe in parables when they will distrust anecdotes. They know that a parable is imaginative, but they expect an anecdote to be literal; and if once they catch the relater tripping, there is an end to their confidence, not only in the speech but in the speaker.

In all our ministry we have to magnify Jesus Christ as the Saviour of the world; and whether it be by figure and parable, or by the plain statement of doctrine, let us be sure that we reach the highest point of our vocation. At the base of your ministry let there be sound, enlightened, fearless, and reverent exposition of the Divine word; without *that* your ministry will be a failure, you will never train men; you may please giddy and shallow listeners, but no manly host will prove the vigor of your teaching. Having laid your foundations, you may call up all your powers and attainments to give scope, massiveness, and beauty to the building. Don't lay an interdict upon your fancy; don't be afraid of the occasional service of humor; don't always put a seal upon your wit; let your whole nature preach; let fancy, humor, wit, sarcasm, contribute their share of help to your ministry; they will be of use as allies, if you be careful to have something stronger on the main line. If you honor Christ in your ministry, you will be honored by Him in return. When the fisherman goes to the river, it is that he may attempt to take fish; are not you a fisher of men? Why not then go to every sermon with the one set purpose of bringing men to the Savior? *That is the one object of the true ministry.* We have to bring men to Christ as a Saviour, and we have also to bring men to Christ as a *Teacher.* Repentance and faith are not the end, they are but the beginning of Christian life. We seek conversion first, then we aim at edification. Throughout the process we are the agents, the servants, the ambassadors of Christ,—He will honor those who wait upon Him, if they forget themselves in the glory of His blessed name.

XIX.

FRAMEWORKS.

I HAVE given you a few hints upon figures; let me now further expose myself to your criticism by offering you a few crude outlines of discourses. I have not spared you; there is no occasion for you to spare me. Use your keenest edge, and give full swing to your young strength. I care less and less for mere outlines, and more and more for a sympathetic and intelligent discussion of the *subject* of any text. Some preachers are outline mad; they are nothing but outline; they plan beautifully, but build nothing. Give them the word *thinking* as a text, and they will see in it: (1) Man in a reduced physical state — *thin;* (2) man in a high social state — *king;* (3) man in a true intellectual state — *thinking.* Give them as a text the word *feeblest,* and they will see in it: (1) a professional income — *fee;* (2) an indication of supreme happiness — *blest;* (3) a description of a human state deserving commiseration — *feeblest.* Give them for a text the words *Come unto Me*, and they will see in them: (1) a state of activity — *come;* (2) activity well directed — *unto;* (3) activity terminating upon the best of beings — *Me.* The outline of which this is hardly an exaggeration is irreverent trifling with the inspired word; it shows off the poor powers of the textual gymnast, and by so much degrades and insults the holy vocation of the Christian ministry. Study the idea of the text; try to pierce to its very heart; and having seized the truth, expound it with all simplicity and earnestness. With these introductory remarks, let me place before you a few outlines which may be quite as useful as warnings as examples.

I. *The Private Ministry of the Gospel.*

"Philip findeth Nathanael, and saith unto him, We have found Him, of whom Moses in the law, and the prophets, did write," etc. — JOHN i. 45–51.

The scene: one man speaking to another about Jesus Christ!

I. EVERY CHRISTIAN HAS A MESSAGE TO THE WORLD: "We have found Him," etc. The message is founded upon matter of *fact*, and is supported by *personal* testimony. The responsibility of *silence.*

II. EVERY CHRISTIAN MAY EXPECT TO ENCOUNTER CONTROVERSIAL INQUIRIES. Nathanael put the question of prejudice: others will start critical, metaphysical, and ethical difficulties. No subject more deeply agitates the mind than Christianity. This is in its favor; so profound and comprehensive a revelation must appeal to all that is highest and mightiest in man.

III. EVERY CHRISTIAN HAS A PRACTICAL ANSWER TO SUCH INQUIRIES: "Philip saith unto him, *Come and see;*" — not discussion, but fact. Jesus adopted the same method with the disciples of John. The works of Christianity are its best defence. We know that the Bible is inspired because of its inspiring influence upon human life. The Christian advocate should always take the inquirer directly to Jesus Christ. A Christian man should be a convincing reply to all scepticism; his *life* should be his argument.

IV. EVERY CHRISTIAN WILL WITNESS THE HAPPIEST RESULTS OF AN ACCEPTANCE OF HIS MESSAGE. It was so in the case of Nathanael. (1) Jesus Christ showed familiarity with his history; *every* man feels that Jesus Christ speaks to him personally; in no case did Jesus Christ require any information respecting those who came to Him. He seemed to carry each man's history in His own great life. (2) Jesus Christ wrought in him the joy of *personal* conviction: "Thou art the Son of God," etc. Christianity is not altogether a matter of *external* evidence; it becomes part of the man's very soul; hence the authority with which men can speak of their Divinest experiences. (3) He gave him the prospect of still fuller revelation; "hereafter ye shall see heaven opened," etc. Acceptance of Christ is not a *final* act; it is the initiation of the soul into an unending course of development of strength and love. The Christian will ever have more to "see" than he has yet seen. "Eye hath not seen," etc. "He is able to do exceedingly above," etc.

Application: Preach to *one man;* preach *Christ* to him; preach Christ to him on the authority of *personal experience.*

II. *The Divine Echo in the Human Heart.*

"Well, Master, Thou hast said the truth." — MARK xii. 32.

God's word may be received controversially, speculatively, or lovingly; men may argue about it, or let it argue with them to their conviction and redemption. Take, for example, the doctrine, *Man is a sinner.* You may make it a matter of controversy, and by all the poor devices of self-conceit may endeavor to escape its consequences; it may be met by flat denial, or received with many modifications. But take it into the heart, when the heart is in its best mood, ponder it when far from the influence of the world's excitement and flattery, and say whether there be not a voice which responds affirmatively to the tremendous charge. Take again the doctrine, *Man needs a Saviour.* It is possible to meet such a doctrine in a captious and resentful spirit; it denies the possibility of self-redemption; it dismisses all the fancies which the soul has been treasuring, and shows man his poverty and weakness. But take it also into the heart, under circumstances which allow it to be fairly considered, when the heart knows most of its own bitterness, and has seen the limit of the world's little power, and say whether there be not a voice answering God's appeal with, "Well, Master, Thou hast said the truth." We do not ask for the acceptance of doctrines which ignore or override the instincts and experience of the world; on the contrary, Christianity addresses itself to the intuitions of every man.

What are the *practical consequences* of our having this responsive faculty? I. MAN IS MADE A CO-WORKER WITH GOD; not a machine, but a co-operating agent. This gives confidence to personal hope, and authority to personal teaching. II. MAN ENJOYS THE RESTRAINTS OF CONSCIENCE. Upon practical morals man is his own Bible; he carries an unwritten law which warns him from forbidden ground. The conscience is God's witness in our apostasy. The Bible appeals to it, and works with its full consent. III. GOD BASES HIS JUDGMENT UPON THIS RESPONSIVE FACULTY: "To him that knoweth to do good," etc.; "Thou wicked and slothful servant, thou knowest," etc. The judgment day will be short, because every man will be his own witness.

Application: Is there nothing in you which responds to the appeals of the gospel, which says, "Master, Thou hast said the truth"? Your treatment of that voice will determine your destiny. "Quench not the Spirit." "He that knoweth his Lord's will and doeth it not," etc.

III. *God's Revelation of Himself.*

"I am the Lord; the God of all flesh; is there anything too hard for Me?"—JER. xxxii. 27.

This is God's revelation of Himself; not the fancy of a speculator, not the dream of a poet, but a Divine and authoritative declaration of personality, relationship, and power. Peculiar importance attaches to the very form of expression, inasmuch as it assumes to be the precise language which has fallen from the lips of the Almighty. No man is at liberty to adopt the words; if they are not what they profess to be, they are the utterance of daring blasphemy. It is our joy to believe in their simple truth, and to govern our lives by the holy principles which they imply.

"*I am the Lord*": here is a direct assertion of *personality;* it is not the voice of creation, but the voice of the Creator; not only life, but the living One. We have need to be assured of God's personality; He never appears to our natural vision; we see the works, but not the Worker; and many a time the heart desires a clearer revelation of the Divine nature than is supplied by the sublimities and beauties of creation. In all ages man has desired to come near his Maker, to get beyond the courts of the temple in which He is enthroned, and to behold Him as it were face to face. Job said: "Oh, that I knew where I might find HIM." It was not enough to live in His light, and to be surrounded by the tokens of His power; he wished to look upon Him and to speak to Him, as a man might speak to his friend. We cannot enter into all the reasons why we are excluded from a sight of God's personality; but we have rest in the belief that in another theatre we shall be satisfied that while in the flesh, oppressed by its guilt and limited by its weakness, we could not have borne the revelation for which, in our ignorance, we have often sighed. Surely God will not reproach us for our desire to look upon Him, if that desire be the expression of filial love and not of sinful audacity. Is it unnatural that a child should wish to see his Father, especially when that Father is so near as to be able to speak to him, often by name and always in the langauge of wisdom and love? The very nearness constitutes a temptation. Were the name announced in distant thunder, as if it were too awful to be uttered in the language of men, we might tremble, and reverently abide the time of more intimate revelation; but when the voice is nigh us, when it is even in our souls, stimulating and comforting us, it is not to be wondered at that we should wish to see the all-gracious and ever-abiding Speaker. Denied this sight, we take refuge in such declarations as the text; we accept the abounding manifestations of goodness as a pledge that when our discipline is complete and our faculties are mature, we shall assuredly see the King in His beauty.

"*I am the Lord.*" Here is a direct assertion, not only of personality, but of absolute *dominion.* God does not announce Himself as *a* lord, one of *many;* but as *the* Lord, the one and only Sovereign, whose glory is incommunicable, and whose empire is the universe. There is no hesitation in the language; it is complete, absolute, and final. To accept it is to be saved from all wandering of heart towards the "lords many and gods many" of pagan superstition or semi-Christian speculation. This gives steadiness of heart; it defines alike the Divine and human position, and develops the strength by showing the weakness of all finite life.

IV. *Christian Experience.*

"I am crucified with Christ."
"I would to God that all that hear me were such as I am."
"By the grace of God I am what I am."

I. Christian experience is *personal.* "*I am*": (*a*) internal; (*b*) intense; (*c*) vital.

II. Christian experience is *benevolent.* "I would to God," etc.: (*a*) Christianity enlarges human sympathies; (*b*) Christianity compels to noble action in behalf of others.

III. Christian experience is *Divine*. "By the grace of God." It is a Divine effect: (*a*) mysterious; (*b*) generous; (*c*) complete.

V. *First Efforts.*

"This beginning of miracles did Jesus," etc. — JOHN ii. 11.

I. The *memorableness* of first efforts (in every department of life).

II. The *determining effects* of first efforts (encouraging, discouraging; beginnings often determine ends).

III. The *modesty* of first efforts (compared with Christ's other miracles, this seems, in many respects, to be the simplest of them all). Encourage men to make first efforts, — first efforts in family prayer, public prayer, Christian service, etc.

VI. *The Mission of Christ.*

"The Son of man is come to seek and to save that which was lost." — LUKE xix. 10.

I. The most magnificent *historical fact:* "*came.*"

II. The most appallingly *significant mission:* "*to seek.*"

III. The most transcendently *beneficent purpose:* "*to save.*"

IV. The most perfect description of the *state of humanity:* "*lost.*"

(*a*) If Christ came, man's responsibility is increased. (*b*) If Christ came to *seek*, then seek ye the Lord while He may be found. (*c*) If Christ came to *save*, then the sinner is without excuse. (*d*) If Christ came to save the *lost*, then the worst may welcome Him. (*e*) Christ will *come*, will come to *seek*, once more.

Such is a handful of outlines. Every man must have his own way of making plans of sermons; there is no *best* way; that way is best which the preacher himself has proved to be best. We should aim at *variety* in division; sometimes the division may be very formal, sometimes it may be quite subordinate. It is not always necessary to describe the outline to the congregation; occasionally it may be specified with advantage. You must judge of the circumstances, and act accordingly. Beware—suffer this word of exhortation—of having an artistic framework and a lifeless expansion. Men will be affected more by your tones than by your heads.

XXI.

EPILOGUE.

THERE can be no doubt that the ministerial market, if the expression may be allowed, is overcrowded. Serious inconvenience arises from this fact. The applications which ministers make to one another for introductions to vacant pulpits are not only excessively numerous, but often most embarrassing. There is, of course, a disposition to be kind to worthy men, and not seldom this disposition sets aside the discrimination which ought to be exercised in relation to the merits of the applicant, and the special necessities of the position to which he wishes to be introduced. The difficulty is much increased by the fact that the applicants are men of excellent character, of good attainments, and of unquestionable orthodoxy: the one thing which is wanting is *pulpit efficiency*. In many cases the defect in this particular is most obvious. I know men whose moral reputation is above suspicion, whose scholarship is sound, and whose doctrine is unexceptionable, men who have college certificates and even university honors, who find it extremely difficult to obtain a livelihood in the ministry. How so? Simply because they can do nearly everything except *preach*. In conversation they have no difficulty in maintaining their ground; in point of information they are decidedly above the average; in manners they are fit for the best society; yet as preachers of the gospel they are utterly incompetent. In looking at such cases we must come back to our old doctrine, viz., ministers cannot be *made*. Let colleges exist for purposes of scholarship, let theology even be taught to all who wish to study that greatest of the sciences, let a special effort be made by the establishment of evening classes for teaching scholars to read the Scriptures in the original languages, — do everything that is possible for the extension of biblical study; but do not continue to multiply a class of able and worthy men having no adaptation to the public work of the ministry. To teach a man that he is a *minister*, simply because he has completed a prescribed curriculum, is to put him into an altogether false position. He is not a *minister* because of that; he may be a scholar, a theologian, a critic, but it does not follow that he is a *minister*. Adaptation to the ministry is quite a distinct question. *Every* Christian should study theology; the study of theology should not be a merely *professional* exercise; *every* Christian, too, should make it his special business, so far as possible, to acquire a knowledge of Greek and Hebrew: *then*, when the highest education has been made available to the whole church, let those men who have the gift of preaching give public utterance to Divine truth. My call is not for a learned *ministry*, but for a learned *church*. Of course, there are difficulties in the way of such extension of education as is proposed: there will be just complaints of want of time, and in some cases want of capacity; but these do not touch the main question at all. *Popularize*, not *professionalize*, theological education; as in classics or mathematics, let the doors be thrown *open to all*, and when it is made clear that certain men can *excel* in this department or that, let an inner circle be established, and the highest advantages be offered to such as have fully shown claim to the most advanced culture which the resources of the church can furnish. To my own mind it is perfectly clear that a considerable proportion of the young men who during the last five and twenty years have undergone preparation for the ministry would to-day have been doing much more good had they never aspired to the pulpit. At the same time it is equally clear that most of them were patient and successful students, and well deserved every commendation and honor accorded to them. The mistake was, in my judgment, to encourage the idea that they were *ministers*, and to set them apart as members of a distinct professional class. In addition to its being a mistake, it inflicted considerable injury upon the men themselves: if they had entered college to become scholars, critics, and theologians, the end would have been answered; but inasmuch as they claimed to be *ministers*, they were compelled to bear the stigma of failure where they might have enjoyed the honor of success. To this there is an obvious answer. The students could not afford the time if they were not by study qualifying themselves to obtain a livelihood by preaching. There is force in the answer; yet instead of putting an end to the difficulty, it rather suggests a further inquiry. Can any other method than that of the ordinary collegiate system be adopted for the extension of theological knowledge and of accurate biblical learning? The university lists clearly show that degrees and honors have been attained by means of *private study*. Is it not possible, then, to encourage private study in theology and related subjects, and to give such recognition of results as shall remove all doubt of the competency of the student? I venture to think that it is quite possible, and possible in this way: let an unsectarian theological council be established, and let all men of all churches, who wish to be examined in any given number of subjects, present themselves for examination at such times as the council may appoint; and in the event of their satisfying the examiners, let them be certificated accordingly. Suppose that such a man as Dean Alford should consent to conduct the examination in the Greek Testament, and should certify that the student had creditably answered all the questions proposed, would not such a certificate carry with it the highest scholastic and social value? So with such a man as Dean Stanley and the Old Testament; so with Henry Rogers and Butler's Analogy;

and so with other competent examiners in various subjects. The council should, of course, be thoroughly unsectarian; no questions need be asked as to the denominationalism of the candidates for examination; even the names of the candidates need not be known until the result was declared; the whole process would have reference exclusively to the merits of the papers returned to the examiners.

To the establishment of such a council it may be objected, that in private study young men lose the advantage of *conversational teaching*, of stimulus, of the discipline of criticism and comparison, enjoyed by those who study in company. True: yet as it is not proposed to compel them to study in solitude, this objection does not apply. In some cases, solitary study would of course be inevitable; but in others, by far the most numerous, existing college systems could be adapted to meet them. Evening classes might be established; small companies of young men might engage the assistance of competent teachers to assist them in special difficulties, — in these ways the objection might be met to a large degree, and if it can be shown that the proposed examination has great counterbalancing advantages, the objection will be removed altogether. Let it be known that twice a year a Theological Council will be held in London for the purpose of examining members of all Christian denominations who wish to have their knowledge of given subjects tested, and the probable consequence would be an instant and powerful stimulus to theological study. The unsectarianism of the council, its indisputable competency, its perfect impartiality, would secure for it profound and universal confidence. Six months beforehand, or twelve, the council might publish the list of subjects for the next examination: for example, in Hebrew, a historical or prophetical book (to be named); in Greek, the Gospel by Luke and the Epistle to the Romans; in theology, six subjects, with textbooks, to be named; and the same with moral philosophy and ecclesiastical history. Students would thus have something before them worth striving for, and by the time they attained it they would have had opportunity of knowing themselves, and forming a tolerably sound judgment as to their fitness for the Christian ministry. For the education of *preachers*, special provision should be made. Their preparations should be superintended by men who themselves excel in preaching, and who are enthusiastic in their convictions respecting the power of the Christian pulpit. Even though an orator cannot reduce to rules the passion which gives him supremacy in the pulpit, he can by that very passion arouse and encourage those who have latent power of public address. The students should be made to feel that their teacher illustrates in his own ministry the grandeur of the vocation to which they have committed themselves. What if their teacher be languid in his appreciation of the pulpit? What if he be a preacher from whose ministry the public have withdrawn? What if he be not a preacher at all, but a layman who could not interest an audience for ten minutes? It is not at all to the point to reply that he is a scholar, a man of taste, and a good judge of literature. Granted that he is all that, what does it prove if he is not a preacher? This kind of service would not be tolerated in any other line of life; why should it be tolerated in the highest of all? Because a man is an excellent judge of leather, and has correct information as to the anatomy of the human foot, is he therefore qualified to teach the art of shoemaking? If a man never played a tune on a piano, would you send a scholar to him to learn the use of that instrument because the man had a fine ear for music and had written some excellent tunes? It does not follow that Shakspeare was an actor, any more than that Garrick was an author. I hold that essay writing and sermon preaching are totally distinct; that literature and oratory are not identical; and that it is as awkward for an orator to consider his oratory a qualification for teaching literature, as it is for a scholar to consider his scholarship a qualification for teaching men how to preach. He can listen to their essays with a critical ear, he can correct their style, he can give direction to their courses of thinking; but all this does not touch the one question of preaching with earnestness, with power, and with success. It will not do to say that good scholarship, sound theology, competent criticism, are to be considered before preaching. I say nothing about their comparative merits; I have to deal with the one fact that students are being sent forth to *preach*. It is as *preachers* that they seek to engage the confidence and support of the churches; it is by *preaching* that they have to maintain themselves; and if they fail in *preaching* they miss the end at which they aimed in offering themselves as candidates for the Christian ministry.

Turning from this point, which I cannot but regard as of growing importance, I may relieve you by indulging in a little speculation. The time will come when Sunday services will be modelled upon a new and better basis. The minister will have to preach less and to preach better. There will be one service in the day, — beginning say at twelve o'clock, and continuing about two hours; in the evening, parents will have time to teach their children; and those members of the household who could not go out in the morning will have opportunity of going to special services here and there in the evening; and it will be matter of surprise if any be present in the evening who attended service in the morning. It is better to have one well-prepared and thoroughly appreciated service, than to drag through two services with the heaviness of indifference. Those who have been at service in the morning will be doing work in the evening. Their children will be instructed, the poor and ignorant will be gathered together, and taught the way of truth; and wherever Christian teaching is needed, it will be eagerly and gladly supplied. The idea of a man hearing two sermons on one day will be considered either a punishment or a waste of time; and the days that are now passing over us will be laughed at for their oddities, or pitied for their endurances. I know of no body of men so hardly worked as the Nonconformist ministers of England. The lawyers are hardly worked, but they are helped by the *variety* of their labors, whereas the ministers are depressed by the monotony of their engagements. It is easy enough to reply that no monotony ought to be felt in Christian service; but human nature is not to be put off or satisfied with a remark which is not sanctioned either by piety or common sense.

It is to me a pleasant conviction that no office is to be compared, for interest, reality, and importance, with the office of the Christian ministry. I have followed the course of many men with most anxious watchfulness, — the lawyer, the statesman, the physician, the dramatist, the poet; and it is the sober conviction of my mind that not one of them is to be compared with the earnest, intelligent, and powerful preacher of Jesus Christ. Having regard to the scope, the urgency, and the far-reaching results of our ministry, we may truly exclaim, "all things are ours." The statesman operates within very narrow limits, so does the lawyer, so does the physician; and whatever there may be of depth, vitality, and inspiration, in the highest intellectual activities, is all at the service of the interpreter of God and the Christian teacher of man. I magnify mine office! Get a low notion of your work, and your soul will go down, you will not bring to bear upon it your passion and your strength; have a high notion of it, if you would work with enthusiasm and success. You must pray to be saved from the service of the mere letter; it is drudgery, it is bondage, it is pain. Preaching should be as natural and as easy as healthy breathing. There is no occasion for it to be a toil. It should be the expression of the heart's best life,—not the effort of a pump, but the blessing of rich and genial rain. Men talk of *making* sermons and *getting off* sermons and begging sermons,—flee from such men as from enemies! Let your acquaintance with the holy word be accurate and profound; let the word of God dwell in you richly; be careful and constant in your study of human nature; live not in the clouds, but in the common experience of the world; rely upon the inspiration of the Holy Ghost; and never submit to the servility of making pretty sentences and preparing for pampered seat-holders packets of fancy confectionery. What some ministers will have to answer for in this particular! Many a sin will be found in well-trimmed rhetoric, in neat couplets, in stanzas forced in for effect, and in perorations intended to elevate the speaker rather than advance the truth. The heart is deceitful above all things! How we catch at any text on which we can show our cleverness! How we cheer ourselves with the anticipated effect of this happy allusion or that telling illustration! How we turn some sentences to please the chief subscriber, and give emphasis to some doctrine we care nothing about, just to keep the old man in the great pew in tolerable sympathy with our ministry! How often our prayers are mere investments, and our tears the price of popularity! Our ministry should be in spirit and in truth, but how often is it formal and practically false! "Many walk of whom I have told you often, and now tell you even weeping, that they are the enemies of the cross of Christ." We are abashed and utterly confounded when we read what was done by the mighty men of old, who led the cause of God, and suffered for it even unto death. They "subdued kingdoms, wrought righteousness, obtained promises, stopped the mouths of lions, quenched the violence of fire, escaped the edge of the sword, waxed valiant in fight, turned to flight the armies of the aliens; they had trials of cruel mockings and scourgings, yea, moreover, of bonds and imprisonments; they were stoned, they were sawn asunder, were tempted, were slain with the edge of the sword; they wandered about in sheepskins and goatskins, being destitute, afflicted, tormented." And are we the self-seeking successors of such men, writing pretty sermons and fattening ourselves with luxury? "We are troubled on every side, yet not distressed; we are perplexed, but not in despair; persecuted, but not forsaken; cast down, but not destroyed; for Thy sake we are killed all the day long, we are accounted as sheep for the slaughter." Are we worthy successors of those princes of God? If we speak of having in any degree been inconvenienced in the discharge of our ministry, how instantly are we rebuked by the testimony of Paul: "In labors more abundant, in stripes above measure, in prisons more frequent, in deaths oft; of the Jews five times received I forty stripes save one; thrice was I beaten with rods, once was I stoned, thrice I suffered shipwreck, a night and a day I have been in the deep; in journeyings often, in perils of waters, in perils of robbers, in perils by mine own countrymen, in perils by the heathen, in perils in the city, in perils in the wilderness, in perils in the sea, in perils among false brethren; in weariness and painfulness, in watchings often, in hunger and thirst, in fasting soften, in cold and nakedness, — even unto this present hour we both hunger and thirst, and are naked, and are buffeted, and have no certain dwelling-place." What is our lot to this experience of pain and sorrow and loss! In the hearing of such heroic words, we feel as if we aggravate our sin by professing to be ministers of Jesus Christ, so poor is our service, so faint our devotions, so deep our self-indulgence. God be merciful unto us sinners! Enter not into judgment with thy servants, O Lord!

My brother, we have now had long converse with each other. Month by month, for two years, I have spoken to you such things as were intended to stimulate, instruct, cheer, and bless you. On some occasions, I have used great plainness of speech; on others, I have taken the liberty of teaching by exaggeration, thereby saying many things which are to be interpreted with charity, and applied with discrimination. We part now. "What is writ is writ; would it were worthier"! Be assured that wherein I have spoken harshly, I have felt the smart of the scourge myself; wherein I have yielded to humor, I have not been unmindful of the reality and sadness of human life; and wherein I have extolled my office, I have desired to magnify only the grace of God. For the present, let us say farewell. When you want to know what I have to say that is intended to help you, read "Springdale Abbey" and "Ad Clerum." In these two books I have exhausted all that is at present in my mind upon church questions, general oratory, pulpit preparation, and ministerial work. I commend you to God and to the word of his grace. "That good thing which was committed unto thee, keep by the Holy Ghost which dwelleth in us." Be steadfast in God. "I charge thee, therefore, before God, and the Lord Jesus Christ, who shall judge the quick and the dead at His appearing and His kingdom, preach the word; be instant in season, out of season; reprove, rebuke, exhort with all longsuffering and doctrine, — watch thou in all things, endure afflictions, do the work of an evangelist, make full proof of thy ministry"; and in the solemn end, when the full light shineth, and we see things as they really are, thou shalt have the abiding honor which cometh from God.

Stereotyped by ALFRED MUDGE & SON, Boston, Mass.

THE GREAT RELIGIOUS BOOKS OF THE DAY.

ECCE HOMO.
ECCE DEUS.

Although it is now two years since the publication of "Ecce Homo," and one year since "Ecce Deus" appeared, the sale of these extraordinary and remarkable books continues quite as large as ever. Some of the ablest and most cultivated minds in the world have been devoted to a critical analysis of them.

The foremost man in England, the Right Honorable W. E. Gladstone, has just published a book devoted entirely to a review of "Ecce Homo," in which he uses the following language: —

"To me it appears that each page of the book breathes out, as it proceeds, what we may call an air, which grows musical by degrees, and which, becoming more distinct even as it swells, takes form, as in due time we find, in the articulate conclusion, 'Surely, this is the Son of God; surely, this is the King of Heaven.'"

Of "Ecce Deus," which may be considered the complement of "Ecce Homo," there are almost as many admirers, the sale of both books being nearly alike.

Both volumes bound uniformly Sold separately. Price of each, $1.50.

Prof. Ingraham's Works.

THE PRINCE OF THE HOUSE OF DAVID; or, Three Years in the Holy City.

THE PILLAR OF FIRE; or, Israel in Bondage.

THE THRONE OF DAVID; from the Consecration of the Shepherd of Bethlehem to the Rebellion of Prince Absalom.

The extraordinary interest evinced in these books, from the date of their publication to the present time, has in no wise abated. The demand for them is still as large as ever.

In three volumes, 12mo, cloth, gilt, with illustrations. Sold separately. Price of each, $2.00.

The Heaven Series.

HEAVEN OUR HOME. We have no Saviour but Jesus, and no Home but Heaven.

MEET FOR HEAVEN. A State of Grace upon Earth the only Preparation for a State of Glory in Heaven.

LIFE IN HEAVEN. There Faith is changed into Sight, and Hope is passed into Blissful Fruition.

From Rev. Samuel L. Tuttle, Assistant Secretary of the American Bible Society.

"I wish that every Christian person could have the perusal of these writings. I can never be sufficiently thankful to him who wrote them for the service that he has rendered to me and all others. They have given *form and substance to every thing revealed in the Scriptures respecting our heavenly home of love*, and they have done not a little to invest it with the most powerful attractions to my heart. Since I have enjoyed the privilege of following the thought of their author, I have felt that there was *a reality* in all these things which I have never felt before; and I find myself often thanking God for putting it into the heart of a poor worm of the dust to spread such glorious representations before our race, all of whom stand in need of such a rest."

In three volumes, 16mo. Sold separately. Price of each, $1.25.

Mailed, post-paid, to any address, on receipt of the price by the publishers.

www.ingramcontent.com/pod-product-compliance
Lightning Source LLC
LaVergne TN
LVHW010230110826
845151LV00004B/1247
* 9 7 8 1 4 2 5 5 2 5 4 6 0 *